# Presidential Saber Rattling
*Causes and Consequences*

The Founders of the American republic believed presidents should be wise and virtuous statesmen consistently advocating community interests when conducting American foreign policy. Yet the most common theoretical model used today for explaining the behavior of politicians is grounded in self-interest rather than community interest. This book investigates whether past presidents acted as noble statesmen or were driven by such self-interested motivations as reelection, passion, partisanship, media frenzy, and increasing domestic support. The book also examines the consequences for the nation of presidential behavior driven by self-interest. Between 1945 and 2008, presidents issued 4,269 threats to 19 countries; Professor B. Dan Wood evaluates the causes and consequences of these threats, revealing the nature of presidential foreign policy representation and its consistency with the Founding Fathers' intentions.

B. Dan Wood is Professor and Director of the American Politics Program at Texas A&M University. He is the author of *The Myth of Presidential Representation* (Cambridge 2009) and *The Politics of Economic Leadership: The Causes and Consequences of Presidential Rhetoric* (2007) and coauthor of *Bureaucratic Dynamics: The Role of Bureaucracy in a Democracy* (1994).

# Presidential Saber Rattling

## Causes and Consequences

### B. DAN WOOD

*Texas A&M University*

CAMBRIDGE
UNIVERSITY PRESS

CAMBRIDGE UNIVERSITY PRESS
Cambridge, New York, Melbourne, Madrid, Cape Town,
Singapore, São Paulo, Delhi, Mexico City

Cambridge University Press
32 Avenue of the Americas, New York, NY 10013-2473, USA

www.cambridge.org
Information on this title: www.cambridge.org/9781107021273

First published 2012

Printed in the United States of America

A catalog record for this publication is available from the British Library.

Library of Congress Cataloging in Publication Data

Wood, B. Dan.
Presidential saber rattling : causes and consequences / B. Dan Wood.
  p.  cm.
Includes bibliographical references.
ISBN 978-1-107-02127-3 (hardback)
1. Presidents – United States – History.  2. Presidents – United States – Language – History.
3. Political oratory – United States – History.  4. Rhetoric – Political aspects – United States –
History.  I. Title.
JK511.W65  2012
352.23'80973–dc23      2011049501

ISBN 978-1-107-02127-3 Hardback

*To Nathaniel David and Rebekah Joy Wood*

# Contents

# List of Figures and Tables

## Figures

Tables

# Preface

This book is about the causes and consequences of presidential threats toward other nations. Of course, history is replete with leaders who threatened other nations in self-defense or out of ambition, passion, revenge, desire for personal glory, partisan compacts, and avarice. Egyptian Pharaoh Seti I threatened and made war on the Hittites in 1298 B.C. in defense of their persistent incursions into Egyptian territory. Persian King Xerxes I threatened and made war against the Greeks in 483 B.C. out of revenge for their interference in the Ionian revolt. Many Roman rulers starting around 800 B.C., and lasting for more than 1,200 years, threatened and made war to extract wealth from surrounding territories. Duke William of Normandy, coveting the throne of England, threatened and defeated English King Harold in 1066, leading to the Norman conquest of England. And King George III threatened American colonists starting in 1774 through a series of Coercive Acts that ultimately resulted in the American Revolution.

Keenly aware of history, the Founders of the American Republic had a very different vision for how presidents would behave while conducting American foreign policy. They believed that presidents should use their foreign policy tools only to achieve *just* foreign policy goals. Presidents should be motivated *solely* by the community interest, rather than self-interest. They should be wise and virtuous leaders, divorced from their passions and personal considerations. Presidents should be beyond the partisan fray and oblivious to media frenzies. Because American presidents reside in a democratic system, they should be attentive to public opinion, but they should not be enslaved by it. In other words, the Founders believed in a "statesman" ideal of presidential foreign policy representation.

As with ancient rulers, modern presidents have often used threats as a tool of American foreign policy. From 1945 through 2008, presidents issued a total of 4,269 distinct threats. Of these, 3,163 were of a general nature directed at no particular country or group. The remaining 1,106 were specific and targeted toward particular countries or groups. There were 508 threats seemingly intended to deter, 398 presidential threats of economic or political sanction, and 200 threats of military action. The targets of presidential threats since World War II have included nineteen countries, as well as various terrorist organizations.

A primary purpose of this book is to evaluate whether modern presidents have lived up to the "statesman" ideal when making threats. Presidential saber rattling is taken as an object of scientific analysis for the purpose of studying the nature of presidential foreign policy representation. Accordingly, this study poses the following research questions. Are the causes of presidential saber rattling rooted primarily in external threats to the nation, or do presidential threats also derive from domestic factors? Do presidents divorce themselves from their passions, partisanship, public opinion, and domestic politics when making threats, or does presidential saber rattling derive from factors such as reelection incentives, partisanship, media frenzies, approval ratings, economic performance, or other factors that might suggest self-interested motivations?

Another purpose of this book is to evaluate the domestic and foreign policy consequences of presidential saber rattling. Domestically, do presidents benefit from making foreign policy threats? If so, how do they benefit, and for how long? Are there unanticipated consequences of presidential saber rattling? For example, do presidential threats affect consumer confidence and economic behavior, thereby affecting U.S. economic performance? With respect to foreign policy, how do those being threatened typically react to presidential threats? Do they bow to the overwhelming power and resources of the U.S. president, or do they fail to respond, or even react negatively to presidential threats? More generally, are public presidential threats toward other nations an effective tool of American foreign policy?

This book addresses all of these research questions through analysis of empirical data. The "take away" themes are the following: (1) Modern presidents are not the pure "statesmen" representatives envisioned by the Founders but are driven by a variety of domestic factors, including reelection, partisanship, and media frenzies. (2) Presidents benefit domestically from their threats through increased public approval, especially among opposing partisans and independents. However, presidential threats also adversely affect the economy. (3) Presidential threats toward other nations are largely ineffective in producing compliance with U.S. interests and often have the undesirable effect of provoking foreign adversaries.

The research reported in this book was initiated in the fall of 2006, with various conference papers delivered in 2007, 2009, and 2011. As with any project of this duration, there are many to whom I am indebted. My work has always centered on issues of representation and responsiveness for various political institutions. However, Jeffrey Cohen (Fordham University) pointed out to me that little work had previously been done on foreign policy representation. Jeff also commented on various conference papers that later became chapters in this book.

The chapter on the domestic consequences of presidential saber rattling benefited from data on presidential approval broken down by partisanship provided by Matthew Lebo (State University of New York at Stony Brook) and updated by Jeffrey Cohen. The chapter on the foreign policy consequences of presidential saber rattling benefited from comments by participants at the 2011 European Consortium for Political Research Joint Sessions Workshop on Political Institutions and Political Violence in St. Gallen, Switzerland. Kristian Gleditsch (University of Essex), Simon Hug (University of Geneva), Matthew Wilson (Penn State University), and Pippa Norris (Harvard University) were especially helpful.

I am also indebted to those who provided research assistance for this project. The data on presidential saber rattling were initially machine-coded using PERL. However, validation of these machine-coded data required considerable human effort. The bulk of the human effort was supplied by Han Soo Lee, Stephen Huss, and Clayton Webb. Note that a more extended treatment of the results reported in Chapter 5 concerning the economic consequences of presidential saber rattling are reported in the *American Journal of Political Science* (Wood 2009b). I also thank three anonymous reviewers for their insightful comments, most of which are implemented in the final manuscript.

In the interest of future research, I encourage replication of the work reported here, as well as further application of the data. Thus, all of the data on presidential saber rattling reported in the empirical parts of the book are available on my Web site at Texas A&M University. The Web address is currently http://people.tamu.edu/~b-wood. However, a Google search for my name should always find the data.

Robert Dreesen of Cambridge University Press was helpful in advising me on how to pitch the manuscript. He encouraged me to write in a style that would be inclusive of readers at all levels. Accordingly, I have focused on substance rather than minor technical issues that might excite those in the methodological community. I hope the materials in this book are not so complex as to deter serious readers. If so, then Robert deserves some credit. He was a pleasure to work with as an editor, especially in securing expert reviewers and facilitating the review and acceptance process.

Financially, this research was supported by Texas A&M University through a College of Liberal Arts Cornerstone Fellowship from 2007 through 2011. I thank former Dean Charles A. Johnson for recognizing the importance of rewarding faculty scholarship. I am also deeply appreciative of my department and university for their supportive intellectual environment.

Finally, I thank those closest to me for their understanding and support for my career and research. My wife Patricia continues to help me in every possible way. I dedicate this book to our two grandchildren, Nathaniel David and Rebekah Joy Wood. If I had known how much fun it is to have grandchildren, I would have had them first.

I

# Presidential Saber Rattling in the Early American Republic

On May 16, 1797, President John Adams delivered a message to a special session of Congress about developing hostilities with France. In his speech the president expressed outrage over French depredation of American shipping. He indignantly described insults by the French government toward the new American ambassador to Paris. The president also accused the French of attempting to "produce [partisan] divisions fatal to our peace." He stated that "Such attempts ought to be repelled with a decision which shall convince France and the world that we are not a degraded people, humiliated under a colonial spirit of fear and sense of inferiority, fitted to be the miserable instruments of foreign influence, and regardless of national honor, character, and interest." Further showing his pugnacity, Adams called on Congress to implement "effectual measures of defense" by increasing U.S. naval power and creating a provisional army capable of repelling any foreign invader (Richardson 1907a).

Of course, the French had earlier been an important American ally. In 1778 the two countries signed the Treaties of Alliance and Commerce, binding them together in perpetual friendship and support. These treaties were the basis for French assistance critical to the success of the American Revolution. The Commerce Treaty established the principle that "free ships make free goods," meaning that neither country would attack the other's maritime commerce. Indeed, the two countries had promised to protect one another's shipping from mutual enemies.

Yet the French were attacking American ships as early as 1793, with intensified hostility as President Adams took office (Elkins and McKitrick 1993, 537–38). What caused this turnabout? The French Revolution, an ensuing European war, and American ratification of the Jay Treaty with Great Britain were all important factors. The French Revolution, which began in 1789, had overthrown the French monarch, Louis XVI, who had originally signed the Treaties of Alliance and Commerce. The new French government may no longer have felt obligated by the treaties.

The upheavals of the French Revolution threatened monarchies across Europe, both philosophically and physically. In April 1792 the new French republic declared war on the Austrian Empire. In January 1793 the French executed their former monarch, and during this same month Spain and Portugal entered the war as part of the anti-French coalition. In February the French declared war on Great Britain and the Dutch. The French revolutionary spirit directly challenged the divine right of sovereigns, and those challenged responded accordingly. All of Europe was engulfed in a war that seemed remote from American interests.

There were, of course, factions in the United States that favored the French in their European war. Democratic-Republicans, mainly from the South, were sympathetic, as were various private Jacobin societies in both the North and the South. French Ambassador Edmund-Charles Genet was sent to the United States to cultivate support by soliciting money, provisions, and even an invasion force to attack Spanish Florida (Elkins and McKitrick 1993, 330–36; Ferling 1992, 337–38; McCullough 2001, 444–45; Sharp 1993, 69–91). American support for the French would, in fact, have been consistent with the Treaties of Alliance and Commerce.

However, most Federalists preferred stronger ties with Great Britain. Such ties were more conducive to commerce beneficial to the mercantile interests of the Northeast. President George Washington also viewed honoring the 1778 treaties as dangerous to a fledgling nation in need of unity and stability. He did not view U.S. involvement in the European war as consistent with these goals, especially with emerging partisan differences about whether to favor the French or British. Therefore, he declared a policy of neutrality, effectively disregarding the Treaties of Alliance and Commerce.

Washington's decision to assert American neutrality greatly offended the French, who believed that the United States should be its natural ally. Their earlier support of the American Revolution and presumption that the American and French Revolutions were similar in spirit formed the basis for this belief. With the failure of Ambassador Genet to secure American support, relations with France deteriorated (Ferling 1992, 339). Rubbing salt in the wound, President Washington sent an emissary to Great Britain to negotiate a treaty with the British. On August 14, 1795, the president signed the Jay Treaty, which effectively normalized trade relations with Britain and resolved various foreign policy disputes. The Jay Treaty was viewed by the French as favoring the British in their European war and as a violation of the principle of neutrality.

In response to these developments, the French Directory (the executive leadership of the new French republic) issued a decree on July 4, 1796. They announced their intention of dealing with neutral vessels in the same manner as London had earlier treated such vessels (Elkins and McKitrick 1993, 537–38; Ferling 1992, 339–42). In other words, American shipping would be seized and confiscated. In the spring of 1797 Secretary of State Timothy Pickering reported that the French had seized more than 300 American ships since the decree. American seamen had been wounded. There were reports that "French captors . . . had tortured [an] American captain in an unsuccessful attempt to make him say that he was carrying British cargo" (McCullough 2001, 486–87). As President Washington left office in March 1797 and John Adams assumed the presidency, the conflict with France had boiled over.

Diplomatic relations had also deteriorated. At the time of Adams's inauguration, Washington had recalled the U.S. ambassador, James Monroe, and appointed Charles Coteworth Pinckney of South Carolina to fill the post in Paris. Upon arrival, Pinckney learned that the French Directory had not only refused to accept him as ambassador but ordered him out of the country as well. He left for the Dutch republic to await instructions from the president (Elkins and McKitrick 1993, 550–51). When President Adams received word of the French treatment of Ambassador Pinckney, there was also word of new French seizures of American shipping. Additionally, the French Directory issued a new decree in March 1797 explicitly abrogating the French-American treaties of 1778 and ordering the seizure of neutral vessels transporting goods bound for Great Britain (Ferling 1992, 342).

This was the foreign policy environment within which President Adams made his address to the special session of Congress. In his message, the president sought to give an impression of strength and resolve in the face of French hostility. However, he did not seek war. He stated, "It is my sincere desire . . . to preserve peace and friendship with all nations; and believing that neither the honor nor the interest of the United States absolutely forbid the repetition of advances for securing these desirable objects with France, I shall institute a fresh attempt at negotiation, and shall not fail to promote and accelerate an accommodation on terms compatible with the rights, duties, interests, and honor of the nation" (Richardson 1907a).

The president's special message to Congress was like the well-known presidential seal, an American eagle with arrows in one talon and an olive branch in the other. The president engaged in saber rattling toward the French, presumably to project American strength and resolve in defending her interests. At the same time he expressed a desire for peace.

President Adams had concluded even before his inauguration that he would send a new mission to France to negotiate an agreement similar to the Jay Treaty. He tried to convince prominent Democratic-Republicans, Thomas Jefferson (his vice president) and James Madison, to undertake the mission. However, partisan Federalists in his cabinet adamantly opposed their appointment. Furthermore, Jefferson, Madison, and other prominent Democratic-Republicans refused to undertake the mission (Elkins and McKitrick 1993, 541–44; Ferling 1992, 341). Democratic-Republicans had strongly opposed the Jay Treaty with Great Britain and believed that Adams was insincere in his effort toward reconciliation with France.

Nevertheless, in the months after his speech the president did send a new set of emissaries to France. The representatives consisted of Charles Coteworth Pinckney (still waiting in the Dutch republic), John Marshall (a Federalist judge from Virginia), and Elbridge Gerry (a trusted friend and Democratic-Republican from the president's home state of Massachusetts). The charge to the delegation was to negotiate an agreement giving France the same commercial rights as had been given to Great Britain under the Jay Treaty. However, the president insisted on an American right to neutral trade with whatever nation it pleased. The diplomats were also told explicitly that the United States would extend neither aid nor loans to France as long as it remained at war, because to do so would involve the nation in that war (Elkins and McKitrick 1993, 555–61, 562–63; Ferling 1992, 344–45). In July and August 1797 Marshall and Gerry sailed to Holland to join Pinckney.

Meanwhile, President Adams left Philadelphia for four months to await word of the outcome. While waiting he hoped for the best but expected the worst. During the third week of November 1797 he returned to the capitol to deliver another message to Congress. His speech indicated little hope for success, and he again asked Congress to approve his request for a naval and military buildup (Richardson 1907b). As with his earlier request, Congress remained unconvinced of the urgency of the situation and did little (Ferling 1992, 348–52).

Then, on March 4, 1798, word arrived from the envoys that they had again been rebuffed. French Foreign Minister Charles Maurice de Talleyrand-Périgord refused to receive the American diplomats without preconditions. Talleyrand asked for an official apology for President Adams's alleged warlike remarks in his May 16, 1797, special message to Congress. Furthermore, he demanded that all unpaid French debts contracted to American suppliers be assumed by the U.S. government. All claims for French spoliations of American commerce were to be assumed by the U.S. government. They sought extension of a $6 million loan before negotiations could begin. There was also an implicit threat of war if America failed to comply with these demands. Finally, and perhaps the worst of it, Talleyrand demanded a bribe of £50,000 sterling as a precondition for negotiations to begin (Elkins and McKitrick 1993, 571–79; Ferling 1992, 352–53).

President Adams was infuriated by what he perceived as French malevolence. His initial reaction was to prepare a militant and raging message to Congress denouncing the outrageous French demands. However, the message he actually delivered struck a more moderate tone. His address to Congress on March 19, 1798, was terse and sought to guard against overreaction. He said, "it is incumbent on me to declare that I perceive no ground of expectation that the objects of [the envoys'] mission can be accomplished on terms compatible with the safety, the honor, or the essential interests of the nation."

The president again urged Congress to adopt measures "for the protection of our seafaring and commercial citizens, for the defense of any exposed portions of our territory, for replenishing our arsenals, establishing foundries and military manufactures, and to provide such efficient revenue as will... defray extraordinary expenses... occasioned by depredations on our commerce" (Richardson 1907c). Contrary to past policy, the president also unilaterally authorized the arming of American merchant vessels. However, what was most important about the president's speech is what it did not say. It did not divulge the insulting nature of the French response to the American peace mission (Elkins and McKitrick 1993, 585–86; Ferling 1992, 353–54).

Congress's reaction was again less than what the president wanted. Jefferson referred privately to Adams's message as "insane." Democratic-Republicans sought to remove the president's discretionary authority to arm merchant vessels. They believed that Adams sought to provoke a war with France and had exaggerated French malevolence. Accordingly, Democratic-Republicans demanded that he release the envoys' actual dispatches. Federalists also demanded the dispatches but for a different reason. They suspected the dispatches would reveal behavior more malicious than the president had depicted (Elkins and McKitrick 1993, 587–88; Ferling 1992, 353–54).

Adams complied and gave the dispatches to Congress. However, he urged in his cover letter that they be considered in private until members of Congress could fully assess their implications. After considering the dispatches, Democratic-Republicans voted to keep them quiet, fearing they would provoke a war. However, Federalists immediately published 50,000 copies and distributed them as handbills across the nation. The threats and insulting behavior of the French became public knowledge (Beschloss 2007, 40; Elkins and McKitrick 1993, 587–88; Ferling 1992, 354–55; McCullough 2001, 496–99).

This episode, known in diplomatic history as the XYZ Affair (with X, Y, and Z representing the concealed names of the three French diplomats delivering the outrageous demands), had important implications for relations with France and the domestic status of the American president. After publication of the XYZ dispatches, Federalists clamored for war. In contrast, many Democratic-Republicans tried to explain away French behavior as a natural response to Adams's earlier bellicosity. The "lower class of people," as Abigail Adams had begun to refer to most Americans, were "now roused" and abandoning their "Jacobean" leanings toward the French republic. A period of intense public acrimony toward the French ensued, as did a sense of national unity and newfound fondness for the president (Elkins and McKitrick 1993, 589–90; Ferling 1992, 354–55; McCullough 2001, 499–502).

Adams's popularity surged as he began to speak hawkishly in public (McCullough 2001, 499–502). Between April and August 1798 the president wrote seventy-one separate responses to patriotic letters he had received. Many of these letters were printed in newspapers or published as handbills. His responses were consistently truculent (DeConde 1966, 80–84; Elkins and McKitrick 1993, 588–89). For example, he suggested that it would be cowardly not to respond to the French insults. He told one group, "[N]either Justice nor

Moderation, can secure us from Participation in the War." To another he said war is "less Evil than national Dishonour." He consistently urged his readers to adopt a "warlike character" and noted that the American people would lose their "Character, moral, political, and martial" if they did not resist (Ferling 1992, 357). French songs and support for French republicanism disappeared and were replaced by Federalist banners and cries for war.

People paraded on Adams's behalf. Patriotic marches were played in the president's honor at concerts and before theater performances. When Adams traveled, he was accorded "every mark of distinguished attention." According to one Federalist, when he went to New York in the summer of 1798, he received the "most splendid" reception ever given a political leader, former President Washington notwithstanding. Some people believed that Adams's stature was now equal to Washington's and that "no man... will go down to posterity with greater luster." President Adams reveled in this adulation and began to appear in a full military uniform with a sword strapped to his side. His public rhetoric consistently referenced the patriotic sacrifices of earlier generations. He noted that these forebearers would feel "disgust and Resentment" if America did not act on his recommendations (Ferling 1992, 356).

Against this backdrop, newspapers published a rumor that an invasion armada was gathering off the French coast and would soon sail for America. They also reported that French operatives were inciting a slave rebellion in South Carolina and that secret agents of the French government had been sent to torch the nation's capitol and assassinate the nation's leaders (DeConde 1966, 84–89; Ferling 1992, 356; Sharp 1993, 174–75).

It was within this hysterical milieu that Congress finally enacted a series of defensive measures. Beginning in April 1798, Congress gave the president everything he had requested, and much that he had not asked for. Provision was made for completion of three large frigates that were already under construction. Congress authorized the acquisition of twelve new sloops of war and ten galleys for the protection of shallow coastal waters. Twelve additional warships were authorized in June and three more in July. Money was appropriated to fortify harbors and to create foundries for the manufacture of artillery. An independent Department of the Navy was established to oversee the development of U.S. naval power. The new navy was authorized by Congress to attack French vessels preying on American shipping and could retake any American ships already captured. Congress also commissioned 1,000 privateers to capture or repel French vessels.

Furthermore, an embargo was imposed on all trade with France and its colonies, and all treaties with France were formally abrogated. A standing army of 10,000 men was created, with provision for increasing it to 50,000 if the president deemed necessary. President Adams was also authorized to call up 80,000 militiamen if the need arose (Elkins and McKitrick 1993, 589–90; Ferling 1992, 356). Congress levied a tax of $2 million to pay for the defensive buildup, a measure that later proved unpopular. The Federalists also enacted legislation to curtail domestic dissent, the Alien and Sedition Acts, which President Adams later used to silence his Democratic-Republican critics (Elkins and McKitrick 1993, 589–90).

The aftermath of the XYZ Affair would have readily enabled President Adams to call for a congressional declaration of war. To be sure, such a request would have been granted because of strong public sentiment in that direction. Federalists controlled Congress and were more inclined toward war than peace (McCullough 2001, 504). However, President Adams from the beginning did not seek war. Rather, the president wanted to produce an image of strength and resolve in the face of French hostility.

Adams favored a strong navy to make the United States independent of European powers. However, he was distrustful of a standing army, fearing it might potentially endanger the republic. Indeed, he saw little need for a standing army. In October 1798 he revealed privately to Secretary of War James McHenry that "[T]here is no more prospect of seeing a French army here, than there is in Heaven" (Ferling 1992, 369). Thus, despite his earlier bellicose rhetoric and success in persuading Congress to build up American defenses, the president actually believed that a French invasion was unlikely (Elkins and McKitrick 1993, 614–15; Ferling 1992, 372–80).

Although there was no declaration of war, a state of "quasi-war" did exist between 1797 and 1800. Before the U.S. naval buildup, the French ravaged American shipping at will. During 1798 several naval engagements occurred in U.S. coastal waters, demonstrating the prowess of the new American navy, but there was still significant danger to American shipping. However, in August 1798 the British navy under Admiral Horatio Nelson defeated French naval forces at the Battle of the Nile. After this, the French were no longer able to muster sufficient naval power to dominate the American coast. There were at least ten ship-to-ship naval actions after this, the last occurring in November 1799 (DeConde 1966, 124–30, 161).

During this same month a change occurred in France that significantly altered relations between the two countries. Napoleon Bonaparte led a successful coup d'état against the French republic that effectively ended the French Revolution. This event changed French policy toward the United States and other neutral powers. Napoleon desired the support of neutral Denmark and Sweden for his upcoming military ventures. Accordingly, he stated a new policy in December 1799 that neutral ships make for neutral goods. French depredations of American shipping fell precipitously after the new policy.

American diplomats in The Hague (William Vans Murray) and Berlin (John Quincy Adams) sent word to President Adams that France wanted to negotiate. Murray reported that a war on the United States would be unpopular in France. Furthermore, it had become clear that French aggression was counterproductive. French malevolence had shifted American public opinion from pro- to anti-French. America had been driven toward the British.

Thus, Talleyrand (still the French foreign minister) sent a letter to President Adams stating that "every plenipotentiary whom the Government of the United States will send to France . . . will undoubtedly be received with the respect due to the representative of a free, independent, and powerful country" (see also DeConde 1966, 174–180; Ferling 1992, 375). In response, President Adams again dispatched official peace envoys to France.

Adams's "about-face" on war with France was politically costly. The president had aroused public passions. He had successfully prepared the nation militarily. As a result, Federalist partisans and the president enjoyed renewed electoral strength. However, the Federalists' presumed leader suddenly reversed course to take away the most potent issue for the 1800 elections. Predictably, many Federalists viewed Adams as a traitor for quenching the flames of a pending war. Adams's turnabout also produced an image of unstable judgment. At one moment the president was saber rattling; at another he was extending an olive branch of peace.

As expressed by Ferling (1992, 372–95), Adams's fellow partisans and much of the public were "thunderstruck." According to Deconde (1966, 181), one Federalist said, "there is not a Sound mind from Maine to Georgia that has not been shocked by it." Adams must have been duped by "the wiles of French diplomacy." Theodore Sedgwick, the Federalist Senate leader, decried Adams's decision as "the most embarrassing and ruinous measure." One Federalist was so angered by Adams's turnabout that he threatened the president's life: "Assassination shall be your lot" (DeConde 1966, 182).

Nevertheless, American diplomats met with Napoleon in March 1800, and negotiations ensued. The Treaty of Mortefontaine was finalized in October to end the "quasi-war" and restore friendly relations. However, word of the successful negotiations did not reach the United States in time for President Adams to benefit in the election of 1800 (Ferling 1992, 407–08). Absent this information the peace mission and resulting treaty were not seen as the success they actually were.

Dissension among Federalists over the need for war, as well as the unpopularity of higher taxes and curtailed civil liberties, cost President Adams significant support. Federalist leader Alexander Hamilton backed Charles Pinckney instead of Adams in the 1800 presidential election, resulting in a split that gave Thomas Jefferson the presidency (Ferling 1992, 396–405). Thus, efforts to resolve the dispute with France were successful but politically costly to the nation's second president.

## President Adams's Saber Rattling as an Object of Scientific Analysis

The preceding vignette describing French and American hostility toward one another during the early American republic provides a theoretical hook for this more general study of presidential saber rattling. Much of what occurred during the Adams administration foreshadows the modern causes and consequences of presidential saber rattling. President Adams's entire adminis-tration was occupied with resolving the French crisis. Thus, his behavior is itself worthy of analysis.

### Was John Adams a "Statesman" President?

President Adams spoke belligerently toward France on many occasions during his presidency. What motivated his behavior? Was his saber rattling grounded in just causes and a strong conception of the national interest, or was it con-trived and rooted in partisanship or self-interest? Did President Adams live up to expectations for presidents behaving in a statesman-like manner?

An argument can be made that John Adams did, in fact, behave as a states-man in his dealings with France. The nation faced *just*, rather than *pretended*, causes for war. John Jay (1788b), writing in Federalist #3, stated, "The JUST causes of war, for the most part, arise either from violation of treaties or from direct violence." America experienced both conditions during the crisis with France. The French disregarded the Treaties of Alliance and Commerce and were attacking American shipping.

Of course, it could be argued that America violated the treaties first by declaring neutrality and not providing support to the French in their European war. However, it is also clear that the treaties were not negotiated with the revolutionaries in France and may not have been binding on either French or American behavior. These arguments aside, France was attacking American shipping, and this was just cause for the president to respond.

The historical record also provides evidence that President Adams's saber rattling was driven by concern for the nation. The president wanted to build a stronger national defense to deter foreign aggression. To do so, he needed to build a case before Congress and the public that there was an external threat. Without perceptions of an external threat, it was unlikely that Congress and the public would have been supportive. Thus, President Adams's bellicosity may have been driven by his oath to defend the nation against foreign enemies.

Along these same lines, the president may have wanted to bolster the nation's foreign policy credibility through saber rattling. Projecting an image of strength and resolve sends a signal to foreign adversaries. The president was saying, "Don't Tread on Me!" Furthermore, it was not only the president who bene-fited from higher presidential popularity and greater national unity because of saber rattling. These domestic outcomes also benefited the nation at large. A popular American president supported by a unified nation is a powerful tool in the president's foreign policy arsenal. Indeed, increased presidential credibility might have potentially deterred French aggression and leveraged his bargain-ing power. Thus, there were also foreign policy incentives for presidential bellicosity.

However, despite there being just cause for belligerence toward France, it also seemed clear to the president that war was not in the nation's best interest. France was a Great Power, whereas America was a fledgling nation with a fragile political and economic system. The outcome of a war with France was, in all likelihood, predetermined. War would have accentuated political divisions. It would have devastated the American economy. It may also have resulted in loss of territory or independence. President Adams recognized these possibilities and behaved accordingly.

Despite his saber rattling, the historical record suggests that President Adams actually sought peace. In his special message to Congress on May 16, 1797, the president spoke with indignation about French behavior and called for defensive measures. However, he also extended an olive branch by expressing his intention to send a new peace mission. President Adams made a strong effort to staff the new mission with representatives friendly to the French. However, he was unsuccessful because of resistance from both political parties.

Then, in March 1798 when it became clear that the new peace mission had failed, the president addressed Congress to report the failure. Despite his personal outrage at the French, he downplayed their malevolence by giving a speech that was more moderate than he initially planned. Upon being required to release the XYZ dispatches to Congress, the president asked that they be considered in private until their implications could be fully considered. It was only after the XYZ dispatches became public that he began to speak more openly of war.

Finally, once the president received word in November 1799 that an accommodation might finally be possible, he pursued this option vigorously. This was despite vitriolic opposition from his own political party and the obvious consequences for his personal prestige and political fortunes.

Viewed in this light, President Adams behaved as a statesman in his dealings with France. He put the interests of the nation at large ahead of passion, personal glory, partisanship, reelection, and the need for domestic support.

### Was John Adams a Support-Seeking Partisan?

An argument can also be made that President Adams's behavior was driven by self-interest and partisanship. Consider some factual evidence in this regard. French treatment of neutral American shipping was barely different from that of the British. Even before the Jay Treaty, "The French had been ignoring the [1778] treaty's 'free ships, free goods' stipulations off and on ever since the outbreak of hostilities in 1793" (Elkins and McKitrick 1993, 538). Furthermore, near the end of the crisis, a story was published showing that, on the basis of insurance claims, "American merchants had actually suffered greater shipping losses at the hands of the British Royal Navy than to the Directory's prowling frigates" (Ferling 1992, 375–76). Yet the president did not talk of war with the British. If both the British and French were attacking American ships, then why were only the French singled out by the president as the enemy?

Consistent with these facts, Democratic-Republicans believed from the start that President Adams was driven by partisanship and an abiding hatred of the French and their revolution. The president was, after all, a Federalist, and

Federalists preferred aristocracy and the British over the anarchical tendencies of the new French regime. Furthermore, Adams disapproved of Roman Catholicism and abhorred the radicalism of the French Revolution (Ferling 1992, 340–41, 364–65). He had earlier written a string of lengthy newspaper essays, titled *Discourses on Davila*, about the evils of an unbalanced democracy such as he believed was occurring in France (Elkins and McKitrick 1993, 536; Ferling 1992, 306–307).

President Adams's assertions that the nation needed to be ready for war seemed to Democratic-Republicans like a provocation to war. In other words, they believed that the president was "INVITING war," rather than attempting to "repress and discourage it" as warned against by John Jay in Federalist #4. After the president's May 16, 1797, special message to Congress, "Republicans blasted the president's course as certain to lead to war." James Madison referred to Adams as "our hot-headed Executive" (Ferling 1992, 344–45). Thomas Jefferson persistently "carped at Adams's pugnacity" (Ferling 1992, 354) and thought he "was conspiring with the 'English faction' to wage a war against France in order to help Federalists at the polls" (Beschloss 2007, 37). Democratic-Republicans generally believed that the president had succumbed to war hawks within his own party (DeConde 1966, 26).

Indeed, it is easy to imagine that if Democratic-Republicans had been the majority party in Congress, then the president's bellicosity toward the French would have been greatly diminished. Under such an institutional alignment there would have been less prospect of attaining the proposed defense buildup. As a result, there would have been less reason for presidential truculence and diminished thrust toward war. In other words, the president may have been emboldened by having strong Federalist support in Congress.

However, there were also disadvantages for the president to having strong Federalist support. Early in his administration, President Adams made a fateful decision to retain the same cabinet members who had served under Washington. He believed that retaining these officials would make the transition easier and less divisive than selecting advisors across emerging party lines (McCullough 2001, 471–72). As a result of this decision, the advice the president received throughout the crisis was more consistent with partisan Federalist preferences than the interests of the nation at large.

The president sought advice from his Federalist cabinet before the May 16, 1797, special message to Congress, and much of that advice was incorporated into the message (DeConde 1966, 21–24). The Federalist cabinet was also important to Adams's selection of representatives for the 1797 peace mission to France. Again, the president first approached Jefferson, his Democratic-Republican vice president and a well-known Francophile. When Jefferson refused, he then suggested another prominent Democratic-Republican, James Madison. Jefferson later reported that Madison had also declined to be part of the delegation. Regardless, the cabinet rejected Madison out of hand, even threatening to resign if Madison or other prominent Democratic-Republicans were members of the delegation. Ultimately, the president was constrained by partisanship, resulting in a peace mission less friendly to the French than the president may have preferred (but see DeConde 1966, 28–29; Ferling 1992, 344–45).

As the crisis escalated after the release of the XYZ dispatches, the president's Federalist cabinet increasingly pushed for war. Then, after the president received word in November 1799 that France was willing to negotiate, Federalists within the cabinet sought to destroy the peace initiative. They first argued against sending a new peace mission to France. They also attempted to halt the mission through administrative delay and excuses (Beschloss 2007, 53–56; Ferling 1992, 383). Once it became obvious that the president would again negotiate with the French, they attempted to "stack" the delegation with Federalists (Ferling 1992, 380). Having had enough of their maneuvers, President Adams fired the two most obstructionist, Secretary of War James McHenry and Secretary of State Timothy Pickering, replacing them with advisors more favorable to peace.

Federalist officials within Adams's cabinet seemingly took their marching orders from Alexander Hamilton, the de facto leader of the Federalist party (e.g., see Ferling 1992, 333–34, 343–44, 352, 381–83). All during the crisis, Hamilton wrote essays for the press warning about the danger the nation faced from the French Directory and beating the drums of war. It was Hamiltonian Federalists in Congress who released the XYZ dispatches to the press and public (Beschloss 2007, 40). Hamiltonian Federalists also succeeded in substituting their program for that of the president (DeConde 1966, 76–77). The Federalist program went much further, including nullification of all treaties with France, an embargo of French goods, the creation of a large standing army, and efforts to quell domestic dissent through the Alien and Sedition Acts. They even blocked efforts to adjourn Congress early so that they could keep the war spirit strong (DeConde 1966, 95). Federalist partisans sought to "destroy whatever remained of the old friendship with France, for after all she was now the enemy" (DeConde 1966, 91).

Joining the Federalist contagion, President Adams intensified his saber rattling after the XYZ Affair became public, perhaps as a result of his own partisan fervor. As stated by Ferling, "But during the spring of 1798 Adams appeared to change. The pressure upon [the president] from within his own party was enormous. . . . The blandishments and the cheers were a heady experience, perhaps too much to resist for one who had so often and so fervently longed to win attention as a soldier" (1992, 355–56).

Beyond influences stemming from passion and partisanship, the president was also buffeted by the press. The press was not neutral during this era but an extension of the political parties. The most prominent among the Democratic-Republican newspapers was the Philadelphia *Aurora*, edited by Benjamin Franklin Bache, a grandson of Benjamin Franklin. In almost daily attacks, the *Aurora* belittled the president as "The President by Three Votes,"

"His Rotundity," a hypocrite, a tool of the British, and "a man divested of his senses" (McCullough 2001, 485). The president's speech to the special session of Congress on May 16, 1797, was labeled a "war speech" (Bache, 17 May 1797). Following the speech the president's selection of representatives for the peace mission was heavily criticized by the *Aurora*: "Can it be supposed that success will attend this negotiation when the persons who are nominated, will carry with them the temper of a British faction, instead of the temper and sensibility of the people of the United States?" (Bache, 2 June 1797).

As the XYZ Affair unfolded, the *Aurora* published a letter from Talleyrand that constituted the French response to Federalist reactions to the XYZ dispatches (Bache, 16 June 1798). President Adams and most Federalists viewed publication of Talleyrand's letter as seditious. Ten days after publishing the letter, Bache was arrested and charged under the Sedition Act. This was despite the fact that the legislation had not even passed Congress to become law.

The president and especially the first lady were incensed by the almost daily attacks of the press. Accordingly, President Adams signed deportation orders under the Naturalization Act for editors from the *Aurora* and *New York Time Piece* (Diggins 2003, 110–13). All total, the Adams administration secured fourteen indictments under the Sedition Act, six against the most prominent Democratic-Republican newspapers. Circulation among these newspapers fell precipitously, and many others moderated their anti-administration tone under the potential for indictment (DeConde 1966, 78–79). The majority of these indictments occurred in 1798 and 1799, with most of the trials occurring just before the 1800 election. This timing may have been strategic, given Federalist efforts to keep the war furor flowing before the election (Ferling 1992, 366–67).

On the other side was an equally partisan and hawkish Federalist press. The Federalist answer to Bache's *Aurora* was the Philadelphia newspaper *Porcupine's Gazette*, owned by an English printer and bookseller who wrote under the pen name "Peter Porcupine." He openly urged war with France, and the alliance with Britain that was likely to result (McCullough 2001, 478–79).

Like the *Gazette*, most American newspapers relied almost exclusively on British sources for their European news. This meant that American readers often saw the crisis as interpreted through a British lens. After the XYZ dispatches broke, public hysteria against France was greatly amplified by the Federalist press. "Federalist newspapers kept the people angry and built up the mood for war. Some extremists, arguing that the best defense is the offense, urged preparations for an offensive war against France" (DeConde 1966, 78).

Within this media frenzy, the president used the press to his advantage. As noted earlier, he wrote numerous published letters and pamphlets urging war, questioning the loyalty of those opposing it, and extolling the patriotism of his supporters. Thus, one could argue that the president used the press to manipulate the ongoing Federalist contagion to his advantage. This interpretation again suggests that the president was caught up in escalating passions and hatred of the French.

Consistent with this interpretation, President Adams seemingly had a strong need for public approbation and the type of fame enjoyed by war heroes. He was accused throughout his career of being vain, overly ambitious, and in a quest for personal glory. He relished the recognition that came from public office and incessantly sought to raise his public standing. He even admitted in his diary that he was compelled by vanity to search for fame (Ferling 1992, 19).

Adams had achieved personal fame as a diplomat and politician, but he also longed for the sort of adulation bestowed on President Washington (Beschloss 2007, 41–42). During the American Revolution he was always dissatisfied with the role he played as a diplomat, secretly preferring to participate as a soldier. The soldier, he said in his diary, will always "Wear the Lawrells." His generation lionized and attributed to soldiers "the traits it esteemed as proper for manly behavior, making the warrior the embodiment of strident masculinity.... Adams shared these views about soldiers... and he yearned for the recognition that was a soldier's reward" (Ferling 1992, 132–33). Thus, the president's pugnacious response to the French crisis may have been an outgrowth of his innate desire for soldierly glory.

Viewed in this light one could argue that President Adams was a support-seeking partisan. He both responded and contributed to the frenzy generated by the media. The president used saber rattling strategically in a quest to achieve personal goals, approbation, and soldierly glory. Thus, the president may have manufactured pretended causes for war, just as Jay admonished against in Federalists #3 and #4.

## The Complex Consequences of Presidential Saber Rattling

The Adams vignette also highlights some of the potential consequences of presidential saber rattling. Some of these consequences are obvious. Presidential saber rattling can increase public, institutional, and media support for the president and policies. Saber rattling can also potentially affect the behavior of nations being threatened. However, these domestic and foreign policy consequences are more complex than is suggested by a simple analysis.

Competing benefits and costs contribute to this complexity. Presidents may benefit from their saber rattling through increased public, institutional, and media support. Increased domestic support can, in turn, bolster the international standing of the president. The president's threats may then be more credible to the nation being threatened. Higher presidential credibility may then increase the likelihood that the threat will be successful in altering an adversary's behavior.

However, these benefits may be offset over the long term by costs if presidents fail to follow through with their threats. A failure to follow through may actually reduce future public, institutional, and media support for the president and policies. Such failures to follow through may also make threats less credible to the nation being threatened. Reduced credibility lowers the likelihood that threats will be effective. Thus, leaders engaging in saber rattling are subject to a complexity of consequences due to competing audience benefits and costs.

Furthermore, it is important to recognize that causality of consequences can be multidirectional in both the domestic and foreign arenas. In the foreign arena, saber rattling may occur within a game of "tit for tat" escalation in which nations threaten in mutual response to one another. A threat by one nation is likely to be answered by a threat from the other nation. As with French-American relations in the early American republic, an escalation of hostility can then occur.

Relatedly, foreign policy threats can have important consequences within the nation being threatened. The nation being threatened can acquire greater national unity and patriotism, and the threatened leader's public standing can improve. Such outcomes bolster the threatened leader's credibility both domestically and externally. In turn, these complex consequences can affect the behavior of the country making the threat. Observing the reaction of the country being threatened, the threatening country may then need to adjust its behavior to produce more optimal outcomes.

### The Complex Consequences of Saber Rattling during the Adams Presidency

The American president and French Directory engaged in a mutual war of words and actions between 1797 and 1799, presumably to accomplish their respective foreign policy goals. Was bellicose French behavior during this period a consequence of American presidential behavior? Or was American presidential behavior a consequence of bellicose French behavior? Did the causal relation run in both directions?

In response to American behavior, the French issued various threatening decrees and demands. After Washington's declaration of neutrality and the Jay Treaty, the French Directory announced its intention to deal with American vessels by seizing and confiscating them. Soon after President Adams assumed office, a second decree was issued by the French explicitly abrogating the French-American Treaties of 1778 and ordering the seizure of neutral vessels transporting goods bound for Britain. Then, after President Adams made his alleged "war speech" to the special session of Congress and sent new peace emissaries, the French Directory again responded with hostile demands, even threatening war if America did not "cave in" to its requirements for monetary support and a bribe.

However, there were unanticipated consequences of French hostility toward America. Following the XYZ Affair Americans held the French and their Revolution in lower esteem. The American press became anti-French. Many Americans who had previously been supportive of the French Revolution became angry at French behavior toward their country. French threats and actions produced more American national unity, a public outcry for war, and stronger support for the president. Furthermore, their behavior ultimately drove America closer to the British. These outcomes from French hostility toward America suggest the important principle that confrontational foreign policy can have adverse consequences. Rather than securing national interests, saber rattling can actually be destructive of national interests.

During this same period, President Adams also issued various threatening remarks in response to the French. On May 16, 1797, the president called on Congress to act forcefully to confront diplomatic insults and French attacks on American shipping. He called for "effectual measures of defense" by increasing U.S. naval power and creating a provisional army capable of repelling any foreign invader (Richardson 1907a). The president addressed Congress again in November 1797 expressing pessimism about French intentions and asking again for a military buildup to prepare for potential war (Richardson 1907b). On March 4, 1798, after it was clear that the peace mission had failed, the president again urgently asked Congress for defensive preparations. Then, after the XYZ dispatches were released, the president embarked on a continuous campaign of war talk.

The president viewed his pugnacity toward the French and the resulting military buildup as an expression of strength and resolve in pursuit of American interests. However, just as there were adverse consequences for French hostility toward the United States, there were also adverse consequences for the American president's posturing toward the French. The French Directory was highly offended by the president's May 16, 1797, special message to Congress. They demanded an official apology for the president's remarks as a precondition for further negotiations. In response to the speech they also issued a battery of new decrees and demands. Additionally, French depredations of American shipping continued and increased through time. Thus it is clear that President Adams's posturing toward the French actually provoked the French Directory, rather than making it more sympathetic to American concerns.

There were both benefits and costs associated with President Adams's saber rattling. The president benefited by rallying his fellow partisans, the press, and public opinion against what he perceived as French malevolence. As a result, he secured all that he had asked for in defensive preparations. The ensuing public and congressional support made the president's foreign policy seem more credible to the French. America was viewed as stronger and more resolute. Accordingly, the French became more receptive to a peaceful resolution of the crisis (e.g., see Beschloss 2007, 59; Ferling 1992, 373–77). Thus, the president accomplished his foreign policy goal through the strategic use of saber rattling.

However, the president also subsequently bore heavy costs from a domestic audience disappointed about the president's failure to follow through with a threatened war. President Adams built up public fervor and expectations for war. When he reversed course, his credibility suffered with fellow partisans and the public. He was judged a failure as an unstable, weak, and vacillating leader (e.g., see Beschloss 2007, 61–64). The result was that the president was punished in the election of 1800. Audience costs from earlier saber rattling made President Adams the first one-term president in American history.

### Research Questions Flowing from the Adams Vignette

This introductory chapter has developed a vignette highlighting presidential saber rattling in the early American republic. The theoretical principles apparent from this vignette foreshadow the more systematic work to be presented in later chapters. Indeed, repeated reference will be made to the theoretical principles emerging from the Adams vignette as we examine the causes and consequences of saber rattling for modern presidents.

A number of research questions flow from the preceding analysis. Why did President Adams engage in saber rattling toward the French Republic? Was he behaving as a statesman or as a self-interested partisan? Were the causes of his saber rattling foreign, rooted purely in malevolent French behavior and a threat to national security? Or were they also domestic, rooted in partisanship, a desire to enhance his personal glory, or both? Did President Adams respond to electoral incentives to potentially increase the likelihood that he and his party would be reelected? Was there an institutional basis for President Adams's saber rattling due to having a strong supportive coalition in Congress? If so, what might have been the tenor of President Adams's remarks if he had faced a Democratic-Republican Congress? How, if at all, did the media frenzy and public opinion shape President Adams's saber rattling?

On the flip side, a complementary set of research questions emerges from considering the consequences of President Adams's saber rattling? Did President Adams's threats toward the French produce more or less French hostility? Did his war talk following the XYZ Affair produce the desirable result of containing French hostility? Or did his behavior actually exacerbate the foreign policy crisis? On the domestic front we can also ask whether President Adams's hostility toward France benefited the president in both the short and long term. Clearly, the president's saber rattling increased short-term partisan, media, and public support. However, that support quickly disappeared when the president turned toward a more pacific approach. In other words, there were costs associated with presidential threats that ultimately proved the president's undoing in the 1800 election.

This chapter has highlighted a set of research questions for a single president. However, case study evidence for a single early president does not enable generalizing about the causes and consequences of modern presidential saber rattling. Thus, later chapters will address and answer these questions more systematically with quantitative evidence for presidents from Truman through George W. Bush.

# 2

# Presidential Saber Rattling and Presidential Representation

Presidents are often described by American government and presidency textbooks, social scientists, and political pundits alike as the nation's chief foreign policy representative. This facile description is generally taken as self-obvious. Yet scholars actually know little about the nature of presidential representation for foreign policy.

Foreign policy representation involves projecting American preferences or interests to the rest of the world. In all of their foreign policy behaviors, presidents act on behalf of the nation at large. Studying presidential saber rattling can potentially provide insight about the nature of the president's foreign policy representation. Does presidential saber rattling always reflect the interests of the nation at large? Or does presidential saber rattling sometimes reflect presidential self-interest or partisanship? These are the overarching research questions of the next three chapters.

In attempting to understand presidential foreign policy representation, the potential causes and consequences relating to both foreign and domestic audiences will be examined. Of course, the causes of presidential saber rattling are inextricably linked with the consequences. Presidents may use saber rattling to achieve particular outcomes, domestic or foreign. The likely outcomes, in turn, may reinforce presidential propensity toward saber rattling. These possibilities are addressed through systematic analysis in later chapters.

In the remainder of this chapter an overarching theoretical framework is developed for understanding presidential saber rattling as an aspect of foreign policy representation.

## The Legal Foundation for Foreign Policy Representation

The Founders did not intend for presidents to be the only national representatives in the area of foreign policy.[1] They envisioned shared authority between Congress and the Executive. Article II of the Constitution gives the president authority (with the consent of the Senate) to appoint ambassadors to other countries. These ambassadors are authorized within those countries to speak on behalf of the president and nation. The president alone is authorized to receive ambassadors from other countries. Article II authorizes the president (with the consent of the Senate) to appoint the nation's foreign minister, the secretary of state, who is also head of the foreign policy bureaucracy. Article II also gives the president the power to negotiate treaties with other countries (which must be approved by two-thirds of the Senate). The president is the commander in chief of the military, which enables a great deal of control over how the United States interacts with other nations. However, only Congress can declare war, and presidents must rely on congressional appropriations for military operations.[2]

Thus, presidents share foreign policy powers with Congress. However, it is also widely understood that presidents exercise significant foreign policy powers independent of Congress. President Washington initiated this tradition early on. As mentioned in the introductory chapter, when war broke out between France and England in February 1793, President Washington viewed entanglement in the European war as dangerous to American unity and stability. Thus, he declared a policy of American neutrality. He did so without consulting Congress. Yet there is no explicit grant of such presidential authority in the Constitution.

Washington's proclamation of neutrality was immediately controversial. Secretary of State Thomas Jefferson and Secretary of Treasury Alexander Hamilton agreed that a policy of neutrality was the best course. However, James Madison questioned the president's authority to issue the neutrality proclamation without congressional approval. Thus, a debate broke out, headlined by a series of articles published in the *Gazette of the United States* labeled *Pacificus vs. Helvidius.*

---

[1] Although presidents were not intended to be the dominant actors in American foreign policy, some scholars claim that they are. For example, Wildavsky (1966) asserted that there are actually "two presidencies," a very powerful foreign policy presidency and a less powerful domestic policy presidency. This assertion has been extensively evaluated and challenged through quantitative research (e.g., see Canes-Wrone et al. 2008; Cohen 1991; Edwards 1986; Fleisher and Bond 1988, 2000; LeLoup and Shull 1979; Lewis 1997; Marshall and Pacelle Jr. 2005; Sigelman 1979).

[2] The War Powers Resolution of 1973 was an attempt by Congress to reassert shared authority after Presidents Johnson and Nixon conducted a lengthy war without an explicit congressional declaration. However, presidents of both parties have often ignored its requirements, some even believing it to be unconstitutional (Feldman 2006, 2007; Grimmett 2001; Nixon 1973; Rumsfeld 2011).

As *Helvidius*, Madison noted the objections to Washington's proclamation of neutrality: it was not authorized by the Constitution, it was contrary to the Treaties of Alliance and Commerce with France, it was contrary to the gratitude owed the French for their assistance in the American Revolution, and it was unnecessary. As *Pacificus*, Hamilton developed the theory that the executive power vested in the president under Article II inherently included the full panoply of rights in foreign affairs possessed by the British Crown and other national sovereigns. *Helvidius* countered that the Congress more rightfully shared these powers.

Most important about this debate, *Pacificus* and *Helvidius* agreed that there were indeed presidential powers, inherent in the idea of sovereignty, not spelled out in the Constitution. Historically, *Pacificus*'s argument has prevailed, yielding a presidency in which authority derives from the broad grant of executive authority in Article II, "The executive Power shall be vested in a President of the United States of America." From this point forward, the president used inherent sovereign powers in foreign affairs, and so they became his.[3]

The courts affirmed early on that as sovereign leaders, presidents are the nation's chief foreign policy representative. Future Supreme Court Justice John Marshall stated in 1800 when he served in the U.S. House of Representatives that "The President is the sole organ of the nation in its external relations, and its sole representative with foreign nations" (10 Annals of Congress 613). Relying on Marshall's "sole organ" doctrine, Supreme Court Justice George Sutherland wrote in 1937 (*United States vs. Curtiss-Wright Export Corp*, 299 U.S. 319), "In this vast external realm [foreign policy], with its important, complicated, delicate and manifold problems, the President alone has the power to speak or listen as a representative of the nation." Although the plenary nature of executive authority in foreign relations is not universally agreed,[4] the modern chief executive relies extensively on the "sole organ" doctrine to define presidential power broadly, and it is now largely uncontested that presidents are the sole representatives of the nation to the outside world.

---

[3] For example, President Thomas Jefferson invoked the theory of sovereign executive authority when he made the Louisiana Purchase from France for $11.25 million in 1803 without congressional consent. The president used $3 million in gold from the treasury as a down payment and financed the remainder with government-issued bonds. Historically, presidents have also issued proclamations and executive orders, negotiated executive agreements, created executive agencies, and claimed executive privilege to withhold information, all without input from Congress (Cooper 2002; Howell 2003; Lewis 2003; Lewis and Howell 2002; Mayer 1999, 2001). More recently, presidents have issued signing statements, claiming executive authority to reinterpret law independent of the courts (Fisher 2007c; Greene 2009; Halstead 2007). Additionally, presidents have claimed authority to suspend civil rights during times of crisis, as well as seized individuals and sent them to other countries for rendition in the name of national security.

[4] For example, see the persuasive arguments by Fisher (2006, 2007a, 2007b, 2007c, 2007d, 2007e, 2008a, 2008b).

## On the Nature of Presidential Foreign Policy Representation

What does it mean to say that presidents are the sole representatives of the nation to the outside world? The concept of political representation has been extensively studied both by political theorists and scholars of American politics. As a result, there is a large literature that offers many different definitions of the concept.[5] Pitkin (1967, 8) offers one of the simplest definitions. To represent is to "make present again." In other words, political representation is making citizens' voices, opinions, and interests "present again" in the policy-making process. The president is the only elected official in the United States who represents the nation at large. Therefore, it is reasonable to argue that presidents should "make present again" the preferences and interests of the nation at large in their foreign policy interactions.

Although this definition is simple, it lacks specificity. How do presidents go about representing the nation in foreign policy? An enduring controversy exists over whether democratic leaders should be delegates or trustees in their manner of representation. Edmund Burke delineated this controversy on November 3, 1774, in a speech to the electors of Bristol:

Certainly, gentlemen, it ought to be the happiness and glory of a representative to live in the strictest union, the closest correspondence, and the most unreserved communication with his constituents. Their wishes ought to have great weight with him, their opinion high respect; their business, unremitted attention.... But his unbiased opinion, his mature judgment, his enlightened conscience, he ought not to sacrifice to you, to any man, or to any set of men living.... Your representative owes you, not his industry only, but his judgment; and he betrays instead of serving you, if he sacrifices it to your opinion. (Burke 1774)

In this passage Burke offered the classic rationale for representatives behaving as trustees. The "mature judgment" and "enlightened conscience" of wise and virtuous public officials is invaluable to constituents who may not possess these attributes. Because of their unique qualifications, democratic representatives are selected as agents of their constituencies. They are chosen specifically because they are better qualified than others to judge the manifold issues affecting constituent interests. Representatives are charged with decision making on behalf of their constituents specifically because of their superior attributes. Thus, representatives who are trustees follow their own understanding of what is in their constituents' best interest. They have autonomy to deliberate and act, even if it means going against the preferences of their constituency.

---

[5] Classic treatments by political theorists can be found in the works of Dovi (2006), Pennock and Chapman (1968), Pitkin (1967), Mansbridge (2003), and Schwartz (1988). Concise reviews of the literature on legislative representation can be found in Box-Steffensmeier et al. (2003), Hill and Hurley (1999), and Wood and Andersson (1998). Presidential representation in the domestic arena has been studied less often. However, see Canes-Wrone (2006), Canes-Wrone et al. (2001), Canes-Wrone and Schotts (2004), Cohen (1999), Erikson et al. (2002), Jacobs and Shapiro (2000), Stimson et al. (1995), and Wood (2009a).

In contrast, representatives who are delegates simply follow the expressed preferences of their constituents. They live in "strictest union" and "closest correspondence" with their constituents and afford their preferences great weight. Delegate representatives sacrifice their own opinions to those of the constituency. They act as a voice for those who literally are not present in the policy process. They are limp translators of constituent preferences and have no autonomy to follow their own judgment.

From this discussion, it follows that representing people's interests and representing their preferences are two distinctly different things. Representing people's preferences implies that presidents should always mirror the public in all of their decisions and behavior. In contrast, representing people's interests implies that presidents may follow their own perceptions about what is in the nation's best interests, independent of people's preferences.

For example, as discussed in the introductory chapter, President Washington proclaimed a policy of neutrality toward France in 1793 based on his perception that to do otherwise would be dangerous to the future of the nation. The president believed that taking sides in the European war would spark partisan divisions internally and potentially entangle the nation in a war endangering a fledgling economy and territory. However, the president faced significant opposition to his proclamation (e.g., see Elkins and McKitrick 1993, 336–41; Sharp 1993, 75–78). The French Revolution was very popular with some citizens, and the ensuing European war was viewed by many as a fight by the French against monarchy and despotism. Yet Washington proclaimed neutrality irrespective of any potential loss in domestic support in the belief that he was representing the nation's best interests.

### The "Statesman" Ideal of Presidential Representation

President Washington's behavior in declaring neutrality was grounded in the "statesman" ideal. He had participated in the constitutional convention and was arguably handpicked to be the nation's first president. As a result, Washington's representational posture was largely consistent with the views of many Founders. They believed that presidents should use their foreign policy tools only to achieve just foreign policy goals. They also believed that the president should always be motivated by the nation's best interests. Presidents should be wise and virtuous leaders, divorced from their passions and personal considerations, beyond the partisan fray, oblivious to the press and whims of public opinion, with behavior motivated solely by the common good.

However, the Founders had little confidence that future leaders could be trusted to live up to this ideal. John Jay, writing as *Publius* in Federalist #4, expressed this skepticism as follows:

But the safety of the people of America against dangers from FOREIGN force depends not only on their forbearing to give JUST causes of war to other nations, but also on their placing and continuing themselves in such a situation as not to INVITE hostility or insult; for it need not be observed that there are PRETENDED as well as just causes of war.... It is too true, however disgraceful it may be to human nature, that nations in general will make war whenever they have a prospect of getting anything by it. (Jay 1788a)

Jay's remarks suggest that presidential foreign policy behavior, like nations' propensities to make war, may be motivated by a variety of causes beyond the "statesman" ideal. Leaders may "INVITE hostility or insult" through "PRETENDED" rather than "JUST causes." In this regard, foreign policy behavior may arise from leaders' passions, ambitions, revenge, desire for personal glory, and to build standing with the public or fellow partisans.

Thus, Federalist #4 recognized that the proclivity for leaders to concoct hostility toward other nations must be constrained:

The people of America are aware that inducements to war may arise out of [economic interest], as well as from others not so obvious at present, and that whenever such inducements may find fit time and opportunity for operation, pretenses to color and justify them will not be wanting. Wisely, therefore, do they consider union and a good national government as necessary to put and keep them in SUCH A SITUATION as, instead of INVITING war, will tend to repress and discourage it. (Jay 1788a)

The Founders viewed "good national government" as a constraint on pretended criteria for hostility toward other nations. In particular, Madison's notes at the Constitutional convention suggest that authority to "make war" was vested jointly in Congress and the president to make war less likely. The Founders saw Congress as slow and contentious, making it difficult to act in haste. The chief executive was viewed by some as too much like a monarch to avoid malevolent behavior. Thus, the power to "declare war" was given solely to members of Congress, whose collective judgment was viewed as more deliberate. The power to "conduct war" was given to the president, who as commander in chief was more adept at responding to emergency and singularly responsible for the military hierarchy (Madison 1911, August 17, 1787).

Beyond these institutional safeguards against malevolent executive behavior, the intention of the Founders was a government staffed by wise and virtuous individuals who would pursue the interests of the nation at large. It was expected that men of good faith and character would be elected to represent the greater good. As expressed by James Madison in Federalist #57,

The aim of every political Constitution is, or ought to be, first to obtain for rulers men who possess most wisdom to discern, and most virtue to pursue, the common good of the society; and in the next place, to take the most effectual precautions for keeping them virtuous whilst they continue to hold their public trust. (Madison 1788a)

Similarly, Alexander Hamilton discussing the presidency in Federalist # 71 stated:

The republican principle demands that the deliberate sense of the community should govern the conduct of those to whom they intrust the management of their affairs; ... it does not require an unqualified complaisance to every sudden breeze of passion, or to every transient impulse which the people may receive from the arts of men, who flatter their prejudices to betray their interests. (Hamilton 1788)

Madison and Hamilton's views were also consistent with President Washington's expressed view of presidential representation. He stated in a letter to the Selectmen of Boston on July 28, 1795:

In every act of my administration, I have sought the happiness of my fellow citizens. My system for the attainment of this object has uniformly been to overlook all personal, local, and partial considerations; to contemplate the United States as one great whole; to confide that sudden impressions, when erroneous, would lead to candid reflection; and to consult only the substantial and permanent interests of our country. (Fitzpatrick 1931)

In other words, Washington believed presidents should reflect the interests of the nation at large while remaining oblivious to personal passions and partisanship. He saw a national interest apart from public preferences, the pursuit of which might involve loss of domestic support. Thus, Washington and many of the Founders viewed the presidency as a trustee of the common welfare, bending to the popular will when it served the nation's interests but deviating when the nation would be better served.

### *"Rational Choice" and Presidential Representation*

The "statesman" ideal of presidential representation espoused by the Founders runs counter to much modern social science theory and research on what motivates politicians. The dominant theoretical model used today to explain politician behavior is grounded in "rational choice." Rational choice argues that *self-interest*, rather than *community-interest*, drives most political behavior.

Specifically, politicians seek to maximize a payoff function that considers their own benefits and costs with respect to their decisions. In maximizing the payoff function, they consistently seek to secure advantages for themselves or their political party.[6] The most commonly espoused approach for accomplishing these goals is for presidents to behave as delegates. They should mirror public preferences as reflected through the median voter. Of course, the median voter is just an analogy for the center of mass preferences.

Downs (1957) first proposed a theory in which self-interested politicians and political parties act strategically to maximize their political support. Davis and Hinich (1966) initiated the seminal spatial modeling literature from this perspective, and median voter theory has manifested itself through

---

[6] An introductory treatment of rational choice theory is contained in Laver (1981). For a more recent treatment, see Shepsle (2010). More generally, the seminal works in this area are Arrow (1951), Downs, (1957), and Olson (1965).

numerous formal analyses grounded in this tradition.[7] Consistent with this theory, a significant body of social science research stresses the importance of mass political preferences to policy outputs from American political institutions (Canes-Wrone et al. 2001; Canes-Wrone and Shotts 2004; Erikson et al. 2002; Page and Shapiro 1985, 1992; Stimson et al. 1995; Wlezien 1996; but see Wood 2009a).

Rational choice posits that politicians are utility maximizers with respect to a set of goals. Politician goals are expressed in terms of the various dimensions of a utility or payoff function. The decision maker seeks to optimize the payoff function by engaging in that behavior that produces a maximum when choosing among alternative goals. Typically, decision makers choose based on unchanging and stable preferences and the constraints facing them. Under this framework, politicians make decisions about how they should act by comparing the personal costs and benefits of different courses of action. Patterns of behavior emerge that reflect their choices as they try to maximize their benefits and minimize their costs.

### The Multiple Dimensions of the President's Payoff Function

Applying this approach to presidential foreign policy representation, we might ask what goals enter into the president's foreign policy payoff function. Clearly, statesmanship and achieving a good foreign policy outcome on behalf of the nation would be important factors. Indeed, most presidents probably have intrinsic preferences that hold the "statesman" ideal in high regard. As noted earlier, high regard for the "statesman" ideal extends all the way back to the Founders. High regard for statesmanship is also apparent from continuing presidential rhetoric.

For example, Theodore Roosevelt, writing in his autobiography about how he had viewed his role as president, said, "I acted for the public welfare, I acted for the common well-being of all our people, whenever and in whatever manner was necessary, unless prevented by direct constitutional or legislative prohibition" (Roosevelt 1913, 197). Franklin Roosevelt expressed similar beliefs about presidential representation when he said, "Government is competent when all who compose it work as trustees for the whole people" (Roosevelt, January 20, 1937). In the same vein, Ronald Reagan, well known for his strong partisan stands, also endorsed the "statesman" ideal when he said, "Our loyalty must be only to this Nation and to the people that we represent" (*Public Papers of the Presidents*, January 21, 1981). Similarly, President Clinton said, "I wanted a Government to represent the national interests, not narrow interests, a Government that would stand up for ordinary Americans" (*Public Papers of the Presidents*, November 8, 1996).

---

[7] This literature is huge and cannot be adequately reviewed here. For expository treatments see Aldrich (1983), Austin-Smith and Banks (1988), Davis et al. (1970), Enelow and Hinich (1981, 1982, 1984), Riker and Ordeshook (1973), or Wittman (1983).

Most presidents have held intrinsic values favoring statesmanship over self-interest. Such values are an expectation of the office. However, it may also be that they value statesmanship because it is in their self-interest to do so. Presidents want to be judged favorably by history. Those perceived as statesmen are more likely to be judged favorably than those perceived as purely self-interested. Therefore, presidents should naturally gravitate toward statesman-like behavior. Additionally, it may be in the president's short-term self-interest to value statesmanship. People may "see through" purely self-interested behavior and judge the president negatively for excessive pandering. Thus, presidents have reasons to prefer at least some degree of statesman-like behavior.

Beyond statesmanship, however, modern presidents seek a multiplicity of other goals. For example, they value domestic support for themselves and their policies. Evidence of support for the president may be manifest through public approval ratings of the president's job performance. Yet another potential source of presidential support is institutional. Presidents need a degree of legislative support to pursue their policies effectively. Of course, higher support of both types implies more presidential power and credibility, potentially resulting in more policy success. Seeking higher public support may also be rooted in presidential vanity, as suggested by the analysis of President Adams's behavior in the introductory chapter. If domestic support enters into the president's payoff function, then the president's foreign policy behavior may also be rooted in whether actions are likely to be well received by the public, Congress, or mass media.

Potential electoral support is a related dimension of the president's payoff function. As suggested by the Adams vignette, presidents seek reelection for themselves and their political party. When elected, it is the party in power that reaps the most benefits. Therefore, presidential foreign policy behavior may be rooted in perceptions that a foreign policy activity will enhance future electoral prospects. The possibility that the president's payoff function depends on electoral factors also suggests a time-dependent feature. Presidents may de-emphasize reelection in foreign policy behaviors when elections are distant; as elections become proximate, electoral factors become increasingly important.

Partisanship may also enter into the president's payoff function. Just as President Adams may have been motivated by his Federalist partisanship in his behavior toward the French, modern presidents may also be motivated by the likes and dislikes of their fellow partisans. Internally, partisanship captures an individual's primary politically relevant beliefs. Viewed from the perspective of the "guns versus butter" trade-off, it is widely believed that Republicans prefer guns over butter, whereas the opposite is true for Democrats. This differential preference ordering is manifest empirically through party platforms and legislative agendas in which Republicans place a higher priority on national defense, and Democrats place a higher priority on social issues such as the health care and the environment. Thus, we might expect Republican presidents to be more aggressive than Democrats in their behavior toward other nations.

As suggested by the Adams vignette, presidents may also be influenced by the alignment of partisan forces. For example, we might argue that as the president's fellow partisans become more supportive of a particular foreign policy behavior, the president is emboldened to pursue that behavior more vigorously. Conversely, as the president's party becomes less supportive, presidents should become less enthusiastic. However, it may also be that when the president faces a majority from the other party, then saber rattling could be a device to bolster public and legislative support. When lacking domestic support, presidents might turn toward foreign rather than domestic policy to play to their strong suit.

### A Graphical Depiction of the Statesman and Self-Interest Models

From the preceding discussion, it should be clear that there are multiple dimensions that can enter into a president's foreign policy payoff function. These dimensions include preferences for statesmanship and a multiplicity of different types of domestic support. Domestic dimensions include the president's job approval, policy approval, legislative approval, partisan approval, and electoral approval. If we assume that presidents always prefer increasing quantities of each factor, and that all types of approval can be considered simply as components of the president's domestic support, then we can collapse the president's preferences into just two dimensions. Assume that presidents hold preferences across two different factors, statesmanship and domestic support. The task then becomes to consider how these factors affect the president's payoff in a third dimension.

Let us begin by graphically depicting the "statesman" ideal of presidential representation. This model is depicted in Figure 2.1. Under the "statesman" ideal, presidents should always prefer representing community interests, regardless of their preference for domestic support. As expressed by Washington, presidents should "consult only the substantial and permanent interests of our country" (Fitzpatrick 1931). Or, as expressed by Hamilton, "The republican principle . . . does not require an unqualified complaisance to every sudden breeze of passion, or to every transient impulse which the people may receive from the arts of men" (Hamilton 1788). Thus, at all levels of preference for domestic support in Figure 2.1, the optimal behavior is for presidents to behave as "statesmen." They are oblivious to any desire to increase their domestic support.

Such a posture and analysis is not to say that presidents do not value domestic support. In theory, practicing statesmanship may be an appropriate strategy through which presidents can gain domestic support. As expressed by Washington, "In every act of my administration, I have sought the happiness of my fellow citizens. My system for the attainment of this object has uniformly been

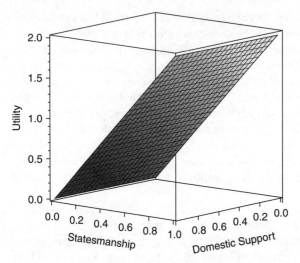

FIGURE 2.1. The statesman ideal of presidential representation.

to overlook all personal, local, and partial considerations" (Fitzpatrick 1931). In other words, presidents who practice statesmanship can expect their desire for domestic support to be rewarded through recognition of their wise and virtuous behavior.[8]

Consider now a model of pure support seeking. This model is depicted graphically in Figure 2.2. Under this model, the optimal behavior is for presidents always to seek greater domestic support, regardless of their preference for statesmanship. Indeed, presidents care nothing about statesmanship, except to the extent that it produces more or less domestic support. Given the uncertainty of this outcome, however, it is plausible that presidents might view statesmanship as an ineffective strategy to build their support. Therefore, the dominant strategy for presidents is always to cater to the median voter. Under this model, presidents become automatons who tailor their policies and behavior to satisfy the electorate. As a result, the president's foreign policy payoff function does not change with respect to their preferences for statesmanship. Presidents limply pursue community preferences to maximize their political support.

---

[8] Although such a posture may have been normatively appropriate for an icon such as Washington, it may not work well for presidents who are mortal and faced with domestic opposition. Indeed, statesmanship did not work well for Washington in increasing his domestic support. Washington's support declined sharply as a function of his foreign policy activities. For example, the negotiation and signing of the Jay Treaty with Great Britain was exceedingly unpopular, even though it may have been in the nation's best interests (see also Beschloss 2007, 1–17; Elkins and McKitrick 1993, 420–421; e.g., see Sharp 1993, 119). Likewise, as noted earlier, Washington's declaration of neutrality did not sit well with much of the public and many Democratic-Republicans.

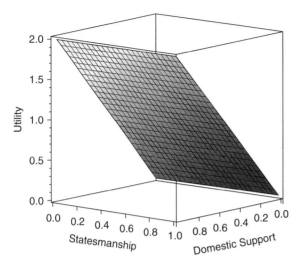

FIGURE 2.2. Pure support-seeking presidential representation.

Although it might seem that such a pure support-maximizing strategy would be normatively nocuous, this approach is consistent with the delegate representation ideal. Delegates always represent by translating community preferences into their own policies and behavior. This strategy pleases constituents, which then translates into greater support. Such a strategy might also achieve community interests. However, such an outcome requires a community that is perpetually wise and virtuous. Indeed, for the support-maximizing model to be deemed normatively better than the "statesman" ideal, the community would need to be wiser and more virtuous than the statesman president.

Of course, the Founders were skeptical of both public and executive wisdom and virtue. As expressed by Hamilton, the public can be subject to "sudden breeze of passion, or to every transient impulse which the people may receive from the arts of men" (Hamilton 1788). Likewise, as implied by Jay in Federalist #4, presidents may invite hostility or insult through pretended, rather than just, causes. Therefore, neither model of presidential representation is likely to be normatively superior.

Moreover, both models are "ideal types." As such, neither is likely to depict realistically all presidential foreign policy behavior. In the real world, presidents are pragmatists whose payoff functions reflect both their preference for statesmanship and their desire to achieve domestic support. Sometimes they may behave as statesmen; at other times they may behave as support seekers. In this regard, statesmanship can produce either gains or losses in domestic support. Furthermore, support seeking can either increase or decrease a president's ability to behave as a statesman. Thus, there is a trade-off between presidential desires to be statesmen and their desire to maintain domestic support.

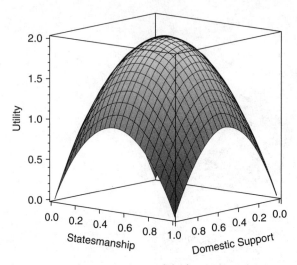

FIGURE 2.3. A pragmatist model of presidential representation.

Said differently, most presidents are willing to give up only a certain amount of statesmanship to achieve domestic support. Furthermore, they are willing to give up only a certain amount of domestic support to enable more statesmanship. Thus, the optimum of the president's foreign policy payoff function probably lies somewhere in between the two extremes of statesmanship and support maximization. Presidents' choices between statesmanship and domestic support should, therefore, be represented by a nonmonotonic function in both dimensions.

One example of the potential trade-off presidents face is shown in Figure 2.3. This hypothetical graph depicts an optimum at the center point in both dimensions. The optimum occurs when presidents pursue a moderate amount of statesmanship because they are unwilling to give up their majority in domestic support. Presumably, presidents who want to be successful require at least a majority to achieve their policy goals and achieve reelection. Therefore, they should be unwilling to give up more in domestic support to pursue more statesmanship.

Of course, optimization across the two dimensions of statesmanship and domestic support may differ both within and across presidencies. Within administrations, presidents may at times pursue statesmanship and at others seek to build their domestic support. Across presidencies, some presidents may be more prone toward pursuing statesmanship and be willing to give up significant amounts of domestic support. Other presidents may prefer more emphasis on domestic support and be willing to give up significant amounts of statesmanship.

Figures 2.4 and 2.5 depict the nature of presidential representation for two hypothetical scenarios in which presidents have different proclivities for statesmanship versus domestic support. A situation in which a president places

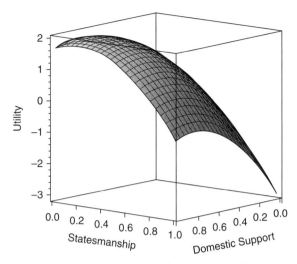

FIGURE 2.4. Strong presidential emphasis on domestic support.

stronger emphasis on domestic support is depicted in Figure 2.4. Note that the maximum for domestic support occurs at 0.8, whereas the maximum for statesmanship occurs at 0.2. This example shows a relatively extreme case in which the president does not become satisfied with domestic support until achieving very high levels. To do so, the president is willing to sacrifice significant amounts of statesmanship.

For example, one might argue that President Adams virtually abandoned statesmanship in 1798 after the failed peace mission to France and release of the XYZ dispatches. He embarked on a campaign of public saber rattling that

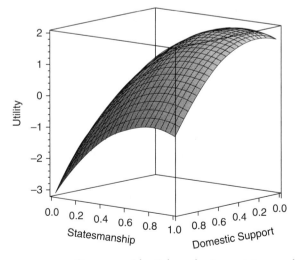

FIGURE 2.5. Strong presidential emphasis on statesmanship.

dramatically increased his popularity and public support for his policies. He also basically discarded any effort to secure peace, choosing instead to prepare the nation for an impending war that would have been costly to national interests.

In contrast, Figure 2.5 depicts a situation in which the president places stronger emphasis on statesmanship. Note that the maximum for domestic support now occurs at 0.2, whereas the maximum for statesmanship occurs at 0.8. This optimum represents a relatively extreme case in which the president pursues statesmanship at a significant cost to his domestic support.

For example, President Adams willingly yielded large amounts of domestic support before the 1800 election to pursue the peace initiative with France. He lost the approval of the public, the mass media, and many of his fellow partisans. Thus, the president gave up much domestic support in the interests of peace and the avoidance of a war that would have been costly to American unity and stability. The president behaved as a statesman, pursuing what he believed was in the community interest.

The examples in Figures 2.4 and 2.5 as they pertain to the Adams presidency are probably the exceptions rather than the rule for modern presidential representation. Most modern presidents have not faced such stark choices.[9] As a result, the more middling model depicted in Figure 2.3 is likely to be characteristic of modern presidential representation. As the nation's sole foreign policy representative to the outside world, presidents do not always behave as the statesmen intended by the Founders. Rather, their behavior is sometimes motivated by a desire to achieve at least a moderate level of domestic support. Evidence of this propensity for presidents to be self-interested is developed in later chapters by evaluating how modern presidential saber rattling has responded to a variety of foreign and domestic factors.

### Saber Rattling as Presidential Representation

Modern presidents use saber rattling as a tool, presumably for projecting American preferences or interests abroad. The overarching questions addressed in later chapters concern how and why they use this tool, and what the consequences are. Do modern presidents behave more as statesmen when they threaten as depicted in Figure 2.1? Are modern presidents the wise and virtuous leaders envisioned by the Founders?

Of course, international relations scholars commonly view leaders' threats from a similar perspective. Foreign policy threats are often considered goal-oriented with respect to the international system (e.g., realism, neoclassical

---

[9] However, consider President Carter during the Iran hostage crisis. He willingly gave up much domestic support in the interest of saving hostage lives and avoiding a war that would have been ill advised over such a trivial issue. At the other extreme, I speculate in Chapter 7 that President George W. Bush may have pursued the Iraq War motivated at least partially by a desire to bolster his support for the 2004 election.

realism; George 2009; Mearsheimer 2001; Waltz 1979). Leaders want to alter the behavior of those they threaten with tools manifesting their relative power. The relative power of two actors in a threat dyad is likely to determine who makes threats and how those being threatened respond.

Does the presidential propensity toward saber rattling derive primarily from the international system? Are presidential threats merely a response to external behaviors directed toward the United States by other nations or actors? Can we explain presidential threats *purely* as a response to the external environment?

Or is presidential saber rattling motivated by domestic support seeking as depicted in varying degrees in Figures 2.2 through 2.5? Do modern presidents use saber rattling out of passion, ambition, revenge, desire for personal glory, or to build standing with the public or fellow partisans? More generally, do domestic factors, such as desire for legislative, media, or public support, affect presidential behavior toward other nations?

Presidents may also act as partisans in their propensity toward saber rattling. Fundamental to this question is whether presidents differ systematically across party lines or individually in their propensity to make threats. If presidents are partisans, rather than statesman representatives (e.g., see Wood 2009a), then the intensity of saber rattling may be a function of the president's intrinsic partisanship or partisan support.

Presidents may also change their saber rattling in response to upcoming elections. As suggested by the Adams vignette, saber rattling may increase public support in the short term, making it more likely that they or their political party will prevail. Do presidents use saber rattling strategically to bolster their prospects for reelection?

Presidential threats may also be encouraged by media frenzies and the resulting excited public. Of course, the mass media has always tended to hyperbolize foreign policy crises. During the Adams administration the Federalist media consistently beat the drums for war with France. Such media pressures were not isolated to the early American republic.

A similar media frenzy occurred after the sinking of the battleship *Maine* in Havana harbor in February 1898, initiating the Spanish-American War. Likewise, the Iran hostage crisis produced a media frenzy that was persistent and strong, potentially pushing President Carter toward threats and military action. Of course, the strongest recent media frenzy occurred after the September 11 terror attacks, pushing President George W. Bush and the public toward wars in Afghanistan and Iraq. Thus, later chapters ask whether media coverage of crises and major foreign policy events amplifies presidential saber rattling through time.

Alternatively, modern presidents may also use saber rattling strategically in an effort to mobilize the media to increase their domestic support. External threats to the nation typically increase media coverage and support for the president. However, do presidents use external threats strategically to amplify the media and public frenzy that often surround external threats?

## Conclusions

The introductory chapter began with a case study of the John Adams presidency and his behavior during the "quasi-war" with France. However, a single case study does not lend itself to systematic understanding of the causes and consequences of presidential behavior. Indeed, scholars can interpret case study evidence differently to yield different conclusions. Therefore, later chapters use quantitative evidence across eleven presidencies and sixty-four years to enable generalizing about the causes and consequences of presidential threats toward other nations.

Why is it important to understand presidential saber rattling? The phenomenon is important in and of itself. Presidential threats are an important tool of American foreign policy. Conducting foreign policy is one of the two or three most important functions of the American presidency. Thus, explaining when and why presidents make threats toward other nations or actors is important to understanding relations in the international arena.

More theoretically, this book takes presidential saber rattling as an object of scientific analysis, because it enables greater understanding of presidential representation. Normatively, presidential saber rattling should be a manifestation of presidents protecting community interests or reflecting the preferences of the American citizenry. Therefore, understanding the causes and consequences of presidential threats toward other nations or actors is an approach to evaluating the nature of presidential representation relative to foreign policy.

Presidential representation has been extensively studied in the domestic arena (Canes-Wrone 2006; Canes-Wrone et al. 2001; Canes-Wrone and Shotts 2004; Cohen 1999; Erikson et al. 2002; Stimson et al. 1995; Wood 2009a). However, there has been no study of presidential representation in the foreign policy arena. This absence of scientific knowledge on the nature of the president's foreign policy representation leaves an important gap in our understanding. Subsequent chapters aim to fill this gap.

# 3

# Measuring Presidential Saber Rattling

Systematic investigation of the causes and consequences of modern presidential saber rattling requires quantitative measures that accurately capture the president's threatening remarks. This chapter describes the methods used to create such measures. It also provides some preliminary statistical and graphical analyses.

Of course, not all bellicose presidential rhetoric explicitly threatens action. For example, President Adams spoke aggressively toward France in a variety of styles and contexts. His May 16, 1797, special message to Congress called for a defensive buildup, as well as a new peace initiative. He made no explicit threat of war. Yet the French were highly offended by the president's remarks. They asked for an apology, issued unfriendly decrees, and stepped up their attacks on American shipping.

In contrast, the president's public rhetoric following the release of the XYZ dispatches did make explicit threats of war. The president issued threats through the news media and in numerous public appearances, seemingly for the purpose of inciting the public and achieving legislative goals. Again, the French were highly offended by the president's remarks and intensified their "quasi-war" against American shipping. In both styles and contexts, presidential rhetoric had serious consequences.

Just as President Adams's bellicosity was varied in style and context, this book is also concerned with a variety of styles and contexts of presidential saber rattling.

## Defining Presidential Saber Rattling

Defined narrowly, saber rattling is "a show or threat of military power, especially as used by a nation to impose its policies on other countries" (Houghton Mifflin 1996). In this book, hostile foreign policy rhetoric of all styles and

TABLE 3.1. *Examples of Presidential Saber Rattling from* Public Papers of the Presidents

---

President Truman, April 30, 1951 – "If the Soviet Union chooses to unleash a general war, the free world must be in a position to stop the attack and strike back decisively and at once at the seats of Soviet Power."

President Kennedy, October 22, 1962 – "It shall be the policy of this nation to regard any nuclear missile launched from Cuba against any nation in the Western Hemisphere as an attack by the Soviet Union on the United States, requiring the full retaliatory response upon the Soviet Union."

President Johnson, August 5, 1964 – "I urge the Congress to enact such a Resolution promptly and thus to give convincing evidence to the aggressive communist nations, and to the world as a whole, that our policy in Southeast Asia will be carried forward – and that the peace and security of the area will be preserved."

President Nixon, August 21, 1969 – "They are the very aggressive North Korean Communists who continue to commit bellicose acts of provocation and infiltration, constantly seeking an opportunity for renewed aggression."

President Ford, March 12, 1976 – "...this country will defend freedom, will be willing to support an adequate defense budget to make America strong, so that we can handle the problem of Soviet and any aggression by the communists."

President Carter, January 8, 1980 – "They know that the consequences to Iran will be quite severe if our hostages are injured or killed."

President Reagan, January 7, 1986 – "In light of this latest evidence of Libya's growing role in international terrorism, it is clear that steps taken so far have not been sufficient."

President George H. W. Bush, September 11, 1990 – "Our quarrel is with Iraq's dictator and with his aggression. Iraq will not be permitted to annex Kuwait. That's not a threat, that's not a boast, that's just the way it's going to be."

President Clinton, December 16, 1998 – "The credible threat to use force and, when necessary, the actual use of force, is the surest way to contain Saddam's weapons of mass destruction program, curtail his aggression, and prevent another Gulf war."

President George W. Bush, September 14, 2001 – "I can hear you, the rest of the world hears you. And the people who knocked these buildings down will hear all of us soon."

President George W. Bush, March 17, 2003 – "Saddam Hussein and his sons must leave Iraq within 48 hours. Their refusal to do so will result in military conflict, commenced at a time of our choosing."

---

contexts will be labeled "saber rattling." The term is used here to imply threats of either a general or specific nature directed toward other nations, actors, or interests.

What does presidential saber rattling sound like? Table 3.1 contains representative examples of modern presidential saber rattling drawn from *Public Papers of the Presidents*. These presidential remarks reflect a variety of responses to foreign adversaries in differing styles and contexts during the various eras of modern American foreign policy. Consider each presidential remark in Table 3.1.

- President Truman's remark on April 30, 1951 was an explicit threat of retaliation if the Soviets invaded Europe.
- President Kennedy's remark was an explicit threat of nuclear war against the Soviets during the Cuban missile crisis.
- President Johnson's remark was a statement of U.S. containment policy in Southeast Asia and is often marked as the start of the Vietnam War.
- President Nixon's remark was reaffirming support for South Korea at a state dinner for the South Korean president.
- President Ford's remark occurred in the context of the 1976 election campaign and affirmed his willingness to defend American interests against communism.
- President Carter's remark was a warning to the Iranians during the hostage crisis.
- President Reagan's remark was a warning preliminary to the U.S. bombing of Libya in April 1986.
- President George H. W. Bush's remark was a warning to Saddam Hussein before the Persian Gulf War.
- President Clinton's remark was a continuation of efforts to contain the Saddam Hussein regime.
- Finally, the two remarks by President George W. Bush were representative of presidential saber rattling after the September 11 terrorist attacks and the buildup to the invasions of Afghanistan and Iraq.

As suggested by the examples in Table 3.1, all modern presidents have faced foreign policy threats and have reacted to those threats with saber rattling. Some of these presidential remarks were made in the formal settings of congressional speeches or addresses to the nation. Others were made in the less formal settings of speeches to groups, news conferences, or even speaking "off the cuff" to reporters. The intents of these presidential remarks were varied, including general statements to deter behavior by foreign adversaries, statements of foreign policy, and overt threats of economic, political, or military action. As reflected in these remarks, presidential saber rattling can range from relatively broad statements about defending our national interests against external threats (e.g., communism, fascism, terrorism, etc.) to more direct expressions of hostility, sanctions, or military action directed toward specific nations (i.e., the former Soviet Union, Russia, Iraq, Iran, North Korea, Libya, Afghanistan, etc.).

Rather than focusing on single presidential speeches or statements, as was done in the introductory chapter, the remainder of this book employs a continuous time perspective to measure the changing flow of presidential saber rattling through time. The measures described in this chapter consist of monthly time series that gauge the relative intensity of presidential saber rattling. The intensity of presidential saber rattling is gauged simply by counting the number of bellicose presidential remarks during each month.[1]

Of course, presidents maintain an extensive public relations apparatus for transmitting a continuous stream of messages. They transmit their messages through multiple mechanisms, including speeches, group appearances, radio addresses, news conferences, policy briefings, news releases, town meetings, and other public appearances. Through these various mechanisms presidents create a continuous stream of messages, intended to affect both foreign and domestic actors.

With respect to foreign actors, the intensity of presidential saber rattling has varied with presidential style and the nature of foreign policy problems. Some presidents have been more prone toward saber rattling than others, and some have faced more troublesome problems. Generally, presidents threaten other actors to deter, to signal intentions, to warn of pending hostile action, or even as a symbolic gesture.

Whether the intended receptors of presidential saber rattling are foreign or domestic, these are potentially important signals. Yet there are no systematic measures of presidential saber rattling currently available to the scholarly community. The next section describes the methods used to construct such measures.

## Measuring Presidential Saber Rattling

The data source for the presidential saber rattling measures is *Public Papers of the Presidents*. This serial set is compiled and published biannually by the Office of the Federal Register, National Archives and Records Administration. All volumes covering presidential administrations from Harry S. Truman through George W. Bush were used to construct the measures. Each *Public Papers* volume contains the speeches and public remarks of the president of the United States that were issued by the Office of the Press Secretary during the specified time period. The appendices to the *Public Papers* contain additional materials previously published in the *Weekly Compilation of Presidential Documents*.

The volumes of *Public Papers* from 1945 through 2008 comprise a massive amount of text. They cover all public remarks by eleven presidents over a time span of sixty-four years. It would be a near impossible task for a single researcher to read and code all saber rattling from this massive amount of text. Therefore, a computer-assisted technology was used for constructing the measures.

---

[1] Of course, one could rightly argue that some presidential remarks should carry more weight than others. Thus, presidential remarks known to be especially hostile might be weighted more heavily. However, there is no objective criterion on which to base such a weighting scheme. Therefore, the measurement scheme used here assumes simply that presidents threaten more often when they want to emphasize a message more strongly.

An electronic file was created containing the *Public Papers of the Presidents* from April 12, 1945, through January 19, 2009. The main electronic file was initially developed for earlier work (e.g., see Wood 2007, 2009a, 2009b; Wood et al. 2005; Wood and Lee 2009) and updated for the present study. The original file was constructed by extracting the ASCII text from a CD-ROM marketed commercially by Western Standard Publishing Company (2000). This medium contained the entire *Public Papers* through 1999, including appendices with supplemental materials from the *Weekly Compilation*. To complete the electronic file to January 2009, the remaining years' materials were downloaded from the Web through http://www.OriginalSources.com (maintained by the same publisher). The resulting electronic file for content analysis of presidential saber rattling contained around 380 megabytes of ASCII text.[2]

With this massive electronic file in hand, a combination of machine and human coding was used to extract the measures. Practical Extraction and Report Language (PERL) was used to manipulate the text contained in the electronic file.[3] In implementing the electronic searches, a PERL program was first developed to extract from the *Public Papers* every sentence spoken publicly by the president containing keywords and phrases indicative of foreign policy. There were 261 foreign policy indicators, including country names, organizational acronyms, international leaders, and words generally associated with U.S. foreign policy.[4] The keywords were validated by human coders to assure that all extracted sentences related to foreign policy.

The resulting foreign policy sentence file contained roughly 400,000 distinct presidential remarks. Having identified the president's foreign policy remarks, the task was then to identify which of those remarks contained saber rattling. Identifying the saber rattling remarks again involved a combination of both electronic and human coding. Initially it was helpful to identify the nations and activities likely to have provoked presidential bellicosity. The Wikipedia Timeline of United States Diplomatic History[5] was used to identify American adversaries and periods of crisis or conflict. Adversaries are more likely to be targets of presidential saber rattling. Therefore, keywords were included to capture when the president was talking about a particular adversary or adversarial activity.

Additionally, a PERL program was developed to list every unique word in the foreign policy sentence file. The word list contained roughly 58,000 unique words and phrases. Human coders were then used to identify those keywords

---

[2] The master text file from this project is available on request from the author.

[3] PERL is a public domain open access code software package for logical manipulation of text. It is a high-level programming language derived from the ubiquitous C programming language and to a lesser extent from sed, awk, the Unix shell, and at least a dozen other tools and languages (Schwartz et al. 1997). A full description of PERL, as well as various user support functions, is available at http://www:perl.com. PERL can be downloaded free from a link on this Web site.

[4] The keywords referenced here and below are contained in PERL programs available on the author's Web site at http://people.tamu.edu/~b-wood.

[5] See http://en.wikipedia.org/wiki/Timeline_of_United_States_diplomatic_history.

and phrases commonly used by presidents when engaging in saber rattling. Around 120 words and phrases were identified and validated as indicative of presidential saber rattling. Validation was accomplished through manual keyword searches in the foreign policy sentence file by recording the percentage of correct hits using the search function in a DOS text editor on restricted segments of the text.

Finally, a PERL program was developed using the saber-rattling keywords to tentatively identify the sentences involving hostile presidential rhetoric. In recognition that machine coding techniques are fallible, human coders were again used to validate the results. The PERL coded saber-rattling file was a starting point that enabled more efficient human identification of presidential saber-rattling sentences. Human coders were used to verify that all PERL extracted sentences were relevant and actually constituted presidential saber rattling. This iterative process effectively identified all instances in which the president made general threats, threats toward specific countries, engaged in deterrence talk, threatened economic or political sanctions, or threatened military action. The final saber-rattling sentence file was country-specific, enabling the work to isolate on specific nations or groups.

Table 3.2 contains representative examples of how the PERL/human coded results appeared when the saber-rattling sentence file was completed. In this coding scheme, the leading set of numbers in each first line entry indicates the year, month, and day respectively of the remark in *Public Papers of the Presidents*. For example, the first remark in Table 3.2 was a sentence spoken by President Nixon on April 18, 1969. This date code is followed by the paragraph number in the *Public Papers* entry, and then the sentence number within each paragraph. In other words, President Nixon's remark appeared in the 72nd paragraph and first sentence of the *Public Papers* entry for this date. This very specific sentence identification scheme generated by PERL enabled human coders to return to the original text when the context was in doubt.

On the same line, each sentence was then coded as a 0 (not saber rattling; the PERL program got it wrong), 1 (aggressive talk of a general nature but not directed toward a specific target), or 2 (a threat directed toward a specific target). The letter attached to this coding was A (threatens economic or political sanctions), B (threatens military action), or C (deterrence talk). If the threat was directed toward a specific target, then this coding was followed by an identifier for the adversary which was the object of the president's saber rattling. When the president's rhetoric was not directed at a particular target, then this identifier was left blank. For example, consider the example sentences in Table 3.2.

- In the first entry, the coding of 0 indicates that the PERL identified foreign policy sentence was not actually saber rattling. President Nixon was merely explaining how he reached a certain foreign policy decision. Having made this determination, the human coder entered this sentence as a zero. The sentence was therefore excluded from further analysis.

TABLE 3.2. *Examples of Coded Presidential Saber-Rattling Sentences*

---

19690418.072.01                                                  0

"I made that decision after I considered all the options that were before me with regard to what was necessary to maintain America's defenses, and particularly the credibility of our national security and our diplomacy throughout the world."

19570322.007.01                                                  1.C

"Today, in the grim necessity of preserving the peace, the free world must turn to the deadly power of the atom as a guardian of freedom and a prime deterrent to aggression."

20010911.010.01                                          1.C.Terror

"America and our friends and allies join with all those who want peace and security in the world, and we stand together to win the war against terrorism."

19960209.032.05                                          2.A.Iraq

"Because of Iraq's failure to comply fully with these resolutions, the United States will continue to apply economic sanctions to deter it from threatening peace and stability in the region."

20011110.022.01                                    2.B.Afghanistan

"I make this promise to all the victims of that regime: The Taliban's days of harboring terrorists and dealing in heroin and brutalizing women are drawing to a close."

19510130.017.03                                          2.C.Korea

"Both France and the United States will support action directed toward deterring aggression and toward preventing the spread of hostilities beyond Korea."

---

- In the second entry, the coding of 1.C indicates generally aggressive talk, perhaps to deter but not directed toward a particular country. President Eisenhower simply expressed the nation's willingness to use nuclear weapons to confront future aggression. Because no particular target was identified from the president's remark, the human coder left the target blank. Nevertheless, this entry was included in the analysis as an indicator of general presidential saber rattling.
- In the third entry, the coding of 1.C.Terror indicates general aggressive talk, seemingly directed toward terrorists or terror supporters. However, this sentence was not explicitly directed toward a specific country or group. President George W. Bush merely expressed determination and unity with the free world in the war on terror. However, because we might be interested in terror-related remarks for future analysis, the human coder entered "Terror" for the target code.
- In the fourth entry, the coding of 2.A.Iraq indicates saber rattling directed toward Iraq with a threat of economic sanctions. In this sentence President Clinton expressed the intent to continue economic sanctions against Iraq for noncompliance with United Nations resolutions. In this coded sentence

the machine correctly identified the saber rattling and target country. The human coder verified that this was actually a threat of economic sanctions and entered the appropriate code.

- In the fifth entry the coding of 2.B.Afghanistan indicates saber rattling by President George W. Bush with a specific threat of military action directed toward Afghanistan. In this case it was necessary for the human coders to return to the original text using the "date.paragraph.sentence" identifier to determine that this was indeed an explicit threat of military action.

- Finally, in the sixth entry the coding of 2.C.Korea indicates saber rattling toward Korea to deter expansion of the Korean conflict. This statement by President Truman was an expression of American policy to stop Korean aggression and contain the conflict to the Korean Peninsula. In this example, the machine correctly identified the saber rattling and target country. The human coder verified that there was no specific threat of economic, political, or military action, and concluded that this presidential remark was primarily intended to deter.

This coding framework identified 4,269 distinct instances of presidential saber rattling from 1945 through 2008. Of these saber-rattling remarks, 3,163 were of a general nature directed toward no particular country or group. The remaining 1,106 were specific and directed toward particular countries or actors. There were 508 threats seemingly intended to deter activities by other countries or groups, 398 presidential threats of economic or political sanction, and 200 threats of military action.

Using the resulting saber-rattling sentence file, the coded presidential threats were then aggregated into monthly time series along each dimension. This was accomplished simply by summing the number of threatening presidential remarks during each month. The resulting measures capture the relative intensity of presidential hostility of each type during each month. Months with a large number of presidential threats are assumed to be periods of intense presidential hostility. Months with few threats reflect periods of relative calm presidential rhetoric.

## Describing the Measures

We can gain a sense of how the intensity of presidential saber rattling has varied through time by examining graphs of the time series measures and calculating some descriptive information. Figure 3.1 contains a plot of all types of presidential saber rattling aggregated together during each month from April 1945 to January 19, 2009. Labels marking some of the most important foreign policy events during this time frame are also included.

The time series covers 766 total months. From these, there were 119 months during which the president made no hostile remarks, 299 months during which

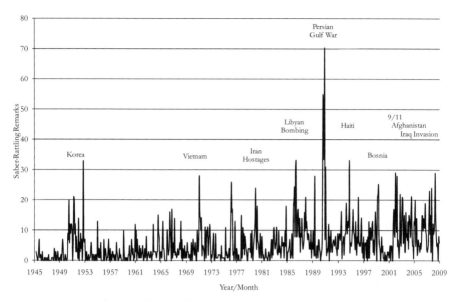

FIGURE 3.1. Presidential saber rattling of any type.

the president made two or fewer hostile remarks, and 641 months during which the president made fewer than ten hostile remarks. The maximum intensity of presidential saber rattling occurred in November 1990 when President George H. W. Bush made 70 threatening remarks toward Iraq over their invasion of Kuwait.

Visual examination of Figure 3.1 shows other intense periods of presidential saber rattling. Peaks are associated with the Korean War, the Vietnam War, the Iran hostage crisis, the Libyan bombing, the Persian Gulf War, Haiti, the Bosnian crisis, September 11, and the subsequent invasions of Afghanistan and Iraq. These graphical results suggest that war and crisis are important causes of presidential saber rattling.

However, visual examination of Figure 3.1 also reveals that presidents engaged in saber rattling during the intervening periods. Considering months during which the president made fewer than ten hostile remarks, the average intensity of saber rattling was roughly 3.5 monthly remarks. These remarks during the intervening periods imply that presidents may have engaged in symbolic saber rattling to bolster their prestige or standing with the public.

Additionally, there are several peaks in presidential saber rattling associated with no specific foreign policy event. For example, during March 1976 President Ford made twenty-six hostile remarks. Examining the saber-rattling sentence file entries for this month shows that these remarks were presidential campaign statements directed at no particular nation but asserting the nation's

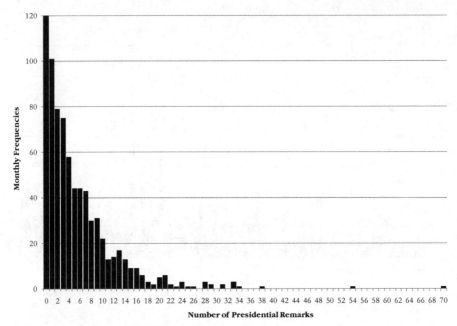

FIGURE 3.2. Frequency distribution of presidential saber rattling, 1945–2009.

willingness to defeat foreign aggression. Similarly, President George H. W. Bush made twenty-eight hostile remarks in May 1989. Again examining the saber-rattling sentence file for this month, these remarks do not seem to have been associated with a specific foreign adversary. President Bush's remarks were aggressive but seemingly for no apparent reason. Again, these peaks suggest that presidents may sometimes engage in saber rattling without a specific foreign policy goal.

More generally, presidents from Truman through George W. Bush made an average of 5.63 hostile remarks per month. The median monthly number of hostile presidential remarks was four. These differences between the mean and median reveal a distribution that is skewed to the right. Consistent with this assessment, the skewness statistic is 3.05. The standard deviation in the number of hostile presidential remarks was 6.67, showing there was substantial variation through time from the mean monthly number of hostile presidential remarks.

We can also directly examine the distribution of presidential saber rattling conditional on particular monthly frequencies. Figure 3.2 contains a frequency distribution of presidential saber-rattling remarks of all types from 1945 through 2008. This plot again confirms a distribution that is skewed right. The modal frequency of hostile presidential remarks is zero. The probability of successively higher frequencies declines sharply toward zero. The decay rate of probable frequencies is not strictly exponential but may be characterized by one of the discrete distributions related to the exponential distribution. Thus, when presidential saber rattling is considered as a dependent variable in the next chapter, we need to use a nonlinear statistical estimator such as Poisson or negative binomial regression.[6]

## Some Preliminary Analyses

### Presidential Style, Partisanship, and Saber Rattling

Have presidents differed in their relative propensity toward saber rattling? Calculating averages for each presidency for the data in Figure 3.1, we find that the average number of hostile remarks for Truman was 3.78, Eisenhower was 1.91, Kennedy was 2.88, Johnson was 4.19, Nixon was 4.69, Ford was 4.79, Carter was 5.08, Reagan was 6.77, George H. W. Bush was 9.66, Clinton was 7.31, and George W. Bush was 9.72. We might expect Presidents Truman, Johnson, Nixon, George H. W. Bush, and George W. Bush to be more threatening because of the presence of war during their administrations. However, these generally increasing numbers also suggest an upward trend through time in presidential propensity toward saber rattling. This trend may reflect the changing foreign policy environment faced by each president, or it may reflect each president's unique foreign policy style.

We can also compare presidents for statistical differences. Table 3.3 reports an analysis in which presidential saber rattling is regressed on indicator variables for each presidency. Using President Truman as the base category, Eisenhower was significantly less hostile than Truman. However, there was no statistically significant difference for other presidents before Reagan. Presidents Kennedy, Johnson, Nixon, Ford, and Carter were about the same in their bellicosity as President Truman. Beginning with President Reagan, however, there was a statistically significant shift in the intensity of presidential saber rattling. Presidents Reagan, George H. W. Bush, Clinton, and George W. Bush were all significantly more bellicose than earlier presidents. Again, this increase after Reagan may reflect the different foreign policy environment faced by these leaders. Or the change in presidential bellicosity may reflect the idea that Republicans are more aggressive than Democrats. Three of four of the post-Carter presidents were Republicans.

Were there also statistically significant differences in presidential saber rattling based on partisanship? Table 3.4 reports a bivariate regression of presidential saber rattling (of all types) on presidential partisanship. On average, Democrat presidents averaged 4.97 hostile remarks per month. Republican presidents averaged 6.21 (4.97 + 1.24) hostile remarks per month.

---

[6] The Poisson distribution counts the number of discrete events in a fixed time period. It is closely connected to the exponential distribution, which measures the time between arrivals of the events. If events occur through time as a Poisson process with parameter $\lambda$, the time between events are distributed as an exponential random variable with parameter $\lambda$.

TABLE 3.3. *Presidency-Specific Effects for Presidential Saber Rattling*

| President | Presidency-Specific Effects |
|---|---|
| Constant (Truman) | 3.78 |
| | (5.86) |
| Eisenhower | −1.87 |
| | (−2.06) |
| Kennedy | −0.89 |
| | (−0.71) |
| Johnson | 0.42 |
| | (0.41) |
| Nixon | 0.91 |
| | (0.91) |
| Ford | 1.02 |
| | (0.77) |
| Carter | 1.31 |
| | (1.18) |
| Reagan | 2.99 |
| | (3.30) |
| George H. W. Bush | 5.89 |
| | (5.31) |
| Clinton | 3.54 |
| | (3.90) |
| George W. Bush | 5.94 |
| | (6.55) |
| *Diagnostics:* | |
| $R^2 = 0.14$ | $N = 766$ |

*Note:* The results in the table are regression coefficients. The results reported in parentheses are $t$ statistics. $t$ statistics larger than 1.96 indicate statistical significance.

TABLE 3.4. *Partisan-Based Effects for Presidential Saber Rattling*

| President | Party-Specific Effects |
|---|---|
| Constant (Democrats) | 4.97 |
| | (13.58) |
| Republicans | 1.24 |
| | (2.55) |
| *Diagnostics:* | |
| $R^2 = 0.01$ | $N = 766$ |

*Note:* The results in the table are regression coefficients. The results reported in parentheses are $t$-statistics.

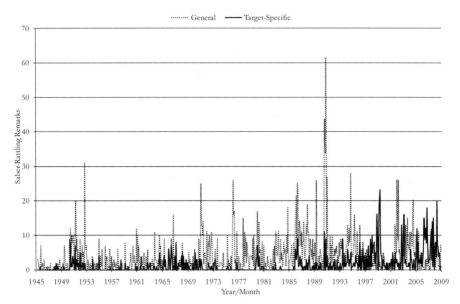

FIGURE 3.3. General and target-specific presidential saber rattling.

These differences are statistically significant at the 0.01 alpha level. These results suggest partisanship effects. However, a definitive claim cannot be made about the importance of presidential partisanship to saber rattling because of the different foreign policy environments faced by each president.

### General versus Target-Specific Saber Rattling

We can further refine our understanding of the data by dividing the time series according to whether presidential saber rattling was general versus target-specific. Recall that Table 3.2 contains representative examples of both general and target-specific saber rattling. The second and third remarks in Table 3.2 demonstrate the nature of general presidential saber rattling. The fourth, fifth, and sixth remarks show the nature of target-specific presidential saber rattling. Figure 3.3 provides an overlay time series plot separating out these two types of saber rattling aggregated by month.

Visual examination of the two plots again shows that significantly more presidential saber rattling was general than was target-specific. There were roughly three times more general than target-specific remarks. Furthermore, the overlay shows that the two time series do not usually line up. The simple correlation between the two plots is only about 0.19. The plots also show that presidents engaged in significant amounts of general saber rattling for prolonged periods without referring to a specific country.

Figure 3.3 also suggests a structural break through time in the types of presidential saber rattling. From 1945 until the mid-1980s, general saber rattling was the predominant mode. Target-specific presidential saber rattling during this period was restricted almost exclusively to the Korean and Vietnam War eras. From the mid-1980s through 2008 the intensity of both general and target-specific saber rattling increased.

More specifically, President Reagan spoke in a consistently hostile manner during the U.S. military buildup occurring in his administration. President George H. W. Bush spewed much bellicose rhetoric before and after the Persian Gulf War, often without referring to a specific target. President Clinton engaged in much general saber rattling during the early 1990s. However, he also directed target-specific remarks toward Iraq, Somalia, Haiti, and during the Bosnian crisis. Finally, President George W. Bush intensified both his general and target-specific saber rattling early in his administration and after the September 11 terrorist attacks and subsequent wars in Afghanistan and Iraq.

When presidents threatened specific targets, there are also interesting differences in the types of threats issued. Figure 3.4 (see color plate after page 50) breaks down target-specific threats according to whether those threats involved deterrence, economic or political sanctions, or military action. Again, note that target-specific threats of any type were significantly less frequent before the late 1980s than after this apparent structural break. Comparing the three plots in Figure 3.4 before the 1980s, we observe that deterrence threats dominated the other two types of threats. This was true even during the Korean War and also during the Vietnam War. However, it also appears that deterrence threats were more prevalent near the start of the Vietnam War, whereas military threats increased near the end of the Vietnam War. Of course, the Cold War era is widely understood to have been an era of deterrence-based foreign policy rather than direct coercion. Therefore, deterrence threats were more prevalent before the late 1980s. It did not make sense for presidents repeatedly to threaten sanctions or military action against the Soviets or Chinese, because such threats would have had little credibility, given the power of these two nations relative to the United States. Consistently, a deterrence-based foreign policy shows up clearly in the data before the 1980s.

This deterrence-based foreign policy initially began to change in the Carter administration, perhaps as a result of two foreign policy crises. Both crises began in late 1979. In November the Iranians took fifty-two Americans hostage in the U.S. embassy in Tehran. In December the Soviets invaded Afghanistan. President Carter responded to both crises with threats of sanction or military action. He issued numerous threats of both types during the Iran hostage crisis. Iran was less powerful, and it made sense to do so in light of his foreign policy goals. His goal was not to deter future Iranian action but the more immediate concern of securing the hostages' release. President Carter also responded to the Soviet invasion of Afghanistan with sanction threats. He levied an embargo on exports to the Soviet Union, which was a major importer of American farm products. He also engaged in significant saber rattling toward the Soviet Union to register American displeasure over Soviet aggression. In both cases President Carter's response initiated a shift in the type of saber rattling commonly used by American presidents.

The Iran hostage crisis also marks the start of an era in which new adversaries emerged apart from the communist bloc nations. These new adversaries were primarily Islamic Middle Eastern countries, all of which were less powerful than the United States. During the Reagan administration the president was responding to both sets of adversaries. Thus, the data in Figure 3.4 show that President Reagan continued President Carter's saber rattling toward the Soviet Union during his first term and intensified his remarks during his second term. Reagan also threatened various Islamic countries as terrorism became an increasingly important concern.

The communist bloc became less threatening after the fall of the Berlin wall, breakup of the Soviet Union, and realignment of Eastern European countries. Presidents since George H. W. Bush have dealt increasingly with the new set of adversaries as they were perceived to be threatening American interests. Thus, Figure 3.4 shows a sharp increase in the number of threats of economic/political sanctions and military intervention after the 1980s.

Which countries were the primary targets of these specific presidential threats? Figure 3.5 (see color plate after page 50) separates out target-specific presidential saber rattling by country. Each country is represented by a different color on the graph. Figure 3.5 again shows a clear break in the intensity of target-specific presidential saber rattling starting in the 1980s. Visual examination of the pre-1980s data shows relatively intense presidential saber rattling toward the North Koreans and North Vietnamese during their respective wars. Of course, it makes intuitive sense that presidents would make hostile remarks toward an adversary during times of war.

If we exclude presidential saber rattling directed toward the North Koreans and North Vietnamese from the pre-1980s data, then the intensity of target-specific saber rattling during this period would be sparse. The other targets of target-specific saber rattling during this era were the Soviets, the Chinese, and the Cubans. However, the intensity of presidential hostility was low compared with more recent times. Before the 1980s the targets of presidential saber rattling were uniformly communist bloc countries.

Again, a shift occurred in which nations were targeted sometime after 1979. Figure 3.5 shows that President Carter directed much threatening rhetoric toward Iran during the 1979–1980 hostage crisis. He also made threatening remarks toward the Soviet Union following their invasion of Afghanistan. President Reagan continued President Carter's bellicosity toward the Soviets early and late in his administration. However, Libya and Iran also became important targets. Saber rattling toward Libya was especially intense before, during, and after the Libyan bombing crisis in April 1986. Interestingly, President Reagan also consistently vilified Iran after the Iran-Contra scandal broke in November 1986.

Figure 3.5 shows that the period from the late-1980s through 2008 was characterized by increasingly intense presidential saber rattling directed toward specific countries. The most obvious targets of presidential threats were Iraq, Iran, North Korea, Afghanistan, Syria, and Bosnia. Many presidential threats were also lumped into a target category labeled "Other." This category included threats directed toward Somalia, Haiti, Zimbabwe, Lebanon, Columbia, and various terrorist organizations such as the Palestinian Liberation Organization, Hezbollah, and Hamas.

Clearly, Iraq was the most important American adversary during the latter part of the time series. Figure 3.5 shows that many presidential threats toward Iraq occurred before and after the 1990–1991 Persian Gulf War, as three administrations attempted to rein in the aggressive tendencies of the Saddam Hussein regime. President George W. Bush also directed significant hostile remarks toward Iraq during the buildup to the 2003 invasion. However, presidential saber rattling toward Iraq basically ceased after the invasion and fall of the Hussein regime. Of course, the stated goals of U.S. invasion were to prevent the spread of weapons of mass destruction and to halt Iraqi support for terrorist Al Qaida. With these alleged goals accomplished, there was no remaining reason for presidential hostility. The focus shifted toward rebuilding Iraq as an ally.

However, the rebuilding of Iraq was also associated with an insurgency and increased saber rattling toward a different set of adversaries. Thus, Figure 3.5 shows that the Iranians and Syrians became much more important presidential targets after the 2003 invasion. Relations with Iran became more intense as evidence emerged that it was supporting the Iraqi insurgency and developing nuclear capabilities. The Syrians were also targets of presidential hostility, because they supported the insurgency, and many former Iraqi Baathists sought refuge in their country.

Additionally, Figure 3.5 shows that the Clinton administration directed a brief but intense campaign of saber rattling toward Bosnia, Serbia, and the former Yugoslav countries starting in March 1999. This episode culminated in a military action to end human rights abuses in this region. Once the conflict was over, presidential saber rattling toward these countries ceased.

President George W. Bush also focused significant threatening rhetoric on North Korea starting with his State of the Union message in January 2002. Presumably, this increased hostility occurred because North Korea was classified as a state sponsor of terrorism. It also abrogated the Nuclear Non-Proliferation Treaty in April 2003. North Korea tested a nuclear device in October 2006. Furthermore, evidence emerged during this period that North Korea sold nuclear

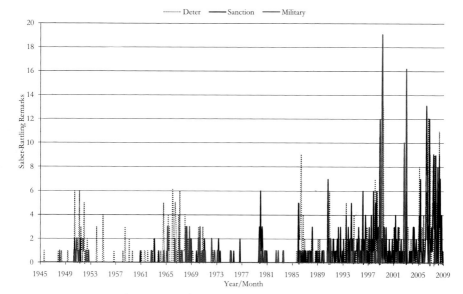

FIGURE 3.4. Types of target-specific threats.

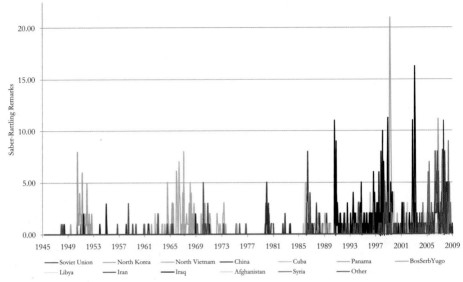

FIGURE 3.5. Targets of country-specific presidential saber rattling.

technology to such countries as Pakistan, Libya, and Syria. Thus, the president may have responded to these developments with threats of increased sanctions to signal American disapproval of these activities.

## Conclusions

This chapter has described the primary measures of presidential saber rattling to be used for statistical analyses in later chapters. Using an approach involving both machine and human coding, several time series were constructed, each representing a different dimension of presidential bellicosity. These time series reflect every hostile public presidential remark of either a general or target-specific nature across eleven presidencies over a period of sixty-four years. Focusing on such an extended time frame allows a more general approach than evaluating a single presidential administration.

Again, the intensity of presidential saber rattling is measured simply by counting the number of hostile presidential remarks of each type during each month. The monthly time series measures gauge the changing flow of presidential saber rattling through time. Using such finely divided time series, we can observe presidential responses to particular crises, as well as how presidents have used saber rattling during the intervening periods. We can also use presidential saber rattling as an independent variable to explore the consequences, both domestic and foreign. Utilizing finely divided time series also enables statistical techniques that are causal, rather than subjective. The goal is to produce generalizable knowledge about the causes and consequences of modern presidential saber rattling through time.

The preliminary descriptive analyses reported in this chapter suggest that the changing intensity of presidential saber rattling may have been presidency- and/or party-specific. Republican presidents threaten more often than Democrats. If this preliminary finding is correct, then this would be consistent with the common belief that Republicans are more aggressive foreign policy leaders than Democrats. In either case, the evidence is not conclusive that there are presidency- or party-specific effects, given the diverse foreign policy environments faced by each president and party.

The graphs in this chapter also provide a first look at how modern presidential saber rattling has varied through time. As should be expected, they show that presidential saber rattling has changed as a function of war, and the various events and crises facing each president. As might be expected, presidents consistently become more hostile during wars and foreign policy crises.

The graphical analyses also suggest that presidential saber rattling has increased through time, perhaps in the form of a structural break starting in the 1980s. The forms of presidential saber rattling also changed about this time. Thus, the end of the Cold War and introduction of new adversaries and foreign policy problems may have produced this change.

Yet knowing that there have been systematic differences and changes through time in presidential saber rattling offers only a start toward understanding the causes and consequences. In the next chapter a theory-oriented approach is applied to explain when and why presidents make threats toward foreign actors.

# 4

# The Causes of Presidential Saber Rattling

This chapter addresses the primary research question, "Why do presidents threaten foreign actors?" More specifically, are presidential threats solely a response to external factors, or do domestic factors also play a role in determining presidential behavior? In answering these questions, the empirical measures of presidential saber rattling described in Chapter 3 are used to evaluate the theoretical models of foreign policy representation described in Chapter 2.

If presidents are pure statesmen responding dispassionately and justly to foreign policy threats, then their behavior should be driven solely by foreign factors. This result would be consistent with the statesman model depicted in Figure 2.1. However, if presidents are also domestic support seekers, then their behavior may also be driven by a desire for personal glory, elections, public opinion, the mass media, partisanship, legislative support, or scandal. This result would be more consistent with the support-seeking models depicted in Figures 2.2 through 2.5. If the latter models are correct, the question then becomes which of these domestic factors is most important.

The descriptive analyses reported in Chapter 3 provided initial insight on the preceding research questions. For example, it is clear from Figure 3.1 that the presence of war and certain foreign policy crises and events correspond with peaks in the intensity of presidential saber rattling. These correspondences suggest that external threats are important to the president's foreign policy behavior.

The preliminary analyses reported in Chapter 3 also suggest that modern presidents may be partisans, rather than pure statesmen in their manner of foreign policy representation. Table 3.3 shows that starting with President Reagan there was a presidency-specific change in the intensity and types of saber rattling. Presidents after 1980 may have been more prone to "cowboy" diplomacy. Table 3.4 also suggests that Republican presidents are statistically more prone than Democrats toward saber rattling.

The graphs in Chapter 3 also suggest that there was a systematic change in the intensity of target-specific saber rattling starting in the 1980s. Was the reason for this change rooted in the foreign policy environment? Did the world become a more dangerous place, thereby causing presidents to become more threatening? Or is the explanation for this change rooted more in domestic factors such as changing media coverage? Just as President Adams may have responded to the media frenzy during the French crisis, modern presidents may have responded to media frenzies associated with the various crises and events starting in the 1980s. The mass media became more adept at "selling" conflict to the public after the Iran hostage crisis. Thus, this chapter asks how media coverage of events and crises affects presidential propensity to threaten other nations.

More generally, like President Adams modern presidents may have altered the tone of their foreign policy rhetoric to gain domestic support. Do presidents use saber rattling strategically for this purpose? For example, does modern saber rattling change as a function of impending elections? Is modern saber rattling a function of the president's public approval ratings or legislative support? How, if at all, does the state of the economy affect the president's propensity to threaten? Does the presence of scandal alter presidential propensity toward threatening rhetoric? This chapter addresses all of these questions.

## Presidential Threats and the International System

International relations scholars have often argued that a nation's behavior toward other nations is primarily a function of the international environment in which that nation resides (i.e., realism, neo-realism; Waltz 1979). The most important factor for explaining a nation's behavior is its power relative to other nations. States seek power and have a strong preference for dominance over other nations (Mearsheimer 2001). As a result, their foreign policy behavior often tends toward coercion (George 2009).

Furthermore, bipolar systems in which power is distributed evenly are viewed as more stable and less prone to conflict. Relations between adversarial nations that are power equals depend on maintaining a balance of power, rather than political, economic, or military coercion. Equals have less incentive to fight, because the cost of doing so is high for both parties. Among equal adversaries coercive foreign policy strategies are less likely to be successful, because effective coercion requires more power than one's adversary. Therefore, saber rattling would not be a preferred foreign policy strategy in a bipolar system of equals.

In contrast, nations that are power-dominant relative to a set of weaker nations have more incentive to pursue coercive strategies. Because their economic and military power is greater, they are more likely to prevail in application of sanctions or war. As a result, coercive strategies are viewed as more credible. Threats perceived as credible are seen as dangerous by the targets of those threats. Therefore, realist theory would predict that stronger nations are more likely use coercion in a multipolar system.

The graphical analyses in Chapter 3 offer tentative support for this theory. Figure 3.4 plotted the intensity of presidential saber rattling toward specific targets from 1945 through 2008. Again, the pre-1980s data show that the only periods of intense presidential saber rattling were periods of war. Excluding wartime threats, the figure showed that presidents made few threatening remarks toward specific nations. For those threats that did occur, the targets were uniformly communist bloc countries (i.e., North Korea, Cuba, North Vietnam, the Chinese, and the Soviets). Thus, before the 1980s the targets of presidential saber rattling were reflections of a bipolar world, and presidents made fewer threats than in the later multipolar world.

The period from the mid-1980s through 2008 was characterized by increasingly intense presidential saber rattling directed toward a multiplicity of nations. The most obvious of these were Iraq, Iran, and North Korea. Of course, these nations also directed significant hostility toward the United States during this period. They were classified by the U.S. State Department as sponsors of global terrorism. Thus, the rise of presidential saber rattling after the 1980s might be linked to perceived threats from these nations.

General theories of international relations might also argue that the demise of a bipolar international system was responsible for the subsequent increase in presidential hostility toward weaker nations. U.S. foreign policy after the 1980s was an effort to consolidate power as hegemon. It might also be argued that altered presidential behavior after the 1980s was a rational response to a fundamental change in the international system. Conflict directed toward the United States from multiple adversaries and the rise of global terrorism basically forced presidents to become more threatening.

### Presidential Threats and Domestic Audiences

A competing theoretical explanation is that changing presidential foreign policy behavior after the 1980s was rooted in stimuli emanating from domestic factors. From this perspective, presidential saber rattling can be viewed as a form of political drama. It is well understood among scholars of American political behavior that political drama such as military actions, foreign policy crises, and other sharp occurrences disturb people's steady-state attitudes about the president. Mueller's (1970) classic study first showed the importance of dramatic foreign policy events to presidential approval ratings. Since then a plethora of other researchers have followed this lead.[1] Indeed, MacKuen (1983) showed that political drama is about equal in importance to economic factors in affecting presidential approval.

---

[1] For example, see Brody (1991), Brody and Page (1975), Chappell and Keech (1985), Clarke and Stewart (1994), DeRouen (1995), Erikson et al. (2002), Fiorina (1981), Fordham (1998a), Haller and Norpoth (1994), Hibbs (1974, 1987), Kernell (1978), MacKuen (1983), MacKuen et al. (1992), Markus (1988), Monroe (1978), Mueller (1973), Norpoth (1996), Ostrom and Job (1986), Ostrom and Smith (1993), and Simon and Ostrom (1989).

Modern presidents understand this relationship. As a result, they use saber rattling strategically to bolster their public support. Presidents play continuously to the mass media, because the media transmit presidential messages to the public and world (e.g., see Brace and Hinckley 1992; Edwards 1983; Kernell 1997). Presidents depend on the media to build images of strength and rectitude that are critically important to public support. Such images may also bolster the president's credibility in the international arena.

Like President Adams, modern presidents may also be caught up in the various media frenzies which have so often occurred since the Iran hostage crisis. For example, Wood and Peake (1998; see also Edwards and Wood 1999) found that the media drive presidential attention to foreign policy issues. However, the reverse relationship did not hold. Presidents do not systematically drive media attention.

Confirming this perspective with qualitative evidence, Andrew Card, former White House official during the Reagan, George H. W. Bush, and George W. Bush administrations, has noted that presidents after 1980 faced a far different media environment than in earlier times. The modern media is relentless in its search for stories that captivate audiences. White House reactions to newly developing stories tend to follow these media-driven efforts, sometimes very quickly, as the administration tries to stay out in front of an evolving process. As a result, the media tends to lead presidential rhetoric through time, rather than merely being responsive to it (Card 2011).

After the late-Carter administration, the media increasingly focused on crisis and conflict. The Iran hostage-taking, Grenada, Libya bombing, Panama invasion, Persian Gulf War, Haiti, Kosovo, September 11, Afghanistan, and Iraq invasion were all periods during which media coverage escalated dramatically. Many of these crises involved significant national security concerns. Under these conditions presidents should speak more loudly to both the media and public (e.g., see Baum 2004). Similarly, the media and public are more interested in what presidents have to say during these periods.

The new audience-oriented (rather than news-oriented) media makes news, rather than merely reporting it. Crisis puts the modern media into a "round-the-clock" mode that bombards the nation with continuous coverage. The crowding out effect of crisis becomes so strong that media coverage spills over to displace other issues. For example, the late evening news show *Nightline* originated to provide the American public with a regular update on the progress of the Iran hostage crisis. In large numbers Americans glued themselves to *Nightline* and other special news programs to keep abreast of ongoing events involving the administration, the government of Iran, and the American hostages. Administration spokespersons frequently appeared on the program, and the president spoke often about the crisis in various public settings.

Because it is a successful news strategy for capturing audiences, this pattern of "hyper-coverage" by the media has been repeated frequently. A major factor for all of these crises was widespread elite and public consensus. Under such conditions, the president's message is transmitted more loudly, perhaps even to the point of the media propagandizing presidential positions (Bennett 1990; Entman 1991). As a result, we should expect presidents to make more public threats during periods of media frenzy.

Beyond periods of media frenzy, there are other periods during which presidents may issue threats strategically to bolster their public support. Presidents seek reelection for themselves and their political party. During election seasons they should be particularly interested in bolstering their support. Elections are periods when presidents and their political party seek future benefits bestowed on them by the electorate. A successful reelection campaign can produce gains for the president in terms of renewed support and political capital. It can also result in material benefits by securing policies favorable to the president and supporters. Presidential saber rattling produces perceptions of strength, which should in turn increase the president's electability.

Furthermore, presidents may be emboldened to make foreign policy threats by having strong public and institutional support. As suggested by the Adams vignette, presidents may feel they are on better footing when they have a supportive public and Congress. Accordingly, high presidential approval ratings and a strong economy might embolden presidents in their foreign policy behavior. For example, Canes-Wrone (2006) finds that presidents are more likely to "go public" on foreign policy when their initiatives are popular. Similarly, the strength of the president's coalition in Congress might also increase the president's propensity toward saber rattling. For example, Howell and Pevehouse (2005, 2007) suggest that presidents are systematically more likely to use military force when their own party controls Congress. Thus, strong domestic political and economic resources should make presidents more prone to issuing threats toward external actors.

However, another line of international relations scholarship suggests the opposite relationship. The diversionary theory of war posits that strategic presidents "embark on risky foreign ventures in an attempt to achieve diplomatic or military gains that will help solve their domestic problems" (Levy 1989, 272). When presidential approval ratings are low, the economy is doing poorly, or the administration is in scandal, the diversionary theory posits that presidents are more likely to involve the nation in conflict. This "folk theory" is commonly invoked by political pundits and is widely believed by the mass public. Historians also commonly posit that leaders are motivated in their foreign policy decisions by domestic conditions (Levy 1987).

The diversionary theory has attracted much scholarly attention but remains in doubt. Quantitative studies have reported mixed evidence on the diversionary theory. Some research suggests the probability of hostile activities directed toward other nations is higher when the United States is experiencing a weak economy or low presidential approval ratings (DeRouen 1995, 2000; James and Hristoulas 1994; James and Oneal 1991; Morgan and Bickers 1992; Ostrom and Job 1986; Russett 1989; Smith 1996). However, other studies seriously undercut this work (Gowa 1998; Meernik 1994; Meernik and Waterman 1996; Yoon 1997). Some researchers have found that presidential use of force is actually more likely when public approval is high than when it is low (James and Oneal 1991; Ostrom and Job 1986) and rarely occurs just before an election. Furthermore, when military interventions do occur, public support for presidents routinely increases in the short term, but support wanes if a conflict becomes long term (Brody and Page 1975; Cotton 1987; Kernell 1978; MacKuen 1983; Mueller 1973).

In yet another line of international relations research, the "signaling" literature suggests another rationale for presidents to make public threats (e.g., see Dorussen and Mo 2001; Fearon 1994, 1997; Gelpi and Griesdorf 2001; Kurizaki 2007; Leventoğlu and Tarar 2005; Partell and Palmer 1999; Ramsay 2004; Schultz 1998, 2001a, 2001b; Smith 1998; Tarar and Leventoğlu 2009; Tomz 2007; Weeks 2008).[2] They seek to bolster their credibility in the international arena by projecting an image of strength and resolve. Public threats are viewed as more credible than private threats by foreign adversaries. Further, public threats may well bolster presidential approval and institutional support, further increasing presidential credibility.

However, there are also potential audience costs that should constrain the propensity of presidents to make public threats. Models of international conflict and cooperation now commonly assume that leaders suffer losses if they issue public threats and fail to follow through. Citizens punish leaders who back down relative to leaders who never commit in the first place. The presence of audience costs and the associated prospect of losing domestic support should therefore discourage leaders from playing to the media and public. Thus, contrary to the earlier predictions, presidents may actually "stay private" in the face of domestic stimuli pushing them toward seeking greater support through "going public" (Baum 2004; Kurizaki 2007).

## Measurement

We cannot know with certainty what motivates presidents in their foreign policy behavior. Such certainty would require psychological data that can only come from within a president's mind. Moreover, presidents can always rationalize foreign policy threats as flowing from a statesman-like desire to protect the nation, project American interests, or increase their foreign policy credibility. Yet outside observers may simultaneously believe that presidential threats are rooted in self-interest, diversionary tactics, or other pretended motivations.

---

[2] This research is discussed further in Chapter 6. Generally, the research cited here focuses on leader credibility when making threats. "Going public" with threats is seen as tying a leader's hands because of potential future costs. Therefore, public threats should become more credible to foreign adversaries, which should, in turn, make them more successful.

As a result of these uncertainties, the best we can do is to develop measures that are indicative of presidential motivations.

With this limitation in mind, this study considers the effect of a variety of foreign and domestic factors on the changing intensity of presidential saber rattling through time. Foreign factors considered in the analyses that follow include the presence of war and the presence of major foreign policy events or crises. Domestic factors include the magnitude and duration of media frenzies, presidential election seasons, partisan alignment of Congress and the president, economic conditions, presidential approval, and scandal. Presidency-specific indicators are also included in the analyses to control for and evaluate hypotheses about how personal differences and partisanship might affect presidential propensities to threaten.

### Foreign Factors

The presence of war is measured using an indicator variable switched on for the Korean War (1950:05–1953:06), Vietnam War (1965:02–1975:03), Persian Gulf War (1990:07–1991:01), U.S. invasion of Afghanistan (2001:9–2001:11), and U.S. invasion of Iraq (2003:2–2003:4).[3] None of these periods involved declared wars but did involve military engagement lasting from several months to many years.

A second indicator time series was included to capture the presence of major foreign policy crises and events from 1945 through 2008. The included crises and events are listed in Table 4.1, along with their respective dates. The 54 listed crises and events range from the dropping of the Atom bomb on Japan in August 1945 to the London tube bombing in July 2005. Also, note that some of the events are actually brief military interventions that might also have been included in the war time series.[4]

Most of the included events were actually independent from war, some preceding, some following, and some substantively unrelated. In a few cases the events time series overlaps with the war time series. For example, U.S. forces crossing the 38th parallel in October 1950 was a critical juncture of the Korean War. However, it was also independently an event that should have produced more presidential saber rattling. Similarly, the Mekong Delta Operation, Tet Offensive, and sending U.S. troops into Cambodia were major events of the Vietnam War that should have had effects independent of the war. Additionally, the United Nations authorization for the Persian Gulf War and United Nations Resolution 1441 were closely connected to their respective

[3] The rationale for ending the measures for the U.S. invasions of Afghanistan and Iraq after November 2001 and April 2003, respectively, is that the United States from those points on became an occupation force. Presidential saber rattling toward these two countries effectively ceased after the successful invasions. Therefore, even though hostilities continued, presidential remarks were directed at the respective insurgencies rather than at the countries themselves.

[4] It makes no difference to the statistical analyses whether the brief military interventions in Table 4.1 are included as war or crisis events.

TABLE 4.1. *Major Events and Crises Affecting U.S. Interests from 1945 through 2008*

| Event | Date | Event | Date |
|---|---|---|---|
| Atom bomb dropped on Japan | 1945:08 | U.S. attacks San Juan del Sur | 1984:03 |
| Start of the Berlin Blockade | 1948:06 | Berlin discotheque bombing | 1986:04 |
| Soviets test first atomic bomb | 1949:09 | Libya bombing | 1986:04 |
| U.S. forces cross 38th parallel | 1950:10 | Iceland summit conference | 1986:10 |
| CIA overthrows Iran government | 1953:08 | Iran Air 655 shot down | 1988:07 |
| Soviets invade Hungary | 1956:10 | Second Gulf of Sidra incident | 1989:01 |
| Suez crisis | 1956:11 | Tiananmen Square | 1989:05 |
| Marines land in Lebanon | 1958:07 | Velvet Revolution in Prague | 1989:11 |
| Bay of Pigs | 1961:04 | United States invades Panama | 1989:12 |
| Cuban missile crisis | 1962:10 | Iraq invades Kuwait | 1990:08 |
| Gulf of Tonkin Resolution | 1964:08 | United Nations authorizes intervention in Kuwait | 1990:11 |
| U.S. troops in Dominican Republic | 1965:04 | Start of NATO intervention in Bosnia | 1992:06 |
| U.S. Mekong Delta Operation | 1967:12 | Iraq refuses United Nations inspection team access | 1992:07 |
| Tet Offensive/Battle of Hue | 1968:01 | U.S. marines land in Somalia | 1992:12 |
| Soviets invade Czechoslovakia | 1968:08 | First World Trade Center bombing | 1993:02 |
| U.S. troops authorized in Cambodia | 1970:04 | Battle of Mogadishu | 1994:10 |
| Signing of SALT I treaty | 1972:05 | Rwanda genocide made public | 1994:04 |
| Munich Olympics terror attack | 1972:09 | United Nations authorizes intervention in Haiti | 1994:08 |
| Fall of Saigon | 1975:04 | Iraq reveals has biological weapons | 1995:07 |
| Iran militants take U.S. hostages | 1979:01 | Iraq suspends United Nations Special Commission cooperation | 1998:08 |
| SALT II treaty signed | 1979:06 | NATO commences Kosovo air campaign | 1999:03 |
| Attack on U.S. embassy in Pakistan | 1979:11 | USS *Cole* terror attack | 2000:10 |
| Soviets invade Afghanistan | 1979:12 | September 11 terror attack | 2001:09 |
| First Gulf of Sidra incident | 1981:08 | Bali Bombings | 2002:10 |
| Start of Lebanese civil war | 1982:06 | United Nations Resolution 1441 on Iraq | 2002:11 |
| Soviets shoot down KAL 007 | 1983:09 | Madrid bombing | 2004:03 |
| U.S. invasion of Grenada | 1983:10 | London train bombings | 2005:07 |

*Note:* All events are switched on at the indicated years and months and off for all other periods.

wars. However, these events should also have coincided with a stark increase in the intensity of presidential saber rattling, beyond normal wartime rhetoric. It should also be noted that some of the entries in Table 4.1 capture discrete stimuli originating from outside the United States, whereas others capture discrete presidential responses to more diffuse external stimuli. For example, the dropping of the Atom bomb on Japan was a U.S.-initiated event in response to the war with Japan. In contrast, the Berlin Blockade was a critical event initiated by the Soviets but was certainly a major determinant of U.S. behavior during 1948. Both types of events require consideration and statistical control.

The decision of which particular events to include in the crises and events time series involved searching http://Spiritus-Temporis.com. Spiritus-Temporis contains a time line of important historical dates in world history. If a crisis or event was listed there, pertained to U.S. interests, and related to foreign policy, then it was included.

### Domestic Factors

Media frenzy was gauged by recording the monthly count of *New York Times* stories associated with each event listed in Table 4.1. Think of each event as an intervention. Then, given a preintervention equilibrium number of stories, a running tally was recorded for every succeeding month after the intervention until the number of media stories returned to preintervention levels. This approach was applied separately for each event. The results were then summed across events to reflect the total media frenzy in each month across the entire saber-rattling time series. Again, the expectation is that greater media frenzy associated with an event should be associated with more presidential saber rattling.[5]

We can obtain insight on the nature of the media-frenzy variable by graphing the resulting time series. Figure 4.1 plots the count of media stories associated with foreign policy crises and events from 1945 through 2008. There are visual similarities between this time series and some of the graphs of presidential saber rattling reported in Chapter 3. Recall again that before the 1980s the target-specific presidential saber-rattling time series was quite sparse. However, after the 1980s the intensity of target-specific saber rattling increased sharply. There appeared to be a break in the time series, perhaps corresponding with the shift from a bipolar to a multipolar world. However, the media-frenzy time series suggests an alternative explanation.

---

[5] Media coverage may not be exogenous, perhaps also responding to the president. Thus, Granger (1969) exogeneity tests were performed to evaluate this possibility. Controlling for events, the tests show that the relation runs from the media to presidential saber rattling, rather than in the opposite direction. The $\chi^2_4$ statistic from the media to presidential saber rattling of all types is 14.49 with $p$ value of 0.01. In the reverse direction, the $\chi^2_4$ statistic from presidential saber rattling to the media is only 2.01 with a $p$ value of 0.73. Note that this finding is consistent with the results reported in Wood and Peake (1998; see also Edwards and Wood 1999). Therefore, the media series is treated as exogenous in subsequent analyses.

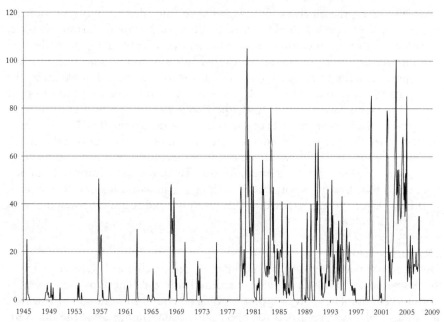

FIGURE 4.1. Media frenzies from 1945 through 2008.

Figure 4.1 shows that media coverage of various crises and events increased sharply after the Iran hostage crisis in 1979. Although the timing is not perfect, it seems clear that the increased incidence of media frenzy corresponds visually with an increase in target-specific saber rattling after the 1980s. Thus, the domestic environment facing the president may have been at least partially responsible for changing presidential behavior after the 1980s.

Election seasons were measured as an indicator variable starting in January and ending in October of each presidential election year. Election campaigns start during the primary season and continue until the election occurs in early November. During these periods presidents attempt to produce images of strength for themselves or their political party. Therefore, election seasons should be ripe periods for increased presidential saber rattling.

Presidents may also respond to incentives flowing from their approval ratings, economic performance, or scandal. As noted earlier, presidents may be emboldened in their foreign policy rhetoric by having high approval ratings and a strong economy. Alternatively, they may use saber rattling strategically to increase their approval ratings when they are low or to divert attention from the economy when it is weak. Similarly, the presence of scandal may weaken a president, resulting in less bellicosity toward foreign adversaries. Conversely, during scandals presidents may use foreign policy rhetoric to divert attention. Thus, theoretical expectations for these three variables are ambiguous.

Presidential approval was measured using the standard Gallup survey measure of public assessments of presidential job performance. The Gallup approval question reads, "Do you approve or disapprove of the way [president's name] is handling his job as president?" The Gallup survey organization has asked this question routinely since March 1949. However, before 1978 the question was asked irregularly with some missing months. After 1978 the question was asked every month but with different timing, and sometimes multiple times in the same month. These potential complications were addressed using the procedure and software WCALC developed by Stimson (1991).[6] The approval time series was lagged by one month to avoid potential problems of reverse causality.[7]

U.S. economic performance was measured using the annualized percent change in the Conference Board's Composite Index of Coincident Indicators. This is an index constructed from four time series chosen by the Conference Board because they are consistently in step with the current state of the economy.[8] The four time series comprising the Coincident Index are employment, personal income, industrial production, and manufacturing/trade sales in 1996 dollars. Using the Coincident Index provides a better measure of current economic conditions than often used individual time series such as Gross Domestic Product (which is released only quarterly and often revised) or unemployment and inflation (which are lagging indicators). According to the Conference Board (2001, 13), the Coincident Index is a "broad series that measures aggregate economic activity; thus they define the business cycle." The Coincident Index was also lagged by one month, again to avoid potential problems of reverse causality.[9]

The presence of scandal was measured using an indicator variable for the three major presidency scandals of modern times. The Watergate scandal (1972:06–1974:08) focused on the crimes of President Nixon and his associates during and after the 1972 presidential election. The Iran-Contra scandal (1986:11–1987:8) confronted the misbehavior of President Reagan and/or

---

[6] The software produced a recursively smoothed monthly time series running from March 1949 through December 2008.

[7] In other words, presidential saber rattling may have affected presidential approval, rather than the reverse. I show in Chapter 5 that there is indeed two-way causality between presidential saber rattling and approval even after controlling for foreign policy events. Thus, it is important to lag the approval variable to avoid possible reverse causality.

[8] The Conference Board is a global, independent research organization working in the public interest that is widely regarded as an objective source of economic and business knowledge. Its research department publishes three widely used indices for gauging the U.S. economy: the Index of Lagging Indicators (for gauging the economic past), the Index of Leading Indicators (for forecasting the economic future), and the Index of Coincident Indicators (for gauging the current economy).

[9] Wood (2009b) shows that presidential saber rattling affects a variety of economic outcomes, including current economic performance. Therefore, it is important to lag the economic variable to avoid reverse causality.

administration officials who violated U.S. law by trading arms for hostages and covertly channeling aid to the Nicaraguan Contras. Finally, the Monicagate scandal (1998:1–1999:2) involved charges against President Clinton, continuously partisan attacks, and impeachment proceedings.

Finally, the partisan alignment of Congress relative to the president may also have affected presidential saber rattling. Partisan alignment was measured using a set of indicator variables to reflect periods when there was unified versus divided government. As suggested by the Adams vignette, presidents could be more prone to aggressive foreign policy stances when they have greater legislative support. Such support should be strongest under unified government and weakest under divided government. Therefore, presidential saber rattling should potentially increase under unified government (e.g., see Howell and Pevehouse 2005, 2007).

However, it may also be that presidents respond to divided government by shifting their attention away from domestic policy toward foreign policy. When presidents are in a weak position institutionally, they may shift to their strong suit, foreign policy, to enable a modicum of success and bolster their domestic support. Therefore, the predicted relationship for the partisan alignment of Congress is again ambiguous.

## Evaluating the Statesman versus Support-Seeking Models

### *Looking for an Electoral Connection: Univariate Spectral Decompositions*

In this section, univariate spectral time series analyses are reported for the six dependent measures described in Chapter 3. Again, the six time series consist of all types of presidential threats (Figure 3.1), general threats (Figure 3.3), target-specific threats (Figure 3.3), and target-specific threats broken down by the three types: deterrence threats, threats of political or economic sanction, and military threats (Figure 3.4).

The intent of these spectral analyses is to evaluate whether presidential behavior changes systematically in response to the electoral cycle. The electoral cycle occurs regularly in the United States with a frequency of 1/48 and a period of 48 months. Because of this regularity we can evaluate the various saber-rattling time series for change at this frequency and periodicity. Spectral decomposition of the six time series into their component frequencies is used for this purpose.

Spectral time series analysis is often used for evaluating physical phenomena such as mechanical vibrations, acoustic patterns, climate change, ocean-driven phenomena, and galactic movements. However, this approach can also be used for evaluating social science phenomena in which one expects regular periodicities (e.g., see Beck 1991; Enders and Sandler 2000). Analyses of this type are also called frequency domain analyses.

Every time series can be expressed as the sum of a set of Fourier frequencies. In spectral time series analysis, the dependent variable is regressed on the set of all sinusoidal frequencies defined by Fourier decomposition. The goal of frequency domain analysis is to uncover the power contained in hidden frequencies within a time series. If a time series is random with respect to the Fourier frequencies, then a spectral decomposition will show that all frequencies contain equal power. However, if some frequencies contain more power than others, then this will show up through spikes at particular frequencies.

Visual analysis of Figures 3.1 through 3.4 in the previous chapter did not reveal any obvious cyclical regularity beyond presidential responsiveness to external events. However, a more systematic analysis of the frequency composition of the various saber rattling time series is appropriate.

Figure 4.2 contains the spectral decompositions of the six saber-rattling time series into their 383 separate Fourier frequencies.[10] The left side of Figure 4.2 contains analyses of saber rattling of all types, general saber rattling directed at no particular target, and target-specific saber rattling. The right side focuses on target-specific saber rattling broken down by deterrence threats, economic or political threats, and military threats.

The large spikes at the low end of the frequency spectrum, toward the left of the graphs in Figure 4.2, show that the series contain more power at the low end of the frequency spectrum. Higher power at this end of the spectrum normally implies a process that is positive autoregressive. However, beyond this autoregressive property, one particular spike near the low end stands out for all six time series. This spike is marked with a dashed vertical line and occurs at frequency 16/766 (i.e., 1/47.875), or about 0.021 cycles relative to the entire series. This higher power corresponds with a periodicity of one cycle every 47.875 months. This number is sufficiently close to 48 months to conclude that there is a strong periodic component to the saber-rattling time series that coincides with the American electoral cycle.

The 48-month periodicity occurs in all six time series with differing amplitudes. The cycle is strongest for the three aggregate time series on the left side of Figure 4.2. The electoral season regularity is clearly present for saber rattling of all types, general saber rattling directed at no specific target, as well as target-specific saber rattling. With lower power, the right side of Figure 4.2 also shows a 48-month periodicity. Among the three right side graphs, the pattern is far strongest for military threats. It is weakest for threats of political or economic sanction. However, presidents increase their target-specific threats for all three measures with a periodicity again roughly corresponding with the 48-month electoral cycle.

---

[10] The time series contains 766 observations. Because of the phenomenon of aliasing, this implies that there are $\frac{766}{2} = 383$ Fourier frequencies.

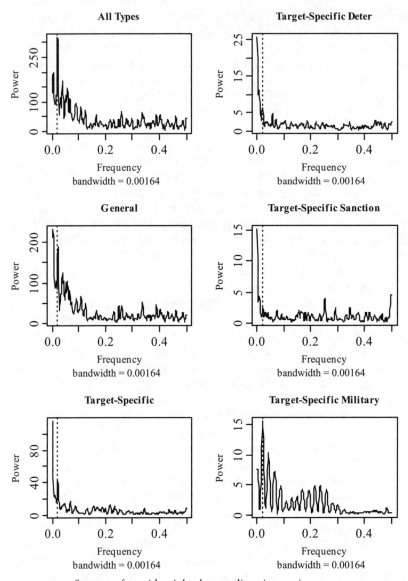

FIGURE 4.2. Spectra of presidential saber-rattling time series.

Thus, the univariate evidence for the dependent variables of this chapter strongly suggests that presidents respond to election seasons.[11] Although this

---

[11] One might reasonably wonder whether this increase in the intensity of presidential saber rattling during election periods is just a function of overall increasing presidential rhetoric during these periods. To evaluate this possibility, I did a machine search of the *Public Papers* on the words

univariate evidence is suggestive, occurring in all six time series, it is not definitive. There are no statistical controls in these analyses. Also, we do not know when the cycle is at its maximum. If the maximum occurs just before elections, then we could draw strong conclusions about presidents using saber rattling for electoral purposes. However, further analysis is required to reach this conclusion.

### A Multivariate Estimation Method

Again, the six measures consist of monthly counts of presidential threats from April 1945 through December 2008. These data are, by nature, always positive integers, characterized by many zeros, with a preponderance of small integers in any given month. Figure 3.2 contained a frequency distribution of the aggregated dependent variable. That plot showed a distribution that is skewed right, with shape similar to an exponential family function. This evidence suggested that we need a Poisson or negative binomial estimator.

However, standard Poisson and negative binomial estimators do not take into account possible interdependence between time series observations. We saw evidence of positive autoregressive interdependence in the preceding spectral analyses. Significant power was concentrated near the low end of the frequency spectrum for most of the six graphs in Figure 4.2.

More theoretically, presidential saber rattling may be inertial, with the counts in a given month being a function of the counts in earlier months. Presidents may engage in streams of saber rattling through time as they deal with various foreign policy issues. This feature of the dependent variable suggests the need to test for and potentially estimate time serial interdependence, but in the context of discrete data.

To begin, standard Poisson and negative binomial models were estimated. The statistical results showed similar coefficients for both estimators. However, the negative binomial overdispersion parameters were large and statistically significant, indicating the need to consider overdispersion in the final statistical specification.

Using the negative binomial estimator, Pearson residuals were calculated from the model predictions.[12] The Pearson residuals were then evaluated using the autocorrelation and partial autocorrelation functions. The results again confirmed positive autoregressive time serial interdependence. Therefore, an

---

"the" and "a" to construct a monthly time series containing the count of most presidential sentences spoken from 1945 through 2009. Using this time series, spectral analysis was again performed to search for periodicities. There was no similar 48-month periodicity in the overall count of presidential sentences. Thus, the result for saber rattling reported in this section is not merely an artifact of increasing presidential rhetoric during elections.

[12] Pearson residuals are calculated by exponentiating the predicted values calculated when all variables were at their means. The exponentiated predictions are then subtracted from the dependent variable and divided by the square root of the exponentiated predictions.

estimator that allows for both overdispersion and autocorrelation was used for the analyses that follow.

A variety of possible estimators can be used under these conditions. Cameron and Trivedi (1998, chapter 7) detail six possibilities. On the basis of their discussion, the quasi-likelihood Markov estimator proposed by Zeger and Qaqish (1988) was used for the following analyses. This specification is sometimes called the conditional model, because it includes a transformation of the lagged dependent variable on the right side. The core of this model is a negative binomial regression to take account of the overdispersion. It also includes a lagged dependent variable, transformed by logging the data adjusted by a small constant to enable the log transformation.[13]

Because this estimator includes a transformed lagged dependent variable, it is somewhat more conservative than other possible estimators. The lagged dependent variable contains all of those historical factors that might have been omitted from the model, thereby producing more conservative statistical tests. The lagged dependent variable also has a substantive interpretation; it models the inertia through time in presidential saber rattling.

*Multivariate Analysis of Presidential Saber Rattling of All Types, General, and Target-Specific*

Consider first a multivariate analysis for three of the six dependent time series: saber rattling of all types, general, and target-specific. Table 4.2 reports the results of these analyses. The numbers in the table are estimated coefficients, with robust *t* statistics in parentheses. We can interpret the coefficients as follows: for a one-unit change in a predictor variable, the difference in the logs of expected counts of the dependent variable changes by the respective regression coefficient, given the other predictor variables are held constant.

However, this interpretation is a bit awkward for imparting meaning to readers. Therefore, a more commonly used metric is to calculate incidence ratios (also called factor changes). Incidence ratios are obtained simply by exponentiating the estimated coefficients. Thus, Table 4.2 reports the coefficients, along with incidence ratios in square brackets.

The incidence ratio for Logged Presidential Threats$_{t-1}$ in the first column and row of Table 4.2 is obtained by $ir = \exp(0.02) = 1.02$. This number is interpreted in terms of percent change over the expected count reported in the first row of the diagnostics section (5.14 threats per month). Thus, the effect of one additional unit of logged presidential threats in the prior month is an increase of about two percent. In other words, presidential threats are only mildly inertial, after controlling for foreign and domestic factors. Of course, the real importance of this variable is in controlling for time serial interdependence. The residuals from all models reported below are non-autocorrelated.

---

[13] Values of zero in the lagged and logged variable were increased by $1 \times 10^{-6}$.

TABLE 4.2. *Statesmanship and Support Seeking in Presidential Saber Rattling*

| Variable | Saber-Rattling Type | | |
| --- | --- | --- | --- |
| | All Types | General | Target-Specific |
| Logged Presidential Threats$_{t-1}$ | 0.02 | 0.02 | 0.03 |
| | (2.27) | (2.72) | (5.04) |
| | [1.02] | [1.02] | [1.03] |
| *Foreign Factors* | | | |
| War | 0.48 | 0.43 | 0.74 |
| | (2.78) | (2.31) | (3.06) |
| | [1.62] | [1.53] | [2.10] |
| Major Foreign Policy Crises and | 0.23 | 0.12 | 0.64 |
| Events | (1.70) | (0.81) | (3.15) |
| | [1.26] | [1.13] | [1.90] |
| *Domestic Factors* | | | |
| Election Seasons | 0.21 | 0.31 | −0.10 |
| | (2.51) | (3.37) | (−0.77) |
| | [1.23] | [1.36] | [0.90] |
| Unified Government | −0.07 | 0.24 | −0.58 |
| | (−0.64) | (1.67) | (−3.11) |
| | [0.93] | [1.27] | [0.56] |
| Economic Conditions$_{t-1}$ | 0.03 | 0.02 | 0.02 |
| | (2.04) | (1.33) | (0.89) |
| | [1.03] | [1.02] | [1.02] |
| Scandal | −0.05 | −0.19 | 0.13 |
| | (−0.40) | (−1.21) | (1.16) |
| | [0.95] | [0.83] | [1.14] |
| Approval$_{t-1}$ | −0.00 | 0.00 | −0.01 |
| | (−0.50) | (0.94) | (−1.18) |
| | [1.00] | [1.00] | [0.99] |
| Media Frenzy | 0.01 | 0.01 | 0.01 |
| | (3.81) | (3.06) | (2.85) |
| | [1.01] | [1.01] | [1.01] |
| *Diagnostics* | | | |
| $\lambda = \exp(\bar{X}\beta_k)$ | 5.14 | 3.83 | 0.87 |
| (Expected Count) | | | |
| N | 717 | 717 | 717 |
| Wald $\chi^2$ | 195.35 | 136.59 | 339.33 |
| $\alpha$ (overdispersion parameter) | 0.65 | 0.78 | 0.97 |
| | (13.02) | (12.58) | (8.82) |

*Note:* The numbers in the table are coefficients, robust *t* statistics (in parentheses), and incidence ratios (in square brackets) from Poisson autoregressive regressions (Zeger and Qaqish 1988) of presidential saber rattling of the indicated types on the variables in the left column. An unreported constant and indicator variables for each presidency were also included in the regressions.

How do foreign factors affect presidential saber rattling across the three dependent variables? The coefficients for the war variable in the second row of Table 4.2 are statistically significant for all three analyses. In the first column, the incidence ratio for the effect of war on all types of saber rattling shows an increase of about 62 percent (i.e., to $1.62 * 5.14 = 8.33$ threats per month). In the second column, the effect of war on general presidential saber rattling is an increase of about 53 percent (i.e., to $1.53 * 3.83 = 5.86$ threats per month). Finally, in the third column, the effect of war on target-specific presidential saber rattling is an increase of about 110 percent per month (i.e., to $2.10 * 0.87 = 1.83$ threats per month). Thus, as was also shown visually in Figure 3.1, war is an important determinant of presidential behavior.

Major foreign policy crises and events produce increases that are more target-specific, rather than general. The results for all types of saber rattling in the first column show a statistically significant increase of about 26 percent (i.e., to $1.26 * 5.14 = 6.48$ threats per month). The second column shows no statistically significant increase in general presidential saber rattling. Finally, the third column reveals a strongly significant increase of about 90 percent in target-specific saber rattling due to the presence of major foreign policy crises and events (i.e., to $1.90 * 0.87 = 1.65$ threats per month). The increase in saber rattling of all types in the first column is clearly due to the effect of target-specific threats in the third column, rather than general threats. Of course, the crises and events listed in Table 4.1 are primarily related to threats directed toward the nation by other countries or actions by the United States directed toward other countries. Therefore, it makes sense that presidential responses would be more target-specific than general (i.e., symbolic) for this variable.

Presidents respond as might be expected to the external foreign policy environment. However, are they also domestic support seekers when conducting American foreign policy? Controlling for inertia, the presence of war, major crises, and events, the results reported in the remainder of Table 4.2 show that they are. The results for election seasons in the fourth row again show that presidents use bellicose rhetoric more during elections. This result is consistent with the spectral time series analysis reported in Figure 4.1. That analysis showed a 48-month periodicity to modern presidential saber rattling in all three time series. The results in Table 4.2 confirm that the peak of the 48-month cycle occurs when presidents are campaigning for reelection.

More specifically, the fourth row of Table 4.2 shows that during election seasons presidential saber rattling aggregated by all types increases by about 23 percent over the expected count (i.e., to $1.23 * 5.14 = 6.32$ hostile remarks per month). The statistical results also suggest, however, that the nature of presidential bellicosity during election seasons does not always pertain to particular targets. The election season coefficient for target-specific saber rattling is not significant. In contrast, general presidential saber rattling increases during elections by about 36 percent (i.e., to $1.36 * 3.83 = 5.21$ threats per month). Presidential saber rattling during elections appears to be more general "chest-pounding" than goal-oriented, probably intended to present an image of strength for the president. Thus, presidents use foreign policy threats strategically to bolster their domestic support. However, their rhetoric appears primarily symbolic, rather than intended to achieve specific foreign policy goals.

How, if at all, does the strength of the president's legislative coalition affect the president's propensity toward threatening rhetoric? The statistical results in the fifth row of Table 4.2 paint a complex picture. The primary argument given earlier was that institutional support might embolden a president in relations with foreign adversaries. However, the reported analysis provides little support for this interpretation. Unified government is not statistically associated with more threatening presidential rhetoric when considering all types. It is associated with a significant increase in general presidential saber rattling directed toward no particular nation or actor. However, unified government is also associated with a significant decrease in target-specific presidential saber rattling. Thus, the two effects offset one another.

For general saber rattling, unified government produces an increase over the expected count of about 27 percent (i.e., to $1.27 * 3.83 = 4.86$ threats per month). However, unified government sees target-specific saber rattling decline by about 44 percent (i.e., $0.56 * 0.87 = 0.49$ threats per month). How can we interpret these inconsistent results? The implication is that two different processes drive the two different types of saber rattling. Presidents increase their general (symbolic) saber rattling when their legislative coalition is strong. However, their target-specific (goal-oriented) saber rattling increases during periods of divided government when their legislative coalition is weak. Thus, presidents play to their strong-suit, foreign policy, when they lack adequate support in Congress.

Next, consider the variables suggesting presidents might be emboldened by a strong economy, high approval ratings, or absence of scandal. Conversely, these same variables might reflect diversionary theory predictions that a weak economy, low approval ratings, or presence of scandal increase presidential threats. The statistical results in the sixth through eighth row of Table 4.2 yield little evidence that presidents respond to these stimuli in a manner supporting either theory.

The coefficient for economic conditions for saber rattling of all types is positive, suggesting that presidents are emboldened by good economic times. However, the coefficients for general and target-specific saber rattling belie this result. These coefficients are not significant, suggesting no relationship between economic conditions and presidential propensity to use threatening rhetoric. The coefficients for scandal and approval are also not significant for all types of saber rattling, as well as for general and target-specific. Thus, the results for these three variables suggest that presidents do not engage in strategic saber rattling to divert attention from their domestic problems. Neither are they emboldened to make threats by strong economic conditions or high approval ratings. Rather, these variables are unrelated to the changing intensity of presidential threats through time.

Finally, the effects for media frenzy reported in the last row of coefficients in Table 4.2 are strongly significant across all three regressions. Each additional news story about a major crisis or event uniformly produces about a 1 percent increase in the count of presidential threats per month. We can obtain insight on what these results mean by considering the average, standard deviation, and maximum of the media frenzy variable. The mean number of stories in this time series is 8.92, with standard deviation 16.91. The maximum number of stories in any single month is 104.

Now, assume that there is no current media coverage of a foreign policy crisis or event. Under this scenario, the expected counts would be 5.05, 3.78, and 0.78, respectively, for the three saber-rattling measures.[14] Then suppose the media is suddenly exposed to an intervention that produces an increase of one standard deviation in media coverage. The increase in the count of presidential threats would then be 16.91 percent across all three measures (given the similar coefficients in the last row). That is, presidential saber rattling of all types would increase to 5.90 threats per month, general saber rattling would increase to 4.42 threats per month, and target-specific saber rattling would increase to 0.91 threats per month.

Of course, this number grossly understates the potential effect of media frenzies because the standard deviation used is calculated on the entire time series, which contains many zeros. Therefore, we might also want to consider the effect at the maximum. Consider the largest media frenzy in which there were 104 stories. It produces a change in the expected count of 104 percent. This change results in presidential saber rattling of roughly 10.30, 7.71, and 1.59 hostile presidential remarks per month, respectively. These are large effects, of about the same magnitude as for war. Thus, presidents are substantially motivated by the mass media when using bellicose rhetoric.

### Multivariate Analyses of Target-Specific Saber Rattling by Type

Now consider a multivariate analysis of target-specific presidential saber rattling broken down by the three types: deterrence talk, threats of political or economic sanction, and military threats. Table 4.3 reports the results of these analyses.

First, note that the expected counts for these three dependent variables are quite small. Threats of each type occur less in continuous streams and are relatively rare presidential behaviors. This rareness is especially true for military threats, which have an expected count of only 0.09 threats per month. Only about one military threat is expected for each year of a presidency.

---

[14] This number is obtained by subtracting 8.92% (i.e., 1% * 8.92) from the expected counts reported in Table 4.2.

TABLE 4.3. *Statesmanship and Support Seeking in Target-Specific Presidential Saber Rattling*

| Variable | Target-Specific Type | | |
|---|---|---|---|
| | Deterrence Talk | Sanction Threats | Military Threats |
| Logged Presidential Threats$_{t-1}$ | 0.03 | −0.00 | 0.04 |
| | (3.58) | (−0.41) | (1.87) |
| | [1.03] | [1.00] | [1.04] |
| *Foreign Factors* | | | |
| War | 0.98 | 0.64 | 2.48 |
| | (3.38) | (1.51) | (3.81) |
| | [2.67] | [1.90] | [11.95] |
| Major Foreign Policy Crises and Events | 0.58 | 0.06 | 1.30 |
| | (1.72) | (0.23) | (3.80) |
| | [1.79] | [1.06] | [3.66] |
| *Domestic Factors* | | | |
| Election Seasons | −0.33 | 0.14 | −0.07 |
| | (−1.90) | (0.77) | (−0.24) |
| | [0.72] | [1.16] | [0.93] |
| Unified Government | −0.24 | −0.38 | 0.11 |
| | (−0.96) | (−1.52) | (0.22) |
| | [0.79] | [0.68] | [1.11] |
| Economic Conditions$_{t-1}$ | 0.05 | 0.05 | −0.01 |
| | (1.55) | (1.42) | (−0.25) |
| | [1.05] | [1.05] | [0.99] |
| Scandal | −0.04 | 0.84 | 0.70 |
| | (−0.12) | (2.73) | (1.31) |
| | [0.96] | [2.32] | [2.01] |
| Approval$_{t-1}$ | −0.00 | −0.03 | 0.02 |
| | (−1.50) | (−3.91) | (1.31) |
| | [0.99] | [0.97] | [1.02] |
| Media Frenzy | 0.00 | 0.01 | 0.03 |
| | (0.07) | (0.90) | (4.22) |
| | [1.00] | [1.01] | [1.03] |
| *Diagnostics* | | | |
| $\lambda = \exp(\bar{X}\beta_k)$ (Expected Count) | 0.43 | 0.18 | 0.09 |
| N | 717 | 717 | 717 |
| Wald $\chi^2$ | 190.01 | 180.70 | 146.84 |
| $\alpha$ (overdispersion parameter) | 1.54 | 1.17 | 4.07 |
| | (6.74) | (5.18) | (5.02) |

*Note:* The numbers in the table are coefficients, robust *t* statistics (in parentheses), and incidence ratios (in square brackets) from Poisson autoregressive regressions (Zeger and Qaqish 1988) of presidential saber rattling of the indicated types on the variables in the left column. An unreported constant and indicator variables for each presidency were also included in the regressions. The Ford indicator was omitted from the Deterrence analysis, and the Eisenhower indicator was omitted from the military threats analysis because of a lack of variation in the dependent variable.

Of course, many fewer than this may occur during the typical year, because these threats are episodic.

The effect of foreign factors on the president's target-specific saber rattling is consistent with the results reported in Table 4.2. War remains important for two of the three threat types. The presence of war increases deterrence talk over the expected count by about 167 percent (i.e., to $2.67 * 0.43 = 1.15$ threats per month). The war coefficient for threats of economic or political sanctions is not statistically significant. However, war, as should be expected, greatly increases the intensity of military threats by about 1,095 percent (i.e., to $11.95 * 0.09 = 1.08$ threats per month).

Major foreign policy crises and events are also important to deterrence talk and military threats but not threats of economic/political sanctions. On average, crises and events increase deterrence talk by about 79 percent (i.e., to about $1.79 * 0.18 = 0.32$ threats per month), whereas they increase military threats by about 266 percent (i.e., to about $3.66 * 0.09 = 0.34$ threats per month). These are again large effects showing that presidential saber rattling responds to external threats.

Now consider the effect of domestic factors on the three types of target-specific saber rattling. As reported in Table 4.2, election seasons do not increase the president's target-specific saber rattling. In fact, the coefficient for deterrence talk suggests that this type of saber rattling actually declines during election periods. Unified government has no statistically significant effect on target-specific saber rattling for any of the three types. This statistical result belies the significant coefficient for target-specific saber rattling reported in Table 4.2. However, similar to the results for target-specific saber rattling reported in Table 4.2, economic conditions do not affect any of the three types of target-specific saber rattling.

The statistical results for scandal and approval in Table 4.3 support the diversionary hypothesis. The results in Table 4.2 showed neither variable to be a significant determinant of the president's target-specific saber rattling. However, the coefficients for scandal suggest that presidents may use threats of economic/political sanction more often when a scandal is occurring. The coefficient for military threats is in the same direction but falls short of statistical significance. Consistent with the diversionary story, the coefficients for approval also suggest an unrevealed dynamic from the aggregate data in Table 4.2. The result for economic/political threats implies that these types of threats are more likely when presidential approval is declining. Also, the coefficient for target-specific deterrence threats has the same sign but again fails to achieve statistical significance. Thus, presidents may or may not use target-specific threats to divert attention from scandal or to bolster their approval ratings. The statistical results are suggestive but not conclusive given the contradictory findings.

Finally, consider again the effects of media frenzy on target-specific saber rattling reported in Table 4.3. The statistical results suggest that presidents do not engage in more deterrence talk or threats of economic/political sanctions during periods of media frenzy. However, presidents strongly increase the intensity of their military threats. Note that the effect of media frenzy on military threats is roughly three times as large as that reported in Table 4.2 for target-specific threats of all types. The significant effect in Table 4.2 is apparently due solely to increased military threats. Thus, we again conclude that the mass media is very important to presidential foreign policy behavior.

### Are Presidents Partisans in Their Use of Saber Rattling?

Finally, let us return to the question of whether partisanship affects the presidential propensity to make threats toward foreign actors. The preliminary analyses reported in Table 3.3 of Chapter 3 suggests presidents differ individually and that Republicans are more aggressive than Democrats. However, that analysis did not control for the differing foreign and domestic policy environments facing each president. The analyses in Tables 4.2 and 4.3 provide such statistical controls.

For the sake of parsimony the coefficients for each president were not reported in Tables 4.2 and 4.3. However, those coefficients have meaning with respect to how partisanship affects presidential behavior. Thus, Table 4.4 reports the presidency-specific coefficients for each of the six regressions reported in Tables 4.2 and 4.3, along with tests of the partisan differences hypothesis at the bottom. Significant coefficients for a president imply effects specific to that presidency after controlling for the foreign and domestic environments. Also, systematic differences across presidents relating to partisanship may imply a partisan bias to the intensity of presidential saber rattling.

The results again show that President Eisenhower was consistently less bellicose than President Truman for four of the six measures. President Kennedy differed significantly from President Truman only on target-specific sanction threats. This difference probably reflects tense U.S. relations with Cuba and the Soviet Union during the Cuban missile crisis. Presidents Johnson, Nixon, and Ford were either similar to or less bellicose than President Truman after controlling for their respective foreign and domestic environments. Presidents Reagan and George H. W. Bush were significantly more prone than Truman toward general saber rattling directed at no particular target. President George H. W. Bush also issued more threats of sanction, probably directed toward Iraq before and after the Persian Gulf War. Finally, Presidents Clinton and George W. Bush made far more target-specific threats of each type than any other president. Thus, there are clearly remaining presidency-specific effects after controlling for the foreign and domestic environments facing each president.

Does partisanship drive presidential bellicosity? The bottom row of Table 4.4 provides statistical comparisons of the Democrat and Republican presidential averages. The third column shows that Democrats were more prone than Republicans toward target-specific saber rattling. However, the coefficients in Table 4.4 show that this result is driven largely by President

TABLE 4.4. *Partisanship in Presidential Saber Rattling*

| President | Saber Rattling Type | | | Target-Specific Type | | |
|---|---|---|---|---|---|---|
| | All Types | General | Target-Specific | Deterrence Talk | Sanction Threats | Military Threats |
| Constant | 1.32 | 0.80 | 0.45 | 0.64 | −2.04 | −4.45 |
| (Truman) | (5.05) | (2.72) | (1.16) | (−1.47) | (−2.43) | (−5.04) |
| Dwight | −0.79 | −0.59 | −1.29 | −0.16 | −0.98 | |
| Eisenhower | (−3.10) | (−2.16) | (−2.66) | (−0.32) | (−0.76) | |
| John Kennedy | −0.34 | −0.45 | −0.01 | 0.57 | 1.91 | 0.18 |
| | (−1.26) | (−1.47) | (−0.02) | (1.31) | (1.89) | (0.15) |
| Lyndon Johnson | −0.49 | −0.81 | 0.34 | 0.83 | −0.54 | 0.53 |
| | (−2.46) | (−3.53) | (1.26) | (2.90) | (−0.44) | (0.97) |
| Richard Nixon | −0.43 | −0.08 | −1.18 | −0.98 | 0.01 | −0.12 |
| | (−1.82) | (−0.30) | (−3.36) | (−2.24) | (0.01) | (−0.18) |
| Gerald Ford | −0.06 | 0.26 | −1.69 | | 1.03 | 1.30 |
| | (−0.21) | (0.79) | (−2.81) | | (1.06) | (−1.48) |
| Jimmy Carter | −0.07 | −0.04 | −0.41 | −1.54 | 2.28 | 0.80 |
| | (−0.28) | (−0.17) | (−1.14) | (−1.68) | (2.88) | (1.15) |
| Ronald Reagan | 0.28 | 0.56 | −0.34 | 0.58 | 1.50 | 0.66 |
| | (1.14) | (2.06) | (−0.85) | (1.39) | (1.58) | (1.00) |
| George H. W. | 0.32 | 0.58 | −0.18 | 0.20 | 2.78 | −0.12 |
| Bush | (1.22) | (1.94) | (−0.45) | (0.42) | (3.03) | (−0.18) |
| William J. | 0.36 | 0.11 | 0.99 | 1.47 | 3.89 | 2.69 |
| Clinton | (1.58) | (0.43) | (2.97) | (4.41) | (4.04) | (5.63) |
| George W. Bush | 0.63 | 0.15 | 1.51 | 2.00 | 3.89 | 2.21 |
| | (2.96) | (0.61) | (4.88) | (5.85) | (4.61) | (3.94) |
| *Comparisons* | | | | | | |
| Average | 1.19 | 0.50 | 0.68 | 0.52 | −0.16 | −3.40 |
| Democrat | | | | | | |
| Average | 1.31 | 0.95 | −0.08 | 0.52 | −0.67 | −3.66 |
| Republican | | | | | | |
| $\chi^2$ *Democrat* = | 0.48 | 6.20 | 10.34 | 0.05 | 0.16 | 1.39 |
| *Republican* | (0.49) | (0.01) | (0.00) | (0.83) | (0.68) | (0.24) |
| (*p* value) | | | | | | |

*Note:* The numbers in the table are coefficients and robust t-statistics (in parentheses) from the Poisson autoregressive regressions (Zeger and Qaqish 1988) reported in Tables 4.2 and 4.3. The last row contains $\chi^2$ statistics for the null hypothesis that Democrats and Republicans are the same, along with their associated *p* values (in parentheses). Eisenhower was excluded from the military threats analysis because he issued no target-specific military threats except during the Korean War. Ford was excluded from the deterrence threats analysis because he issued no target-specific deterrence threats.

Clinton. The second column shows that Republicans were statistically more prone than Democrats toward general saber rattling directed at no particular country. However, the coefficients in Table 4.2 suggest that this result is driven largely by Presidents Reagan and George H. W. Bush. Thus, the statistical comparisons suggest that presidency-specific effects, rather than partisanship, were more important in affecting presidential behavior. Of course, it is difficult to separate presidents after Reagan from their partisanship, so one might also argue that partisanship has also been important.

## Conclusions

As noted in Chapter 2, presidents have been described by American government and presidency textbooks, social scientists, and political pundits alike as the nation's chief foreign policy representative. Yet past research has yielded little about the nature of presidential representation in the area of foreign policy. The research presented in this chapter has filled this gap using presidential saber rattling as an object of analysis.

We have asked whether threatening presidential rhetoric can be explained purely as a function of external threats. If it can, then we would have definitive evidence that modern presidents are statesmen justly protecting the nation at large from foreign danger. We have also asked whether domestic factors enter into the president's payoff function for foreign policy. If they do, then modern presidents may also be self-interested support seekers who deviate from statesman-like behavior.

The analyses reported in this chapter show that presidential saber rattling increases during times of war or crisis and in response to dramatic events such as terror attacks. Such responses are understandable, given that presidents are charged with protecting the nation at large from external treats. The presence of such threats justly evokes responses from the president consistent with the circumstances faced by the nation at large.

This study also provides evidence that presidents issue threats when war, crisis, and dramatic events are not present. Some of these unprovoked threats might be justifiable in the sense that the nation faced ongoing dangers from communism before the late 1980s and from terrorism starting in the mid-1980s. Presidents may issue threats with the intention of deterring certain behaviors by foreign adversaries. They may also issue threats to bolster their credibility in the international arena. In this capacity, presidents may be acting as statesmen to protect the nation from external dangers.

However, this chapter also revealed regularities suggesting that presidents use pretended bellicose rhetoric to bolster their domestic support. The empirical evidence is strong that during election seasons presidents increase their saber rattling. The spectral time series analyses reported in Figure 4.2 show a 48-month periodicity for all six measures of presidential saber rattling. The multivariate analyses reported in Table 4.2 confirm these increases due to elections, after statistical controls, for saber rattling of all types and general saber rattling but not for target-specific threats. Still, the evidence is strong that presidents use bellicose rhetoric to build their domestic support when elections are approaching.

The preceding analyses also yield evidence of presidency-specific and potentially partisan effects. Presidents starting with Reagan were considerably more bellicose than earlier presidents. Controlling for their respective foreign and domestic environments, Presidents Reagan and George H. W. Bush used more general saber rattling directed at no particular foreign actor. These findings suggest that presidents since Reagan may have engaged more in symbolic saber rattling, perhaps to bolster their domestic support. Presidents George H. W. Bush, Clinton, and George W. Bush also made far more target-specific threats than earlier presidents.

A final regularity revealed by this chapter concerns the effect of the mass media on presidents' use of threatening rhetoric. The multivariate results for media frenzies were strong and statistically significant for presidential saber rattling of all types, as well as for general and target-specific saber rattling. Indeed, the effect of media frenzies on the intensity of presidential saber rattling was similar in magnitude to that for war. The magnitude of this effect suggests that the media have an outsize effect on presidential behavior. Such responses probably reflect presidential efforts to appease the press and public by appearing strong in the excited environment created by media.

The larger implication of this chapter is that presidents are not the dispassionate statesmen suggested by Founders' model of presidential representation. They are also not the crass support seekers suggested by Downsian explanations emphasizing a relentless presidential thrust toward building domestic support. Rather, the truth lies somewhere in between these two extremes. Presidents are pragmatists, sometimes responding on behalf of the nation to external threats and at other times seeking to maintain and increase their domestic support. Whether this presidential posture is normatively appropriate is a question for others to answer. Future research should evaluate other dimensions of presidential foreign policy behavior to obtain a better understanding of presidential representation in this area.

# 5

# The Domestic Consequences of Presidential Saber Rattling

Does modern presidential saber rattling increase the president's domestic support, as seemed to occur for a time during the Adams administration? If so, then who among the president's domestic audiences is most responsive? Are the president's fellow partisans most responsive, perhaps because they are naturally predisposed toward supporting the president? Or do independents and members of the opposing party respond more to the president's foreign policy threats? What is the duration of changing domestic support for the president as a result of threats issued toward foreign actors?

Beyond these questions, this chapter is also concerned with the mechanisms through which presidential saber rattling affects domestic support. The case study evidence in the introductory chapter suggested that President Adams increased his domestic support, partially by affecting media coverage. At one level, he did so through intimidation of the opposition media and the Alien and Sedition Acts. At another level, President Adams inflamed the partisan Federalist media into greater bellicosity through rhetoric mirroring his own transitory foreign policy stance.

However, modern presidents lack the legal or moral authority for intimidating the modern press. Moreover, it would be inconsistent with modern democratic norms for presidents to attempt doing so. Furthermore, given that the modern media is very diverse, it is unlikely that presidents can uniformly coerce them into parroting presidential positions. Without such potent tools as those possessed by President Adams, do modern presidents somehow succeed in shaping media coverage of major crises and events, thereby affecting presidential support?

This chapter also explores potential unanticipated consequences of presidential saber rattling. Presidents are psychological leaders looked to by domestic audiences for guidance about the U.S. position in the world. As such, presidents can also affect the economic future. Specifically, presidential foreign policy leadership can affect the confidence people have in future economic outcomes. Uncertainty about economic outcomes can affect people's willingness to assume risk, which can, in turn, affect their economic behavior. Wood (2009b) examines these linkages in great detail, showing that presidential saber rattling affects a range of economic outcomes. This chapter takes a more general view, exploring mutual relationships among presidential threats, domestic support for the president, and people's economic confidence.

## Why Should Presidential Rhetoric Matter to Domestic Outcomes?

Because of their unique status in the American system, presidents are potent psychological leaders. The presidency is the most esteemed office in the land and has been since the early republic. Although the office was initially weak, President Washington set a heroic tone for the presidency that resulted in an office revered by most citizens. Since Washington, the presidency has evolved through time to be the most visible and important political and economic actor in the United States. As symbolic representative of the nation at large, presidents are expected to lead internationally and domestically. They are problem identifiers, policy purveyors, managers of the public welfare, and unifying representatives of all the people. People look to the president both to represent them and to provide leadership on important issues.

As a result, what presidents say in public is virtually always important. Because of their exalted role in the American system, people and the mass media listen when presidents speak. Indeed, presidents don't even have to speak to receive system-wide attention. Virtually every television newscast has at least one segment on the president or the administration. Regardless of topic, whether it is the president's pets, family, health, administration policy, scandal, the economy, or foreign policy, the media covers the presidency broadly and intensely. This lofty status of presidents in the American system increases the likelihood that their messages will be transmitted and heard.

During times of crisis the nation's symbolic leader becomes even more prominent in the scheme of information transmission. Evidence from Chapters 3 and 4 showed that presidential saber rattling is often associated with foreign policy crises and media coverage. Crisis typically puts the media into a pattern of hyper-coverage of events and presidential responses. This pattern of media attention has been repeated consistently through the years for multiple crises (e.g., see Figure 4.1). A major factor for all of these periods has been bellicose presidential rhetoric before, during, and after a crisis (e.g., see Figure 3.1). As a result of the information-rich environment that surrounds foreign policy crises, presidents should more readily influence people's behavior and evaluations.

Of course, crisis can also independently affect people's behavior and evaluations. Amplifying this potential effect, saber rattling by the nation's leader can

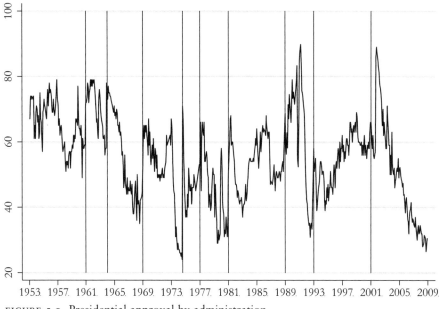

FIGURE 5.1. Presidential approval by administration.

intensify the sense of crisis, making it more imminent and credible. As a result of visible presidential involvement, people have a heightened understanding that the future is uncertain. This uncertainty may hold implications for individuals' behavior, producing responses rooted in emotions, rather than normal evaluations.

*Presidential Threats and Domestic Support*

Because of their exalted status in the American system, presidents and their advisors commonly believe they can shape public support for their policies and ongoing job performance (e.g., see Edwards 2003, 3–8). As a result, modern presidents engage in a permanent campaign throughout their administrations (Blumenthal 1982; Edwards 1983; Gergen 2000; Kernell 1997; Ornstein and Mann 2000; Tulis 1987). Yet political scientists have generally been quite skeptical of presidents' ability to shape their own support through rhetoric (e.g., Edwards 2003; Wood 2009a).

For example, Figure 5.1 graphs presidential approval from 1953 through 2008 with markers for the start of each presidential administration. This graph shows clearly that most presidents have experienced a sharp increase in public support upon taking office. However, what is also clear from Figure 5.1 is that presidential approval has usually declined after this initial jump. Every modern president except Clinton left office with approval ratings lower than they entered with. This well-known empirical regularity raises a question about whether presidents can successfully affect their own public support. Moreover, the many variations in approval within presidencies suggest that they may instead be victims of an expectations gap, the economy, and various crises and events that occur through time.

Nevertheless, saber rattling may be a tool for increasing the president's public support. Why should saber rattling matter to public assessments of the president? The answer is rooted in the American psyche. As mentioned in Chapter 4, a heuristic for thinking about people's responses to political information is placing them in the context of a political drama. Edelman (1964) observed that most people view politics as a sort of moving panorama on a national and international stage. In affecting presidential support, if the political drama unfolds to depict the president as strong and heroic, then people's assessments move in a positive direction. If the political drama depicts the president as weak, indecisive, or shrinking from core expectations, then people's assessments move in a negative direction. Edelman's political drama is primarily about manipulation of symbols and emotions, rather than rational analysis of information.

Since the earliest days of research on presidential approval, scholars have understood that political drama is important. However, past research has only considered political drama to be major events such as crises, military actions, scandals, and other sharp occurrences (e.g., see Brody 1991; Brody and Page 1975; Chappell and Keech 1985; Clarke and Stewart 1994; DeRouen 1995; Erikson et al. 2002; Fiorina 1981; Fordham 1998a; Haller and Norpoth 1994; Hibbs 1974, 1987; Kernell 1978; MacKuen 1983; MacKuen et al. 1992; Markus 1988; Monroe 1978; Mueller 1970, 1973; Norpoth 1996; Ostrom and Job 1986; Ostrom and Smith 1993; Simon and Ostrom 1989).

This chapter expands on the definition of political drama to include public presidential threats toward foreign actors. Why should these threats matter to public support for the president? Again, political drama evokes emotional responses apart from people's normal mode of information processing. It sparks sentiments such as anxiety, fear, patriotism, anger, and loyalty that trump information processing based on normal calculations. People's emotion-based responses to political drama may, therefore, be dissimilar to their responses under normal information-processing conditions.

Past research has consistently demonstrated that the events associated with international crises and events can drive evaluations of the president. Such occurrences as terrorist attacks, military interventions, or assassination attempts are highly visible and can produce anxiety, fear, anger, patriotism, loyalty, and other emotions among the media and public. Regardless of the source of the initial stimulus, presidential rhetoric can either amplify or mute the associated responses. As chief U.S. foreign policy leader, the president can choose when to speak, and how loudly. If the president does not direct significant attention toward critical events, then there will be much less attention from the media and public. In turn, the stimulus to people's emotions is diminished, producing responses rooted less in emotion and more in normal evaluation.

Presidents may also receive increased domestic support simply because there is a crisis. People naturally rally toward their symbolic leader during such times. However, presidents are also expected to lead during times of crisis, with a calm resolve that assures Americans the nation is in good hands. Thus, the president's rhetorical response to a crisis may also be important to people's evaluations. Projections of presidential strength and competent leadership are more likely to produce positive evaluations. Projections of weakness and incompetence are likely to be costly for the president's domestic support.

Thus, presidential saber rattling contributes to the ongoing political drama, above and beyond the critical events considered by past research. Presidents can through their rhetoric affect people's emotions, which may in turn alter their support. Presidents may well engage in saber rattling for the specific purpose of evoking such responses, although we found no evidence of this effect in the previous chapter. Alternatively, presidential saber rattling may actually be intended to achieve foreign policy goals but have the side effect of evoking emotional responses. In either case, understanding how people respond to presidential threats is important if we are to fully understand changing support for the president through time.

### Who Responds to Presidential Threats?

People commonly evaluate political objects through a lens filtered by their ideology, self-interest, and partisanship. As a result, people differ in their relative propensities to support the president. We shall focus only on shared partisanship in evaluating these propensities. People who share a common partisanship with the president are more likely to be supportive. Those who share an opposing partisanship are less likely to be supportive. Those individuals who neither share nor oppose the president's partisanship should fall between these two extremes. We shall call these three groups In-Party, Out-Party, and Independent evaluators, respectively.

Figure 5.2 graphs presidential approval through time broken down by these three groups. Visual examination of this graph shows that In-Party, Out-Party, and Independent evaluators have differed systematically in their support for the president. Clearly, In-Party evaluators have been most supportive. Out-Party evaluators have been least supportive. Independent evaluators have fallen between these two extremes. However, we are more interested in how these three groups have responded to information stimuli (i.e., saber rattling), which might alter their relative support for the president.

Evaluating the magnitude of the respective responses of the three groups requires theory and analysis. Theoretically, there is a long social science

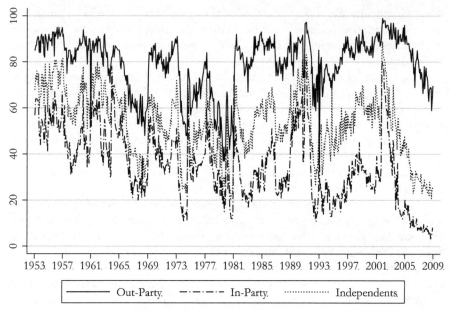

FIGURE 5.2. Presidential approval by partisan affiliation.

tradition arguing that people are biased information processors.[1] From the classic works of Berelson et al. (1954) and Campbell et al. (1960) to later analyses by Markus and Converse (1979, 1982) and Finkel (1993) to more recent work from a Bayesian perspective (Bartels 2002; Wood and Vedlitz 2009), social scientists have consistently found that people's evaluations of new information are colored by their values and partisanship. Their responses are strongly determined by predispositions toward the political object they are evaluating. As stated by Zaller (1992, 23), "predispositions are the critical intervening variable between the communications people encounter . . . and their statements of political preference." As a result, people are less likely to receive and accept new information that runs counter to their predispositions.

This dominant perspective is reinforced by work in social and political psychology that advocates a theory of motivated reasoning (Kunda 1987, 1990; Lodge and Taber 2000). The theory of motivated reasoning posits that people form lasting political judgments based largely on their affect toward political objects, rather than through rational evaluation of new information. As expressed by Lodge and Taber (2005, 456), "All political leaders, groups, issues, symbols, and ideas thought about in the past become affectively charged – positively or negatively – and this affect is linked directly to the

---

[1] I use the term "biased" loosely here to indicate differential information processing in the sense alluded to in the early political science literature. Whether people are indeed biased is subject to the definition of what "biased" means. See Bartels (2002), Bullock (2009), and Gerber and Green (1999) for discussion.

concept in long-term memory. This evaluative tally, moreover, comes automatically and inescapably to mind upon presentation of the associated object, thereby signaling its affective coloration."

As a consequence of this affect toward political objects, people often believe what they want to believe based on their predispositions. Most people most of the time find it hard to evaluate new information in an even-handed way (Redlawsk 2002). They process information so that it conforms to their pre-existing viewpoints. Individuals who are strongly disposed toward liking a political object attempt to maintain that disposition. Those who are strongly disposed toward disliking an object seek ways to continue disliking it. Empirical support for this perspective is abundant (Conover and Feldman 1989; Jacoby 1988; Lodge and Hamill 1986; Lodge and Taber 2005; McGraw et al. 1996, 2002; Rahn 1993; Taber and Lodge 2006) and could be argued as constituting an established paradigm.

If this established paradigm is true, then we should observe systematically different responses to presidential saber rattling across In-Party, Out-Party, and Independent evaluators. In- and Out-Party evaluators should attempt to maintain their predisposed evaluations and therefore be relatively unresponsive to presidential threats. In-Party evaluators are already supportive of the president and should maintain their strong support. Out-Party evaluators are unsupportive of the president and should maintain their lack of support. Independent evaluators are predisposed in neither direction and should, therefore, be most receptive to new information in the form of presidential saber rattling.

Although the theory of biased information processing yields some plausible hypotheses, other scholars have argued that people are actually Bayesian information processors. That is, they exhibit little bias when exposed to new information. For example, Gerber and Green (1999) claim that "most of the studies purporting to demonstrate biased learning are either theoretically indeterminate or consistent with a Bayesian model of rational information processing" (1999, 192). As evidence for their assertions they note that "Only the faintest traces of selective perception are evident from partisan trends in presidential approval [e.g., see Figure 5.2]. All three partisan groups move together – sometimes markedly – as party fortunes change...Beliefs and evaluations do change, and they change to approximately the same degree among those with different political allegiances" (1999, 205). Furthermore, Gerber and Green argue that their findings accord with their earlier analysis of panel survey data, in which Democrats, Republicans, and Independents moved together in their evaluations of which party was best able to handle the nation's economy (Gerber and Green 1997). They also claim that the Bayesian model is in accord with Page and Shapiro's (1992) "evidence that the opinions of opposing ideological, social, and economic groups seldom polarize over time" (1999, 206–07).

If Gerber and Green are correct that people are unbiased information processors, then presidential saber rattling should produce parallel movements in changing public support across In-Party, Out-Party, and Independent evaluators. No particular group should be any more or less responsive to presidential saber rattling than the other. The only thing that should matter is the signal, with emotions playing no role in people's evaluations of the president.

Yet another possibility is a two-state theory of information processing arguing that people sometimes rely on their predispositions but other times deviate from those predispositions when there is an appropriate countervailing stimulus. One version of the two-state theory is the theory of affective intelligence proposed by Marcus, Neuman, and MacKuen (2000; see also Marcus 1988; Marcus and MacKuen 1993; MacKuen et al. 2007). They posit that how people process new information is determined by a cognitive system operating in either a dispositional or surveillance mode.

In the dispositional mode, enthusiasm about a message or its sender leads people to rely on habitual cues such as ideology, party identification, or self-interest. People's past evaluations largely determine their current evaluations in the dispositional mode. The dispositional mode is consistent with the biased information processing model discussed earlier.

The surveillance mode is brought on by anxiety. In the surveillance mode, people seek out answers that resolve stimulus-induced anxiety about the object of interest. In this secondary mode people rely less on habit and more on evaluation of new information. In other words, people become more rational. Using cross-sectional survey evidence from various National Election Studies, Marcus et al. (2000) show that the probability of partisans defecting from their predispositions grows when there is anxiety about their naturally preferred issue stances or candidates.

A more general version of the two-state theory is espoused by Lodge and Taber (2000; see also Lebo and Cassino 2007) and is again based on motivated reasoning. They identify two types of motivated reasoning, directional and nondirectional. Directional motivated reasoning involves the tendency of individuals to process information so as to reach a predetermined conclusion. This may occur if people have strong attitudes and choose to ignore information, to receive the information but interpret it skeptically, or to reinterpret the information to support their own predisposed evaluations. Strong affect toward a political object biases information processing toward acceptance of preexisting evaluations and rejecting contrary information.

In contrast, nondirectional motivated reasoning occurs when a stimulus of sufficient magnitude and valence causes individuals to be uncertain about their preexisting evaluations.[2] People engaging in nondirectional motivated

---

[2] Affective intelligence is one example of nondirectional motivated reasoning. However, the theory of affective intelligence's surveillance mode always causes people to become more rational. This may not be a plausible outcome, given the range of emotions beyond anxiety that might activate a secondary mode (e.g., see Conover and Feldman 1986). Researchers have questioned whether emotions such as anxiety, anger, sadness, and hope uniformly produce the same cognitive responses (e.g., see the discussion in Huddy et al. 2007).

reasoning may or may not defect from their natural evaluations. Defection should depend on the valence and strength of the stimulus. Under nondirectional motivated reasoning, other emotions beyond anxiety can produce defection from one's predispositions. The crucial point about nondirectional motivated reasoning is that people are no longer tightly bound to their predispositions and may be driven by a range of emotions when assessing new information.

If the two-state theory of political evaluation is correct, then saber-rattling stimuli may produce different response patterns than predicted by either the biased or Bayesian information processing models. First, saber rattling may activate emotions that reinforce the predispositions of In-Party evaluators. As a result, In-Party evaluators should remain in the first state and continue or increase their already strong support for the president. Second, saber rattling may activate emotions for Out-Party evaluators that are inconsistent with their predispositions, thereby inducing uncertainty. Out-Party evaluators are the group most challenged by the saber-rattling stimulus and should, therefore, be most susceptible to entering the second state. As a result, saber rattling might actually produce the largest increase in presidential support among the Out-Party group. Out-Party evaluators may be willing to disregard their predispositions to instead support the president on the basis of patriotism or anger. Finally, saber rattling should also activate emotions for Independent evaluators, but these individuals hold weak predispositions that are less challenged by the stimulus. Therefore, their responses should lie somewhere between the In-Party and Out-Party groups.

### Presidential Threats and Economic Confidence

The psychology of public responses to presidential threats is not confined to changing support for the president. Presidential threats can also produce anxiety which affects people's economic confidence. The mechanisms through which presidents affect people's economic confidence are similar to those discussed above. People become emotional upon exposure to a threat stimulus. The induced emotional state causes them to be more analytical and uncertain about the economic future. The result of this uncertainty is altered economic attitudes and behavior.

Of course, economists have long emphasized the role that uncertainty plays in explaining current spending, borrowing, and saving decisions. Early work emphasized an expected income stream (e.g., see Friedman 1957; Modigliani and Brumberg 1954), but uncertainty implied the importance of the expected variance of the income stream. Once uncertainty about future income was incorporated into models of economic behavior, this factor was consistently demonstrated to have an impact on consumption, borrowing, and saving decisions (Caballero 1991; Carroll 1994, 1997; Carroll and Samwick 1997, 1998; Kimball 1990).

Again, uncertainty factors into people's decisions by altering the psychology of their behavior. Here it is the psychology associated with an individual's willingness to assume risk that is important.[3] Uncertainty about future income and employment alters the risks that an individual is willing to take in current economic decisions. For example, the individual may at times be willing to assume more risk to finance current spending through borrowing or reduced saving. At other times the same individual may become risk averse choosing not to spend but rather to pay down debt or save for the future. Confidence in personal finances and the economy produces a greater propensity to consume and willingness to take on risk. Uncertainty about finances and the economy produces greater reluctance to spend and risk aversion.

Individuals attempt to calculate their current and future economic status when making economic decisions. However, the processes used by most economic actors for deciding whether and how much to spend, borrow, and save are often more fragmented than coherent and may display internal inconsistencies (Simon 1947; Souleles 2001). Their ability to interpret economic and political events is limited by their beliefs, environment, education, intellect, exposure to information, and available time. These limitations mean that economic actors use shortcuts when deciding how to allocate their income. They do the best that they can by relying on a wide range of cues and information from their environment.

Economic actors take cues and information about current and prospective economic conditions from a variety of sources. They can derive from personal experience, the experiences of others, economic reports, the news, or elite economic and political actors (including the president). The thesis of the argument here is that presidents can through their saber rattling create an atmosphere of greater apprehension.

As a result of visible presidential involvement, people have a heightened understanding that the future may hold adverse economic and social consequences. American economic resources devoted to hostile foreign policy actions imply money diverted to nonproductive endeavors. Such diversions may have consequences for macroeconomic outcomes, including higher taxes, increased government deficits and debt, or reduced government services. Furthermore, most major military actions since World War I have been followed by recession or other adverse economic conditions.[4]

Additionally, presidential saber rattling heightens the realization that American sons and daughters may soon be in harm's way. The specter of Vietnam-like outcomes, with daily body counts and graphic images of blood and death, may temper American appetites for normal economic activities. With potential

---

[3] This perspective was developed in the early work of economic psychologist George Katona (1951, 1960, 1964, 1975), the originator of the University of Michigan's Survey of Consumers. See economist Richard Curtin (2000) for an overview of Katona's contributions.

[4] The National Bureau of Economic Research dates the start and end of recessions. The data show that there were recessions following World War I, World War II, the Korean War, Vietnam, and the Persian Gulf War (see http://www.nber.org/cycles.html).

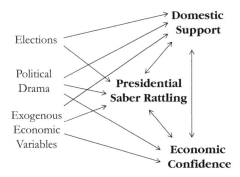

FIGURE 5.3. Potential paths of influence among presidential saber rattling, domestic support for the president, and economic confidence.

blood and death, it may seem inappropriate to visit local shopping malls and purchase major items. Thus, the prevailing economic mood is to wait until the crisis has passed before engaging in normal economic activities.

Of course, we have already noted that presidents may have incentives to drive attention toward a foreign policy crisis. This should be especially true when the nation is experiencing poor economic conditions. Presidential support suffers during periods of economic decline (e.g., see Clarke and Stewart 1994; Edwards et al. 1995; MacKuen 1983; MacKuen et al. 1992; Monroe 1978; Mueller 1970, 1973; Ostrom and Smith 1993; Wood 2000). As a result, the president may choose to amplify a crisis through saber rattling to divert attention from domestic problems (e.g., see DeRouen 1995; Fordham 1998a, 1998b, 2002; Gowa 1998; Howell and Pevehouse 2005; James and Oneal 1991; Meernik 1994; Mueller 1970; Ostrom and Job 1986). Again, we found little or no evidence for this diversionary hypothesis in Chapter 4, but it is still important to consider possible two-way relations between presidential saber rattling and people's economic confidence.

*Formalizing the Theories Graphically*
Figure 5.3 contains a path diagram depicting predicted relations from the preceding discussion. The arrows indicate theoretical connections among presidential saber rattling, domestic support for the president, and economic confidence, while controlling for political drama, the economy, and other exogenous variables. The core of the graph is the three nodes in boldface type for presidential saber rattling, domestic support, and economic confidence. These three nodes are the core because the preceding discussion posits that presidents, because of their exalted status in the American system, can have potent psychological effects on multiple behaviors, including political and economic evaluations.

The double-headed arrows for these three linkages also indicate the possibility that relations between each pair of nodes can be two-way. Presidential saber rattling may cause and be caused by domestic support and economic confidence. Also, the double-headed arrow between domestic support and economic confidence is important to the theory. This set of linkages suggests a common psychological connection between people's evaluations of the president and their evaluations of the economy. People's evaluations of the president and their evaluations of the economy are part of a common behavioral process.

The single-headed arrows in Figure 5.3 imply exogenous linkages. Past theory and analysis suggests that the factors impinging exogenously on the three core nodes share some similarities. However, these factors are not identical. For example, consider the three single-headed arrows from the left to presidential saber rattling. The analyses in Chapter 4 evaluated these linkages in great detail. We found through statistical analyses that presidential saber rattling is strongly determined by political drama (used here generically to encompass war, crises, critical foreign policy events, and media coverage of those crises and events), as well as election seasons. However, saber rattling was found to be relatively oblivious to economic performance.

In contrast, past research suggests that the two single-headed arrows impinging on domestic support for the president include economic performance, political drama, and elections. However, the political drama associated with changing domestic support is not the same as that for presidential saber rattling. The same foreign policy events considered earlier should still be important. We must also consider domestic drama. Such domestic events as attempted presidential assassinations, scandals, broken promises of "no new taxes," and "haircuts on runways" can strongly affect the president's standing with the public.

Finally, the two single-headed arrows impinging on economic confidence should be strongly determined by economic variables (e.g., see Wood 2009b). However, the impact of political drama is less assured. Little past research has investigated this connection. Phenomena such as 9/11 are obvious candidates for affecting people's economic confidence in the short term. However, it is unclear that events of less magnitude are important. Thus, we now investigate this linkage further.

## Research Design

### *Measurement*

The statistical analyses reported in this chapter use one or more measures to represent each node in Figure 5.3. Some of these measures were discussed in the previous chapter. For example, the same variables as were used in Chapter 4 to explain presidential saber rattling are used again here. These same variables are also appropriate as partial explanations for changes in the president's domestic support and people's economic confidence. However, we must include additional variables for a complete explanation.

Consider first the variables for the linkages to explain the president's domestic support in Figure 5.3. The dependent variable for this node is the president's monthly job approval ratings reported by Gallup as graphed in Figure 5.1. The explanatory variables for this node include the same measures as were used in Chapter 4, including foreign policy events and crises, the media, scandal, and the current state of the economy. However, on the basis of past research (e.g., see Erikson et al. 2002; MacKuen et al. 1992), the approval analysis also includes a lagged dependent variable to control for inertia, additional economic variables, a measure of domestic drama, and indicators to reflect bumps in approval after elections.

Specifically, in addition to the variables considered in Chapter 4, the approval analysis also includes the annualized monthly percent change in the unemployment rate and the annualized monthly inflation rate, both as reported by the Bureau of Labor Statistics. The measure of domestic drama includes an indicator for the attempted assassination of President Reagan (1981:04, coded positive), the budget deal announcement in which President George H. W. Bush went back on his "no new taxes pledge" (1990:10, coded negative), and the media report that President Clinton stopped runway traffic at Los Angeles International Airport for a haircut (1993:05, coded negative). Indicators are also included for the first poll taken after the start of a new presidential administration. A measure of economic confidence (discussed subsequently) is also included, reflecting the double-headed arrow between domestic support and economic confidence in Figure 5.3. Controlling for these relationships, the pertinent question is whether presidential saber rattling independently affects the president's approval ratings.

In a separate analysis, we also consider domestic support for the president broken down by In-Party, Out-Party, and Independent identifiers. The presidential approval data broken down by partisanship were initially compiled by Lebo and Cassino (2007) and updated by Jeffrey Cohen through 2008.[5] Indicator variables were created for periods when the presidency was occupied by Democrats and Republicans. Using the partisan approval data and these indicator variables, measures were constructed for whether survey respondents shared the incumbent president's party identification. In-Party approval is defined as the product of Democrat presidents with Democrat respondents' approval plus the product of Republican presidents with Republican respondents' approval. Out-Party approval is defined as the product of Democrat presidents with Republican respondents' approval plus the product of Republican presidents with Democrat respondents' approval. Independent approval is simply the approval of respondents who self-identified as independents.

Now consider the variables for the linkages associated with people's economic confidence in Figure 5.3. Economic confidence is measured using the University of Michigan's Index of Consumer Sentiment (ICS). The ICS is constructed from five questions about current and expected personal finance and

[5] Thanks to Matthew Lebo for collecting the original data and to Jeffrey Cohen for providing the updated data.

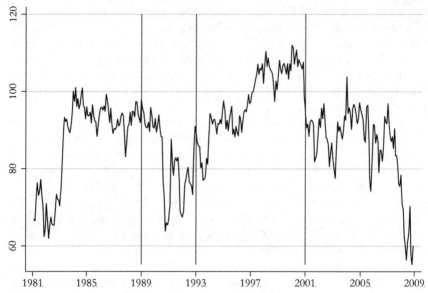

FIGURE 5.4. Economic confidence by administration.

business conditions.[6] It combines both retrospective and prospective evaluations of the economy into a single measure. This measure was chosen over the specific questions comprising the ICS to enable parsimony. Past research suggests that both retrospective and prospective evaluations may be important to presidential approval but is divided over which is more important.[7] Therefore, the combination measure was deemed appropriate. Figure 5.4 contains a graph of the economic confidence measure from 1981 through 2008, along with markers for the start of each presidential administration.

Note that the monthly version of the ICS was only initiated in 1978. This meant that if we are to include this variable, presidents before Carter could not

---

[6] The five questions are as follows: 1) "We are interested in how people are getting along financially these days. Would you say that you (and your family living there) are better off or worse off financially than you were a year ago?" 2) "Now looking ahead – do you think that a year from now you (and your family living there) will be better off financially, or worse off, or just about the same as now?" 3) "Now turning to business conditions in the country as a whole – do you think that during the next twelve months we'll have good times financially, or bad times, or what?" 4) "Looking ahead, which would you say is more likely – that in the country as a whole we'll have continuous good times during the next five years or so, or that we will have periods of widespread unemployment or depression, or what?" 5) "About the big things people buy for their homes – such as furniture, a refrigerator, stove, television, and things like that. Generally speaking, do you think now is a good or bad time for people to buy major household items?"

[7] Including both separately introduces multicollinearity and is unnecessary given the ambiguity of past research (e.g., see MacKuen et al. 1992; versus Clarke and Stewart 1994).

be included in the analyses. Prior research suggests that the ICS is extremely important, so the period of analysis is restricted to more recent presidents. There are also theoretical reasons to restrict the analysis to this later time frame. The descriptive analyses in Chapter 3 showed that presidents became much more aggressive starting with Reagan. Furthermore, there were wild swings in presidential approval during the Iran hostage crisis. For these reasons, all of the following analyses consider only presidencies starting with Reagan.

This temporal restriction enables a critical test of whether recent presidents have affected their own approval ratings and people's economic confidence through foreign policy threats. Presidents Reagan and Clinton were widely known for their strong communications skills. President Reagan especially employed an extensive staff of political consultants to project a positive image. As noted by Blumenthal (1982, 329), "The president who spent his entire adult life as a media performer, understands as Jimmy Carter never did the use of the media as an instrument of policy." If presidential rhetoric made no difference for this later subset of presidents, then it probably never made a difference.

Similar to the analysis for domestic support, the analyses for economic confidence include a lagged dependent variable to control for inertia and various additional measures of the state of the economy. As in the other two analyses, the Conference Board's Composite Index of Coincident Indicators is included. As in the domestic support analysis, unemployment and inflation are included. The analysis for economic confidence also includes the same measure for foreign policy drama as in the other two analyses. The measure of domestic drama is omitted, because there is no theoretical reason that such events should affect consumer confidence. Furthermore, Figure 5.4 suggests no reason to include indicator variables for each presidency. Although there is a sharp break in economic confidence perhaps associated with the George W. Bush administration (e.g., see Wood 2007), this change also corresponds with the onset of a mild recession early in his administration.

### Estimation Method

The double-headed arrows between the three core nodes in Figure 5.3 imply the possibility of two-way effects. There is also a strong possibility of inertia associated with presidential saber rattling, domestic support, and economic confidence. Vector autoregression (VAR) analysis (Freeman et al. 1989; Sims 1980) is ideally suited for modeling such a system. However, as discussed earlier, the three dependent variables do not have identical explanatory variables. For this reason, the system in Figure 5.3 is treated as a Near-VAR with estimation by Seemingly Unrelated Regressions (Zellner 1962).

VAR modeling has important advantages over the usual regression approach, including the natural treatment of possible two-way relations, strong controls for inertia, and the ability to track temporal dynamics through time. Concerning two-way relations and inertia, each dependent variable is regressed on multiple lagged values of itself, as well as multiple lagged values of the other

variables.[8] Including multiple lags of the dependent variables ensures that inertia is not a confounding cause for relationships. The direction of causal relations and dynamics for the system is assessed through moving average response
(MAR) simulations.

Including multiple lags of all variables enables tracking relationships dynam-
ically through time. The dynamic simulations take into account feedback across
variables that can either suppress or accentuate relationships. Using the MAR
simulations one can observe the direction, magnitude, polarity, and time path
of each relationship. Simulations are accomplished by shocking each variable
mathematically to produce an implied response in the other variables in the
system.[9] Confidence boundaries for the MAR simulations are obtained using
Monte Carlo integration and the fractile method recommended by Sims and
Zha (1999).

## Evaluating the Effect of Presidential Saber Rattling
## on Domestic Audiences

### Some Basic Analyses

As a preliminary to the Near-VAR analyses, basic autoregressive regressions
were run investigating the determinants of domestic support for the president
and people's economic confidence. Table 5.1 contains regression coefficients
with *t* statistics in parentheses for these analyses.

Observing the second and third rows of Table 5.1, the statistical results
show that both dependent measures are highly inertial. The lagged dependent
variables are highly significant in their own regressions, with *t* statistics of
39.09 and 21.83 respectively. People's evaluations of the president and their
evaluations of the economy are very persistent through time.

Furthermore, economic confidence is strongly related to domestic support
for the president, and domestic support for the president is strongly related
to economic confidence. Each one unit increase in the ICS produces about
a 0.07 percent increase in the president's approval ratings. In the reverse
direction, each one percent change in the president's approval ratings produces about a 0.06 unit increase in the ICS. These results are consistent and
again highly significant, suggesting that the links between domestic support and
economic confidence in Figure 5.3 are two-way. Thus, a common psychological

---

[8] Based on Akaike's Information Criterion (1973), the analysis included four monthly lags in
each of the equations constituting the Near-VAR. In all analyses the relationships were stable
and consistent regardless of changing the lag length. Residuals from all final analyses were
non-autocorrelated and normally distributed.

[9] The resulting innovations are orthogonalized using Choleski factorization because such innovations have the convenient property that they are uncorrelated across both time and equations.
With Choleski factorization the ordering of the variables can make a difference to the results
if there is a high contemporaneous correlation among the variables. The contemporaneous
correlation between presidential saber rattling and public approval was −0.02. Thus, the order
of the variables made no difference to the results reported here.

TABLE 5.1. *Presidential Saber Rattling, Domestic Support, and Economic Confidence*

| Variable | Dependent Variable | |
|---|---|---|
| | Domestic Support | Economic Confidence |
| Presidential Saber Rattling$_{t-1}$ | 0.06 | −0.06 |
| | (1.64) | (−2.33) |
| Domestic Support$_{t-1}$ | 0.92 | 0.06 |
| | (39.09) | (2.88) |
| Economic Confidence$_{t-1}$ | 0.07 | 0.79 |
| | (1.68) | (21.83) |
| ΔUnemployment$_{t-1}$ | −1.35 | −2.56 |
| | (−0.84) | (−1.81) |
| Inflation$_{t-1}$ | 0.28 | −0.53 |
| | (1.52) | (−3.28) |
| Current Economic Conditions$_{t-1}$ | −0.12 | 0.53 |
| | (−0.70) | (3.56) |
| Scandal | 0.26 | 0.57 |
| | (0.27) | (0.68) |
| Major Foreign Policy Crises and Events | 1.87 | −0.66 |
| | (2.14) | (−0.87) |
| Domestic Drama | 14.92 | |
| | (6.03) | |
| Media$_{t-1}$ | 0.02 | 0.02 |
| | (1.55) | (1.34) |
| Constant | −3.42 | 15.88 |
| | (−1.02) | (5.40) |
| *Diagnostics* | | |
| N | 334 | 334 |
| $\sigma_e^2$ | 4.19 | 3.68 |
| Adjusted $R^2$ | 0.89 | 0.90 |

*Note:* The numbers in the table are coefficients from dynamic regressions of presidential approval and consumer confidence on the variables indicated in the left column. The numbers in parentheses are *t* statistics. Indicators for the first month during which a poll was taken for a new presidency were also included in the presidential approval regression. However, the new presidency indicators are omitted from the economic confidence regression.

process affects both the president's domestic support and people's economic confidence.

The other economic variables in the fourth through sixth rows are not statistically related to the president's domestic support. This nonfinding is consistent with MacKuen et al. (1992; see also Erikson et al. 2002) who find that once people's evaluations of the economy are taken into account, no other economic variables matter to presidential approval. However, the other economic variables are strongly related to people's economic confidence. Higher unemployment and inflation produce lower economic confidence, and an economy that is currently stronger produces higher economic confidence.

Consistent with past presidential approval research, major foreign policy crises and events and domestic drama, reported in the eighth and ninth rows, are strongly associated with domestic support for the president. However, major foreign policy crises and events do not appear related to people's economic confidence. Additionally, media coverage of major crises and events is not significantly related to the president's domestic support or people's economic confidence.

Finally, consider the estimated results for the links in Figure 5.3 from presidential saber rattling to domestic support and people's economic confidence. The first row of Table 5.1 shows that both are statistically significant in the predicted direction. Each additional presidential threat produces an increase of about 0.06 percent in the president's approval ratings. For example, consider the average month from 1981 through 2008 when presidents issued about 8.19 threatening remarks. This translates into an average boost in presidential approval of about 0.49 percent due to presidential bellicosity. Or consider the peak month when George H. W. Bush issued 70 threatening remarks. This peak translated into a boost in presidential approval of about 4.2 percent.

Each presidential saber rattling remark also produced a decline in people's economic confidence of about −0.06. The economic confidence variable ranges from 55.2 to 112, with an average of 89.07. Thus, during the average month of presidential saber rattling, economic confidence was depressed by about 0.49 units because of presidential threats. More interesting is the effect at the peak. When George H. W. Bush issued 70 threatening remarks toward Iraq in November 1990, economic confidence was depressed by about 4.2 units, or about 7 percent of the total ICS scale. This is a sizeable effect.

*Evaluating the Role of the Media*
As noted earlier, President Adams successfully altered media coverage of the crisis with France through public rhetoric and intimidation. Do modern presidents also affect media coverage of major events and crises, perhaps also bolstering their public support? Table 5.2 reports two regressions intended to answer this question. The first column contains an analysis in which media coverage is regressed on presidential saber rattling, along with other explanatory variables. The second column considers the effect of presidential saber rattling conditional on the president's domestic support.

Again, the lagged dependent variables for these analyses are highly inertial, with $t$ statistics slightly greater than 20. The previous month's media coverage is by far the strongest predictor of the current month's media coverage. Controlling for this inertia, the major crises and events themselves are also strong predictors of media coverage. However, the coefficients and $t$ statistics for presidential saber rattling in both columns suggest that presidents do

TABLE 5.2. *The Media, Presidential Saber Rattling, and Domestic Support*

| Variable | Dependent Variable | |
|---|---|---|
| | Media | Media |
| Media$_{t-1}$ | 0.73 | 0.73 |
| | (20.29) | (20.17) |
| Major Foreign Policy Crises and Events | 19.90 | 19.92 |
| | (7.88) | (7.87) |
| Presidential Saber Rattling$_{t-1}$ | 0.11 | 0.22 |
| | (1.25) | (0.59) |
| Domestic Support$_{t-1}$ | 0.02 | 0.03 |
| | (0.31) | (0.43) |
| Presidential Saber Rattling$_{t-1}$ *Domestic Support$_{t-1}$ | | −0.00 |
| | | (−0.30) |
| Constant | 0.63 | −0.42 |
| | (0.21) | (−0.09) |
| *Diagnostics* | | |
| N | 336 | 336 |
| $\sigma_e^2$ | 12.34 | 12.36 |
| Adjusted $R^2$ | 0.62 | 0.61 |

*Note:* The numbers in the table are coefficients from dynamic regressions of media coverage of major foreign policy crises and events on the variables indicated in the left column. The numbers in parentheses are *t* statistics.

not successfully alter the intensity of media coverage either independently or conditional on their public support.

Furthermore, Granger (1969) causality tests were performed between presidential saber rattling and the media variable, with the other variables entered exogenously. Controlling for major crises and events, these tests show that the relation runs from the media to presidential saber rattling, rather than in the opposite direction (see the specifics in footnote 4 in Chapter 4). On the basis of the regressions in Table 5.2 and the Granger tests, the media is treated as exogenous in all subsequent analyses. More substantively, the statistical evidence shows that, unlike President Adams, modern presidents do not successfully alter media coverage of major crises and events.

Nevertheless, it may be that media coverage amplifies or mutes the responses to presidential saber rattling shown in Table 5.1. Do the media moderate the relationship between presidential saber rattling and public support or economic confidence? Table 5.3 reports regressions similar to those in Table 5.1 but containing an interaction between presidential saber rattling and media coverage of major events and crises. The statistical results show a moderating effect by the media for changing domestic support but not for changing economic confidence. Each additional media story coupled with an additional saber-rattling

TABLE 5.3. *The Media, Presidential Saber Rattling, Domestic Support, and Economic Confidence*

| Variable | Dependent Variable | |
| --- | --- | --- |
| | Domestic Support | Economic Confidence |
| Presidential Saber Rattling$_{t-1}$ | −0.06 | −0.07 |
| | (−1.17) | (−1.64) |
| Domestic Support$_{t-1}$ | 0.91 | 0.06 |
| | (39.22) | (2.84) |
| Economic Confidence$_{t-1}$ | 0.08 | 0.79 |
| | (1.91) | (21.74) |
| $\Delta$Unemployment$_{t-1}$ | −1.94 | −2.57 |
| | (−1.21) | (−1.82) |
| Inflation$_{t-1}$ | 0.20 | −0.53 |
| | (1.13) | (−3.25) |
| Current Economic Conditions$_{t-1}$ | −0.19 | 0.57 |
| | (−1.18) | (3.55) |
| Scandal | 0.31 | 0.57 |
| | (0.34) | (0.68) |
| Major Foreign Policy Crises and Events | 1.99 | −0.65 |
| | (2.30) | (−0.86) |
| Domestic Drama | 15.16 | |
| | (6.23) | |
| Media$_{t-1}$ | 0.00 | 0.02 |
| | (−0.99) | (1.11) |
| Presidential Saber Rattling$_{t-1}$*Media$_{t-1}$ | 0.004 | 0.00 |
| | (3.00) | (0.17) |
| Constant | −2.17 | 15.99 |
| | (−0.65) | (5.30) |
| *Diagnostics* | | |
| N | 334 | 334 |
| $\sigma_e^2$ | 4.13 | 3.69 |
| Adjusted $R^2$ | 0.90 | 0.90 |

*Note:* The numbers in the table are coefficients from dynamic regressions of presidential approval and consumer confidence on the variables indicated in the left column. The numbers in parentheses are $t$ statistics. Indicators for the first month during which a poll was taken for a new presidency were also included in the presidential approval regression. However, the new presidency indicators are omitted from the economic confidence regression.

sentence produces about a 1 percent increase in public approval of the president. For example, consider a one standard deviation increase in each. Such a change produces about a 1.53 percent increase in presidential approval. These results suggest that presidents benefit not only from the events themselves, and their own saber rattling but also from the increased media coverage associated with major crises and events.

### Near-VAR Analyses

The preceding analyses are limited in that they do not fully consider the possible two-way relations in Figure 5.3 between presidential saber rattling and domestic support and between presidential saber rattling and people's economic confidence. The preceding regressions also consider only the instantaneous effects of each variable.[10] Yet the effects may well be distributed across time.

Accordingly, Near-VAR analyses were performed that fully implement the model shown in Figure 5.3. Four lags of the three core variables are included in each analysis. Other than this expansion, the estimated equation for presidential saber rattling is the same as that reported in Chapter 4. The estimated equations for domestic support and people's economic confidence are the same as those reported above.

Figure 5.5 reports the impulse responses from this analysis. The approach is to introduce simulated shocks into the Near-VAR system and then to trace out the responses in the other variables based on the estimated coefficients. The variables being shocked are along the diagonal of the graphs in Figure 5.5. The responses are traced out in the rows from left to right.

The top row of graphs in Figure 5.5 shows the responses to a one standard error simulated increase in presidential saber rattling (row one, column one). One standard error is about 7.4 additional saber-rattling remarks per month. The results in the first row and column show that presidential saber rattling dies out fairly quickly after such a shock, lasting for about five months. In other words, presidential saber rattling is moderately inertial, continuing in streams after an initial one-shot stimulus.

However, moving to the right along the top row, the responses to presidential saber rattling for domestic support and economic confidence are shown to be sustained for many months. These sustained responses again suggest that the theory discussed earlier is correct. Presidential saber rattling jointly affects the psychology of domestic support and people's economic confidence.

Consider first how presidential saber rattling affects domestic support, shown in row one, column two. The dynamics of this response show there are long-term payoffs for presidents who issue threatening rhetoric. The positive effect on domestic support begins soon after the shock and peaks at about the fourth month at an increase of about 0.80 percent. Following this, there is a steady decline in the effect through time. The average effect across all lags is about 0.50 percent. Another perspective is to translate this average effect to the peak in presidential saber rattling. The peak effect (70 threats in November 1990) is roughly nine times larger than the simulated shock used here. Thus, there was an increase of about 4.50 percent in the president's domestic support

---

[10] The dynamic effects are constrained to the coefficient on the lagged dependent variables.

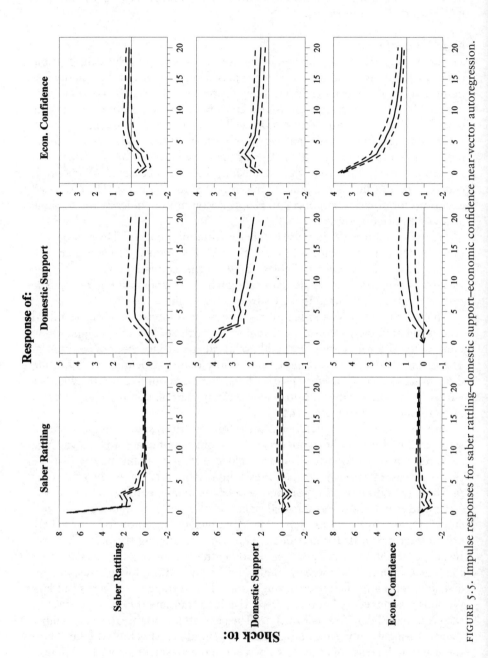

FIGURE 5.5. Impulse responses for saber rattling–domestic support–economic confidence near-vector autoregression.

following this peak effect. Of course, this increase is about the same as that reported in Table 5.1. More generally, the dynamics shown in the first row and second column reveal that increased domestic support from a one-time shock in presidential saber rattling can last for more than a year.

Although presidents benefit from their threats through increased domestic support, the results in Figure 5.5 also show that such threats have the undesirable effect of depressing people's economic confidence. As shown in Wood (2009b), declining economic confidence also has deleterious implications for people's economic behavior and macroeconomic performance. Consistent with those findings, the first row and third column shows that a one standard error shock in presidential saber rattling produces an immediate decline in people's economic confidence lasting for about four months. The maximum decline occurs in the second month after the shock at about −0.80 units. The average effect across the first four lags is about −0.70 units. Translating this change again to the peak of presidential saber rattling, this result implies a decline in economic confidence of −6.30, or about 11 percent of the total scale. Again, this is a sizeable effect.

The second and third rows of Figure 5.5 also imply indirect effects from presidential saber rattling to domestic support and economic confidence. Consistent with the theory in Figure 5.3, the president's domestic support and economic confidence are strongly connected, as demonstrated by the impulse responses in the second and third rows and columns. A one standard error shock in domestic support for the president (i.e., about a 4.0 percent increase shown in the second row and column) produces about a 1.25-unit change in economic confidence (shown in the second row and third column). This increase is rapid and distributed across many months. In the other direction, a one standard error increase in economic confidence (i.e., about a 3.8-unit increase shown in the third row and column) produces about a 0.8 percent increase in domestic support (shown in the third row and second column). Again, the effect of economic confidence on domestic support is distributed across many months.

In other words, good feelings about the president translate into good feelings about the economy. When people feel good about the economy, they also feel good about the president. However, presidents may also hurt their own support over the long term by making people feel economically uncertain.

### Partisan Responses to Critical Events

The earlier theoretical discussion posed a set of competing hypotheses about how people might differ in their responses to political drama, manifest through critical events and presidential saber rattling. Are people consistently biased information processors in responding to the president? Are they unbiased Bayesian information processors who respond in parallel? Or does their response to critical events and presidential saber rattling suggest a two-state model in which people are sometimes driven by their predispositions and at

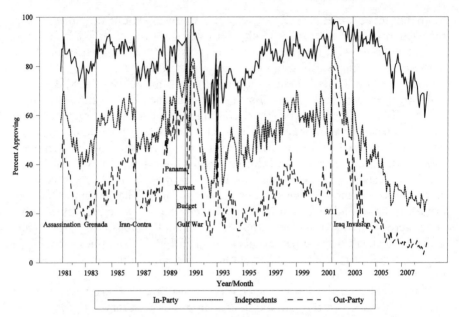

FIGURE 5.6. Drama and partisan presidential approval, 1981–2009.

other times by their emotions? The stimuli reflected in critical events and presidential saber rattling enable evaluating these competing theories.

Consider first how people of different partisan persuasions respond to various critical events. Figure 5.6 graphs partisan presidential approval again from January 1981 through January 2009, along with markers for various events included in the preceding analyses.

As suggested by Gerber and Green (1999), there are similarities in the dynamics of the In-Party, Out-Party, and Independent approvals. The three groups are widely separated in their support for the president, suggesting biased information processing. The three groups move largely in parallel, also suggesting Bayesian updating. However, contrary to Gerber and Green's assertions, a closer inspection of the three time series shows large disparities in partisan responses to many of the critical events.

An exception to this generalization is the Reagan assassination attempt in April 1981. It produced roughly equal increases in presidential approval across all partisan groups. Given the equality of these three movements, the responses do not appear rooted in ideology, partisanship, or self-interest. Rather, these responses must have been an emotional reaction felt consistently by all Americans (perhaps due to sadness, anger, or anxiety).

In contrast, the partisan responses to various foreign policy crises (Grenada, Panama, Kuwait invasion, Gulf War initiation, September 11, and United States invades Iraq) show large disparities only explicable through a two-state theory of information processing. In-Party respondents' evaluations were seemingly dominated by their predispositions. The information reflected in these events did little to change the already strong support for the president among In-Party respondents.

However, the new information from these events caused many Out-Party and Independent respondents to abruptly improve their evaluations of the president. Interestingly, the largest improvements were among Out-Party respondents, with Independents following closely behind. The rapid responses for both groups to these foreign policy events are undoubtedly based on emotions such as patriotism, loyalty, anger, and anxiety. With aggregate data it is impossible to know which particular emotion was at work. Nevertheless, the movements are consistent with nondirectional motivated reasoning in which emotions cause reevaluation of a political object, and, in the case of Out-Party respondents, a higher rate of defection from their normal partisan evaluations.

Consider also the critical events that resulted in decreased presidential approval. Sharply declining presidential approval occurred with the onset of the Iran-Contra scandal in October 1986 and with the announcement of the budget agreement violating the "no new taxes" pledge by President George H. W. Bush in November 1990. On both occasions the declines in presidential approval were again largest among Out-Party and Independent respondents. However, the declines among In-Party respondents were also substantial. Republican support for President Reagan declined sharply by about 12 percent after the revelation of the Iran-Contra deal. Similarly, Republican support for President Bush dropped by about 18 percent after the budget agreement violating the "no new taxes" pledge. Both changes suggest that even In-Party respondents are capable of nondirectional motivated reasoning. When faced with new information that challenges their prior beliefs and values, and stimuli of the proper valence and magnitude, even fellow partisans can reevaluate their support for the president.

### Partisan Responses to Presidential Saber Rattling

The statistical analyses reported in Figure 5.5 used aggregate public approval data to show that presidential saber rattling can produce large increases in public support that last for many months. However, they did not reveal who responds or whether those responses vary across partisan groups. Does presidential saber rattling also produce disparate responses across partisan groups? If so, then are the disparities in partisan responses again consistent with the two-state model of information processing?

Figure 5.7 answers these questions. Each row of graphs contains the first row impulse responses from three separate Near-VARs for In-Party, Independent, and Out-Party respondents. The three graphs in the left column of the figure contain the autoregressive dynamics of a one-time shock to presidential saber rattling. The three graphs in the middle column contain the different partisan

**Response of:**

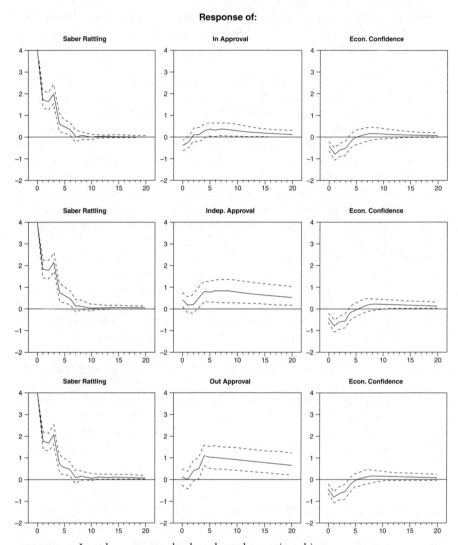

FIGURE 5.7. Impulse responses broken down by partisanship.

responses in presidential approval to a one standard error increase in presidential saber rattling. The three graphs in right column contain the impulse responses for economic confidence.

What is immediately apparent from examining the middle column of graphs in Figure 5.7 is that In-Party respondents are much less responsive to presidential saber rattling than Independents and Out-Party respondents. Although the responses for the three groups are all statistically significant, the response for Out-Party respondents is roughly three times the response for In-Party respondents, with Independents falling between these extremes.

Why do we observe these disparities? Again, the results are consistent with the two-state theory of information processing. Directional motivated reasoning characterizes In-Party respondents. The information contained in presidential saber rattling provides little that would move In-Party respondents away from their predispositions. Most presidential partisans are already committed to the president. However, the president gains some additional support among In-Party respondents, evidenced by the significance of the responses in the top middle graph of Figure 5.7.

The larger changes among Independent and Out-Party respondents suggest nondirectional motivated reasoning. In particular, some Independent respondents, who are not strongly committed to either party, are emotionally activated to support the president. Presidential saber rattling produces uncertainty and reevaluation of their past assessments of presidential performance. Similarly, many Out-Party respondents rally toward the president as their emotions come to dominate their predispositions. As with the critical events discussed earlier, the largest number of converts comes from the Out-Party group.

## Conclusions

As the sole foreign policy spokesperson for the United States, presidents are ultimately responsible for conducting relations with other nations. Presidential rhetoric and actions directed toward other nations should secure U.S. interests internationally. However, this chapter shows that they also have domestic consequences. Presidential saber-rattling affects domestic support for the president, as well as people's economic evaluations.

Why does presidential saber rattling matter to domestic outcomes? Presidents exert a strong psychological influence on the American public. People look to the president for strength and leadership. Making threats projects an image of strength and leadership. Thus, controlling for important foreign policy crises, media coverage, and economic variables, the results reported here show that presidents significantly increase their public approval ratings by using threatening rhetoric. Furthermore, these increases in domestic support are not short-term deviations but can last for many months.

The strong psychological influence of presidential saber rattling on the American public also has unanticipated and undesirable consequences. Economic actors are not fully rational and rely on cues from their information environment to inform their economic decision making. They make forecasts of the economic future and its relative certainty based on these cues. Under normal conditions, presidents are a major source of economic cues. However, they are even more so during times of foreign policy crisis. Increased presidential saber rattling produces greater uncertainty for economic actors. In turn, they become more apprehensive about the economic future and more reluctant to spend and borrow. Because the U.S. economy depends on a continuous flow of consumption and borrowing, such behavioral changes can adversely affect U.S. economic performance.

Beyond the core question of whether presidential saber rattling matters to domestic outcomes, this chapter has also been concerned with "why" and "for whom" it matters. The answer to the "why" question is that presidential saber rattling sparks human emotions such as patriotism, loyalty, anger, or anxiety. These emotions naturally draw domestic support to the president who is our symbolic leader. Thus, a factor much stronger than ideology, partisanship, or economic self-interest is at work during periods of political drama and presidential saber rattling. Emotions trump evaluations of the president based on people's predispositions.

The answer to the "for whom" question is that presidential saber rattling matters for all audiences. The president's fellow partisans and many independents and opposing partisans rally behind the president when threats are issued. However, what is most interesting is how these rally effects differ across groups. The most pronounced movements are among those who are *not* the president's natural supporters. Of course, it is not surprising that Independents become more supportive, given their weak predispositions. However, most additional support comes from Out-Party respondents who often have strong predispositions against the president.

These interesting results suggest that presidential saber rattling is a unifying force in American politics. People of all political persuasions rally behind the president after the president makes threats. Those who naturally oppose the president suddenly become the president's supporters. Those who are undecided about the president rally to the president's side. Those who are the president's natural allies continue to be supportive. As discussed in the next chapter, this more unified domestic audience holds potential implications for the credibility of foreign policy threats and their likely success.

More generally, this chapter shows that the foreign and domestic dimensions of the president's rhetorical leadership do not function in isolation. The president's foreign policy pronouncements can alter domestic outcomes. They can be destructive because saber rattling results in apprehensive consumers and risk-averse economic behavior. They can also be constructive because saber rattling results in greater presidential support and a more unified domestic audience. Therefore, prudent presidential leadership requires cautious foreign policy rhetoric, and careful consideration of the trade-offs between foreign policy goals and domestic consequences.

# 6

## The Foreign Policy Consequences of Presidential Saber Rattling

Does presidential saber rattling increase cooperation or reduce conflict with other nations? Or does it have just the opposite effect, as seemed to occur with the Adams vignette in the introductory chapter? In recent times, presidents have sought to diminish other nations' support for terrorism. Does presidential saber rattling diminish other nations' support for terrorism or the frequency of terrorist acts? Generally, does modern presidential saber rattling produce a world friendlier to American interests? Or does it have the opposite effect? These are the core research questions of this chapter.

As shown by Figure 3.4 in Chapter 3, presidential saber rattling toward weaker adversaries is a relatively recent foreign policy strategy. At the turn of the twentieth century, presidents commonly pursued a policy of "speak softly and carry a big stick" (Roosevelt 1901). Before World War II, American foreign policy was isolationist, not attempting to interfere in the affairs of other nations. Until the 1980s presidents did not commonly threaten other nations unless there was an impending or ongoing war. However, recent presidents have been more likely to threaten other nations without a war. Saber rattling has become a prevalent tool of American foreign policy. Yet little is known about consequences of this shift.

In studying the foreign policy consequences of presidential saber rattling, the analyses in this chapter are restricted to U.S. relations with three adversaries, Iraq, Iran, and North Korea after 1990. These nations have been persistent U.S. adversaries over various time frames. By examining relations for these three critical cases, this chapter seeks to generalize more broadly about the efficacy of presidential saber rattling as a foreign policy strategy.

## Why Should Presidential Threats Matter to Foreign Policy Outcomes?

### The Consequences Side of Realist Theory

As discussed briefly in Chapter 4, realist and neo-realist theories of foreign policy (e.g., Waltz 1979) hold that threats by one nation toward another are driven primarily by the international system. However, these theories also speak to the relative probability of success for a nation's threats. The international system is an environment in which nations often compete for power and benefits. More power implies more control of resources and economic advantages. Weakness implies potential exploitation by stronger powers and economic disadvantages. Within the realist framework, hegemonic states' foreign policy behavior tends toward coercion (George 2009). Weaker states are more vulnerable to coercion. Thus, threats reflect the relative power of nations, as well as the likelihood of threat success.

In a system where power is distributed unequally (such as has existed since the 1980s), threats by hegemons are more likely – and more likely to succeed. Nations that are power-dominant relative to a set of weaker nations have greater incentive to pursue coercive strategies. Their economic and military power is greater, so they are more likely to prevail in application of sanctions or war. As a result, coercive strategies are viewed as more credible. Threats perceived as credible are seen as dangerous by the targets of those threats. Therefore, realist theory would predict that weaker nations are more likely to be coerced and comply in such systems.

The graphical analyses in Chapter 3 offered tentative support for the "causes" side of the realist explanation for presidential threats. Figure 3.5 plotted the intensity of presidential saber rattling toward specific nations from 1945 through 2008. The graph showed a clear break in the intensity of presidential saber rattling toward specific nations starting in the 1980s (i.e., near the end of the Cold War). Visual examination of the pre-1980s data (a period of bipolar power equals) showed that the only periods of intense presidential saber rattling were during the Korean and Vietnam Wars. Excluding these periods, the figure showed that presidents made few threatening remarks toward specific nations, with a few notable exceptions.

President Carter directed threatening rhetoric toward Iran (a weaker nation) during the 1979–1980 hostage crisis and toward the Soviet Union (a power equal) following their invasion of Afghanistan. President Reagan was also quite threatening toward Libya (a weaker nation) during the Libyan bombing crisis and toward the Soviet Union (a power equal) early and late in his administration. Excluding periods of war and these few exceptions, the period from 1945 to the 1980s was characterized by relatively pacific presidential rhetoric.

In contrast, the period from the 1980s through 2008 (when there was greater inequality in the international system) was characterized by increasingly intense presidential saber rattling directed toward a multiplicity of weaker nations. The most obvious of these were Iraq, Iran, and North Korea, the objects of analysis in this chapter. Of course, these nations also directed significant hostility toward the United States during this period. They were also classified by the U.S. State Department as sponsors of global terrorism.[1] Thus, the rise of presidential saber rattling during and after the 1980s might be linked to antagonistic relations with these nations. It might also have been due to their alleged support for terrorist activities.

Figure 3.5 showed that much presidential saber rattling toward Iraq occurred before and after the Persian Gulf War, as three administrations attempted to rein in the aggressive tendencies of the Saddam Hussein regime. Indeed, one could argue that Iraq was the nation's primary adversary from 1991 through 2003. However, hostile presidential remarks toward Iraq basically ceased after the 2003 invasion and fall of the Hussein regime.

U.S. hostility toward Iran and North Korea was also rooted in a historical context dating from the 1979 revolution against the U.S.-backed Shah of Iran and Korean War, respectively. During the period of American hostility toward Iraq, presidential saber rattling toward Iran and North Korea declined. Relations with Iran became more adversarial following the 2003 Iraq invasion, as evidence emerged that it was supporting the Iraqi insurgency and developing nuclear capabilities. North Korea also became a renewed focal point of presidential saber rattling starting with the George W. Bush administration

Thus, the demise of an international system of power equals was followed by a subsequent increase in presidential hostility toward a multiplicity of weaker nations. Realist theory would argue that the change in U.S. foreign policy after the late 1980s was an effort by the United States to consolidate its power as hegemon relative to a weaker set of nations. Furthermore, it might also be argued that the altered presidential behavior was a rational response to a fundamental change in the international system. Conflict directed toward the United States from multiple adversaries and the rise of global terrorism basically forced presidents to become more threatening. The question for this chapter is whether this new strategy resulted in a successful American foreign policy.

### Threat Credibility and Threat Success

Realist explanations provide a major international relations framework for understanding when leaders are likely to make threats, as well as their relative probability of success. In this regard, the concept of "threat credibility" is important. As discussed earlier, the relative power of two adversarial countries is one element of threat credibility. Stronger countries can issue more credible threats than weaker countries because they have more resources to back them up.

[1] Iraq was added the U.S. State Department's list of terrorism-sponsoring nations in December 1979 but removed in 2004 after the Iraq invasion. North Korea was added in 1988 after the bombing of a Korean Airlines Flight but removed in June 2008. Iran was added to the list in January 1984 and remains on the list. See U.S. Department of State (2011).

However, threats should also be perceived as more credible when the leader making a threat is in a stronger position domestically. Of course, the introductory case study of the Adams administration, as well as the statistical analyses in Chapter 5, showed that presidents can bolster their domestic status by making public threats. Presidential approval ratings increase over the long term as a result of such threats. The resulting increases in domestic support should, in turn, make presidential threats appear more credible to the target country. Such domestic changes should increase the probability that a threat will be successful.

Similarly, perceptions of national unity can also increase the credibility of presidential threats. The introductory case study of the Adams administration suggested that people became more unified in their support for the president in standing up to the French. Similarly, the statistical analyses in Chapter 5 showed that Out-Party respondents rally more toward the president when threats are made toward foreign actors. In turn, this increased unity should make presidential threats more credible to those being threatened, which should, in turn, increase the probability of threat success.

Economic factors may also affect perceptions of presidential strength to foreign adversaries. A stronger economy places the president in a better position to follow through with threats. In contrast, a nation in recession, economic decline, or scandal will be perceived by the target country as weak and unable to pursue economic or military action. Thus, a variety of domestic factors should bolster presidential credibility and therefore increase the probability that threats will be successful.

### Audience Costs and Threat Credibility

Many international relations scholars have also argued that threats should be perceived as more credible when leaders "go public," rather than "staying private." For example, Fearon (1994) draws on work by Schelling (1960) to argue that foreign policy success depends critically on making *public* foreign policy commitments. Public commitments "tie the hands" of a nation's leaders, and may have domestic audience costs if leaders fail to follow through. Public threats are powerful signals to target countries. Thus, public presidential saber rattling that threatens economic, political, or military sanctions should be viewed by target nations as commitments toward future action.

Furthermore, Fearon theorizes that leaders of democratic nations (e.g., the United States) are more successful at generating audience costs than leaders of autocratic regimes (such as the former Iraq, Iran, and North Korea). Democratic leaders depend more on their domestic audience and elections for continuation in office. If they fail to follow through with their threats, democratic leaders face potential punishment through lost support and regime turnover. In contrast, Fearon posits that leaders of autocratic nations face fewer adverse consequences. Their continuation in office depends less on popular support and more on raw power. Fearon's analysis, therefore, suggests that democratic leaders such as the American president should be able to signal their intentions more credibly and clearly than leaders of autocracies.

However, others suggest that Fearon underestimates the audience costs associated with autocratic regimes. Weeks (2008) contends that a theory of audience costs should also take into account that authoritarian leaders require the support of domestic elites who act as audiences much in the same way that an electorate does in a democracy. According to Weeks, the critical questions for generating credibility are whether the relevant elites can and will coordinate to sanction a leader and whether the potential for sanctioning is visible to external actors. When these attributes are present, Weeks theorizes that democracies have no advantage over autocracies in generating audience costs and producing the external perception of credible commitment.

Further, while autocratic leaders may not be critically dependent on popular support for continuation in office, they do fear the consequences of being perceived as weak. Such perceptions can embolden the opposition, leading to civil unrest, organized opposition, and potential regime failure. Internationally, perceptions of weakness can diminish regime legitimacy. Autocratic leaders depend on support from other nations to bolster their internal authority. A loss of international support can produce isolation and fewer resources for remaining in power. Thus, under Weeks's framework democracies may be no more successful than autocracies in getting the other nation to back down.

The concept of domestic audience costs has now become central to international relations scholarship (e.g., see Dorussen and Mo 2001; Fearon 1994, 1997; Gelpi and Griesdorf 2001; Kurizaki 2007; Leventoğlu and Tarar 2005; Partell and Palmer 1999; Ramsay 2004; Schultz 1998, 2001a, 2001b; Smith 1998; Tarar and Leventoğlu 2009; Tomz 2007; Weeks 2008). Game theoretic models of international conflict and cooperation now commonly assume that leaders suffer domestic audience costs if they issue threats publicly and fail to follow through. Citizens punish leaders who back down relative to leaders who never commit in the first place. The presence of audience costs and the associated prospect of losing domestic support should discourage leaders from pursuing empty threats and promises.[2] However, when democratic leaders do make threats, the associated audience costs should make those threats especially credible.

More specific to the American case, threats toward U.S. adversaries can come less visibly from lower-level officials or through private channels. Threats may also be issued less visibly through diplomacy. However, presidential saber rattling *by definition* entails threats made publicly by the president. The presidential threats contained in this measure are drawn from *Public Papers of the Presidents*. Because such threats come publicly from the U.S. president, the democratic leader of the free world, they are often highly publicized.

[2] Of course, presidents may prefer to "stay private" by conducting foreign policy out of the public eye (Baum 2004).

As a result, public threats from the president should be viewed by targets as highly credible. According to the theory of audience costs, then, such threats should be an especially effective tool for altering the behavior of foreign adversaries.

### A Critique of Audience Cost Theory

Although audience cost theory is prominent in the field of international relations, there are a number of problems in empirically evaluating it. First, the theory posits that leaders' public threats toward other nations should have more credibility than their private threats. However, private threats are *by definition* unobservable, or they would not be called private. Therefore, it is impossible to evaluate which type of threat, public or private, has more credibility with foreign leaders. Scholars can construct arguments in either direction. For example, Kurizaki (2007) constructed a game showing that private threats can be equally compelling relative to public threats. Still, neither argument is falsifiable, because empirical data do not exist on private threats.

There is also a psychological dimension to audience cost theory that, again, cannot be tested. The theory posits that public threats have more credibility with the leaders of threatened countries. Yet the perception of threat credibility by foreign leaders is not an observable phenomenon. Perception of threat credibility is a psychological phenomenon that requires psychological evidence to verify. Again, such evidence is not commonly available to international relations scholars. One can only observe the behavior of foreign actors.

Additionally, audience cost theory posits that leaders making threats will suffer losses at home if they do not follow through with their threats. This part of the theory might be testable with the right kind of data.[3] Such a test would need to focus on individual threats as the unit of analysis. An analyst might then observe public responses when leaders fail to follow through with their threats. However, such an analysis is again problematic for at least three reasons.

First, there is a strategic selection bias problem that is widely recognized by international relations scholars (Schultz 2001b; Tomz 2007). If leaders anticipate that domestic audiences will react harshly to their backing down after making a public threat, then they will not take that path in the first place. Thus, strategic behavior by leaders leaves little or no opportunity ever to observe a public backlash.

---

[3] For example, Tomz (2007) used experimental data. However, experimentation always raises questions about generalizability. Additionally, it is unclear that his experiment effectively controlled for such factors as history or alternative real-world explanations. In a real-world setting people may not remember that the president made a threat in the distant past. Therefore, they may not punish the president for failure to follow through. Furthermore, presidential evaluations are always subject to a number of factors beyond whether the president made a single empty threat.

Second, there is a measurement problem associated with the concept of "following through" with threats. When would one know whether a leader had failed to follow through with a threat? Is a failure to follow through just a matter of sufficient time passing to deem the threat empty? Is a failure to follow through an explicit repudiation of the threat, such as occurred during the Adams administration when the president reversed course to seek peace with the French? If the first interpretation, then there is a problem in recognizing the stimulus timing; if the second interpretation, then it would be difficult ever to observe the stimulus, because presidents rarely repudiate a public threat.

Third, there is also a data problem in gauging public responses to an empty threat. How does one go about measuring public responses, given that public opinion data relative to particular threats is sporadic at best? Such data are largely unavailable to empirical researchers. From these arguments we must conclude that public responses to presidents who fail to follow through with their threats will remain largely unobserved and unobservable.

Another nuance to audience cost theory is that there are actually two audiences to consider: the threatening leader's domestic audience and the audience within the nation being threatened. Domestic audiences tend to view strong leaders who seem to be protecting national interests favorably. Similarly, foreign leaders may also gain domestic strength by standing firm. These effects were observed in the introductory case study of the Adams administration when French threats bolstered the status of the American president. Furthermore, as demonstrated in Chapter 5, presidential approval ratings go up when presidents project a strong image. Thus, "rally effects" in the targeted nation, such as commonly occurs in the United States, may reduce the effectiveness of a leader's threats.

Perhaps because the theory is untestable, the audience cost literature has focused largely on "storytelling" about leaders who face high audience costs generating credible commitments, which in turn affect the behavior of foreign adversaries. However, we can easily tell an opposing story. U.S. presidents have often paid a high price for actually following through with their threats. President Carter lost significant support by following through on his threat to impose economic sanctions on the Soviet Union after their invasion of Afghanistan. Many U.S. farmers were angry that they had to pay the price of Carter's foreign policy. Furthermore, three American presidents (Truman, Johnson, and George W. Bush) suffered significant loss of long-term public support for involving the nation in protracted military interventions. These actions became increasingly unpopular with domestic audiences because of perceptions of needless lives lost and diverted economic resources.

For all of these reasons, audience cost theory has remained largely untested by international relations scholars (but see Gelpi and Griesdorf 2001; Schultz 2001a; Tomz 2007). The theory will remain untested here. However, we will gain a sense of whether public threats by the democratically elected leader of the free world toward a weaker autocratic adversary are generally successful.

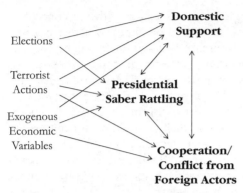

FIGURE 6.1. Potential paths of influence between presidential saber rattling, domestic support for the president, and cooperation/conflict with foreign actors.

## *Formalizing a Theory Graphically*

Figure 6.1 operationalizes many of the preceding hypothesized relationships in path diagram form. Again, the arrows indicate hypotheses about potential relationships among presidential saber rattling, domestic support for the president, and cooperation or conflict from foreign actors. The core of the graph is again the three nodes in boldface type. The double-headed arrows for these three linkages indicate possible two-way relations between each pair of variables. Some of these linkages were already discussed and evaluated in Chapters 4 and 5. Again, the prior analyses showed that presidential saber rattling is strongly determined by elections, war, and major crises and events (including terrorist actions) and may also relate to domestic support and economic variables. The president's domestic support is strongly determined by economic variables, foreign and domestic political drama, and presidential saber rattling.

The single-headed arrows in Figure 6.1 running from economic variables and terrorist actions to cooperation/conflict with foreign actors represent two new hypotheses. First, a stronger U.S. economy should produce perceptions of American strength. Threat credibility is higher when the United States has the economic power to follow through with its threats. Therefore, foreign adversaries should be more cooperative and less conflictual during periods when the U.S. economy is strong.

Second, terrorist actions directed toward U.S. interests may produce more or less cooperation/conflict from the target nation. If the target nation is supportive of terrorist acts, then we should see less cooperation and more conflict toward the United States. If the target nation is unsupportive of terrorist acts, then the relation should either be neutral or run in the opposite direction. In either case, this linkage can provide a sense of whether the target nation is sympathetic of terrorist actions.

The double-headed arrows running between presidential saber rattling, domestic support, and cooperation/conflict from foreign actors represent the core of the theory. In Chapter 5 we considered in some detail the double-headed arrow between presidential saber rattling and domestic support for the president. The analyses there showed that presidents benefit from saber rattling through increased domestic support. However, the analyses showed little evidence that the relation runs in the opposite direction. Nevertheless, we shall continue to evaluate these relations as potentially two-way.

Consider now the double-headed arrow between domestic support for the president and cooperation/conflict from foreign actors. In the vertical up direction the hypothesis is that increased cooperation and decreased conflict with a foreign adversary should produce greater support for the president. In other words, when the president's foreign policy is more successful, the president should benefit through increased domestic support. In the vertical down direction the hypothesis is that greater domestic support for the president should increase the president's credibility. Greater presidential credibility should, in turn, produce a higher probability that presidential threats will be successful.

Finally, consider the double-headed arrow running between presidential saber rattling and cooperation/conflict from foreign actors. In the upward direction, the hypothesis is that presidential saber rattling should respond to changing levels of cooperation and conflict by the target nation. Decreased cooperation and increased conflict should result in increased presidential saber rattling through time.

In the downward direction, if the preceding theories are correct about how relative power, threat credibility, and audience costs affect threat success, then saber rattling by the U.S. president (i.e., by a strong and powerful democratic leader with high audience costs) should systematically affect cooperation/conflict with the targets of those threats (i.e., weaker autocratic leaders with low audience costs). It is through this linkage that we should be able to determine whether increased presidential threats since the 1980s have been a successful foreign policy strategy.

## Measuring the Foreign Policy Concepts

### Terrorist Actions

Figure 6.1 posits that presidents may also issue threats toward foreign actors in response to terrorist actions directed toward U.S. interests. Terrorist actions are yet another form of political drama relative to what was considered in earlier chapters. Earlier, political drama was defined as comprising war, major crises and events, domestic drama, scandals, and saber rattling. We continue to include those variables in the analyses. However, in this chapter the definition of political drama is again expanded to include a list of terrorist actions against U.S. interests.

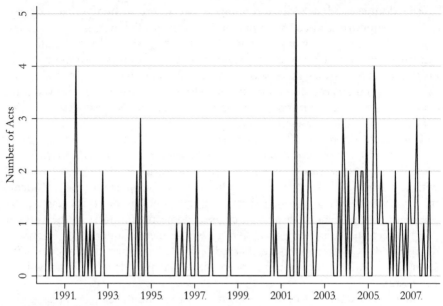

FIGURE 6.2. Terrorist acts against U.S. interests.

Terrorist actions are measured using three new variables. First, terrorist actions against U.S. interests were extracted from the Global Terrorism Database (GTD; accessed on February 7, 2010). The National Consortium for the Study of Terrorism and Responses to Terrorism (START) makes these data available via an online interface at http://www.start.umd.edu/gtd. The GTD is an open-source database that includes information on terrorist events around the world from 1970 through the present.[4] All extracted events occurred between 1990 and 2008 and were again aggregated into monthly time series counts for statistical analysis.

Figure 6.2 contains a graph of this time series. Visual inspection of the graph suggests that the number of terrorist actions increased during and for a period after the 1991 Persian Gulf War. The frequency of terrorist acts declined during the Clinton administration. Observe also the increase in the frequency of terrorist actions following September 11 and the 2003 invasion of Iraq. These ocular indications suggest that war and the resulting presidential bellicosity may be covariates of terrorist actions. However, estimating a simple correlation between presidential saber rattling toward Iraq, Iran, and North

---

[4] The GTD includes data on domestic as well as transnational and international terrorist incidents that have occurred during this time frame and includes more than 80,000 cases. Terrorist acts against U.S. interests in Latin America and non-Islamic Africa are excluded because these are not relevant to the nations under investigation.

Korea reveals correlations of only –0.09, 0.02, and 0.07 respectively. None of these correlations is statistically significant. Furthermore, the simple correlation between war and terrorist actions is only 0.01, again suggesting the unpredictability of terrorist acts.

However, not all terrorist events are created equal. Therefore, the most important terrorist events are captured with two other variables. First, the most important terrorist events, excluding September 11, were identified over this period.[5] These include the first World Trade Center bombing (1993:02), the Saudi Riyadh bombing (1995:11), the Saudi Khubar Towers bombing (1996:06), the African embassy bombings (1998:08), and the USS *Cole* bombing (2000:10). An indicator variable was created to capture these five events separately and labeled "Big Terror" in the analyses that follow. An indicator variable was also included separately for September 11 (2001:09) because of its overarching importance.

### Cooperation/Conflict from Foreign Actors

The measure for cooperation/conflict from foreign actors in Figure 6.1 was created using machine-coded events data developed commercially by Virtual Research Associates (VRA). The VRA data use lead sentences from Reuters Business Briefings to code the actions of one state toward another.[6] These actions are then categorized using a framework laid out in the Integrated Data for Events Analysis (IDEA) coding manual, which again was developed by VRA.[7] A summary of the IDEA event frames used to code the cooperation/conflict data is given in the appendix to this chapter. These event categories are then weighted using Goldstein (1992) scores that range from –10 to 8.3. Cooperative actions are scored positively, with a weight assigned to reflect the relative degree of cooperation. In contrast, extremely aggressive acts, such as an armed attack, are coded negatively and weighted more heavily than rhetorical statements by political leaders. The cooperation/conflict measure is defined as the sum of all Goldstein scores for all events between the different states for a particular month. From the list of cooperative and hostile acts directed toward the United States, only those initiated by the states of interest for this chapter – Iraq, Iran, and North Korea – were extracted from the database.

---

[5] I used the website http://www.spiritus-temporis.com as an initial filter and then validated the major terrorist events list against other U.S. foreign policy chronologies.

[6] For a more detailed discussion of the data, see Bond et al. (2003).

[7] The IDEA coding framework is an extension and a refinement of, and congruent with, the World Event/Interaction Survey (WEIS). Like WEIS, IDEA is nominally scaled. The congruence with WEIS is in the WEIS "cue" categories numbered 1 through 22. The extension of WEIS is the addition of additional event categories beginning with number 23 and extending (with breaks) to 99. According VRA, IDEA event forms represent the lowest level of specificity that machine coding can accomplish with precision at least equal to large-scale human coding exercises. Equivalent events for the major ordinally scaled alternative framework, COPDAB, are generated using a weight applied to each nominal event form as in Goldstein (1992).

The measure for cooperation/conflict from foreign actors is restricted to the period from 1990 to 2008. This temporal restriction is for two reasons. First, the VRA database for the cooperation/conflict measure was unavailable before 1990 and after January 2008. Second, this restricted time frame is reasonably consistent with the theory we need to evaluate. As noted in Chapter 3 and elsewhere, presidential bellicosity toward weaker adversaries increased starting in the 1980s. Thus, the period from 1990 onward captures much of the relevant period.

The resulting cooperation/conflict time series contains 308 positively coded cooperative events from Iraq (121), Iran (39), and North Korea (148). There were 587 negatively coded conflict events from Iraq (365), Iran (104), and North Korea (118). Observe that there are roughly three times more conflict than cooperative events associated with Iraq. There are about 2.5 times more conflict than cooperative events associated with Iran. However, the number of cooperative events associated with North Korea exceeds the number of conflict events.

## Evaluating the Foreign Policy Consequences of Presidential Saber Rattling

### Evaluating Iraqi Cooperation/Conflict Graphically

As a preliminary to statistical analyses, it is useful to visually examine and study the time series plots of cooperation and conflict from Iraq, Iran, and North Korea. Presidential saber rattling toward these three countries is also superimposed onto these plots. During the period from 1990 to 2008, presidents made 233 public threats toward Iraq, 105 public threats toward Iran, and 43 public threats toward North Korea. Obviously, relations were much more intense with Iraq than with Iran and North Korea.

Figure 6.3 contains the plots for Iraq. The vertical line corresponds with the September 11 terror attacks. Examination of the cooperation/conflict time series (dashed line) shows that during the entire period of analysis Iraq directed significantly more conflict than cooperation toward the United States. However, the U.S. president through this period also directed significant amounts of saber rattling toward Iraq (solid line). The most intense periods of presidential saber rattling were between 1991 and 1999 and again immediately before the 2003 Iraq invasion. Presidential threats effectively ceased after the successful 2003 invasion. The inverse relationships through this period suggest that presidential saber rattling had little or no effect on Iraqi behavior.

More specifically, during the three-month buildup before the 1991 Persian Gulf War, President George H. W. Bush made numerous threats toward Iraq. Obviously he wanted to persuade Saddam Hussein to withdraw his forces from Kuwait to avoid military action. However, presidential threats were not successful, and the Persian Gulf War commenced in August 1990. In April 1991, as part of the permanent cease-fire agreement ending the war, the United

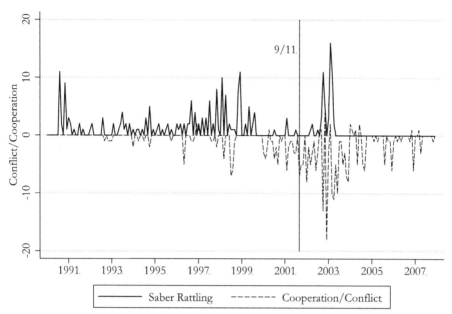

FIGURE 6.3. Iraq cooperation/conflict.

Nations (U.N.) Security Council ordered Iraq to eliminate, under international supervision, its biological, chemical, and nuclear weapons programs, as well as its ballistic missiles that could reach Israel and other countries. Economic sanctions imposed on Iraq by the Security Council in 1990 after its invasion of Kuwait were to remain in place until Iraq had fully complied with these requirements (Arms Control Association 2011b).

Saddam Hussein agreed to these conditions. However, between 1991 and 1999 Iraq deceived, obstructed, and threatened U.N. inspectors seeking to verify the dismantling of its banned programs. A systematic Iraqi effort to conceal began almost immediately when Baghdad lied about its existing programs in the initial declarations. Iraq continued to frustrate U.N. inspectors until late 1998 when they withdrew from Iraq just hours before the United States and the United Kingdom launched three days of airstrikes. Under threat of further attack, Iraq permitted limited inspections of declared nuclear sites, but did not allow more intrusive inspections to verify that it had lived up to its commitments (Arms Control Association 2011b). Thus, as shown in Figure 6.3, from 1991 to 1999 the relative intensity of presidential threats toward Iraq was high as presidents attempted to force Iraqi compliance with U.N. requirements.

Between 1999 and 2002 the intensity of presidential saber rattling went sharply lower. Interestingly, during this same time frame Iraq directed more conflict toward the United States. Perhaps Saddam Hussein was emboldened during this period by his success at thwarting U.N. inspections and U.S. efforts at enforcing compliance. For whatever reason, the Iraqi dictator seemed to be thumbing his nose at the United States.

The visual evidence in Figure 6.3 also shows that conflict from Iraq toward the United States increased after the September 11 terror attacks. We might speculate that this increase suggests Iraqi sympathy with the attacks on their arch-enemy. What is also clear from Figure 6.3 is that the increase in Iraqi conflict toward the United States during this period was not due to increased presidential saber rattling. There was no corresponding increase in the intensity of presidential threats toward Iraq. Rather, the president's rhetoric was directed more toward Afghanistan, pursuing Al Qaida, and constructing a war on terror.

However, attention ultimately returned to Iraq in 2002 when in his State of the Union address President George W. Bush labeled that country part of an "axis of evil," along with Iran and North Korea (*Public Papers of the Presidents*, January 29, 2002). The president's speech was the beginning of a stream of administration statements on the dangers posed by Iraq, many of which advocated the overthrow of Saddam Hussein. On September 12, 2002, amid increasing speculation that the United States was preparing to invade Iraq, President Bush delivered a speech to the U.N. General Assembly calling on the organization to enforce its resolutions for disarming Iraq. The president strongly implied that if the U.N. did not act, then the United States would (*Public Papers of the Presidents*, September 12, 2002). After the president's speech, the level of Iraqi conflict directed toward the United States increased sharply.

The Bush administration continued to press the U.N. for a new resolution calling for Iraq to give weapons inspectors complete access and authorizing the use of force for noncompliance. After considerable debate, the U.N. Security Council adopted a compromise resolution, Resolution 1441. However, Resolution 1441 did not unequivocally authorize the use of force. Nevertheless, in October 2002 the U.S. Congress passed a "Joint Resolution to Authorize the Use of United States Armed Forces Against Iraq" (P.L. 107–243). This resolution authorized the President to "use any means necessary" to enforce Iraqi compliance.

In February 2003 U.S. Secretary of State Colin Powell again addressed the United Nations Security Council, continuing administration efforts to gain U.N. authorization for an invasion (Powell, February 5, 2003). As a follow-up to Powell's presentation, the United States, United Kingdom, Poland, Italy, Australia, Denmark, Japan, and Spain proposed a resolution authorizing the use of force in Iraq. However, NATO members Canada, France, and Germany, together with Russia, strongly urged continued diplomacy. Facing a losing vote at the U.N., as well as a likely veto from France and Russia, the resolution was withdrawn (Arms Control Association 2011b).

After the secretary's address the president embarked on a continuous campaign of public threats toward Iraq. Finally, on March 17, 2003, President Bush addressed the nation and demanded that Saddam Hussein and his two sons,

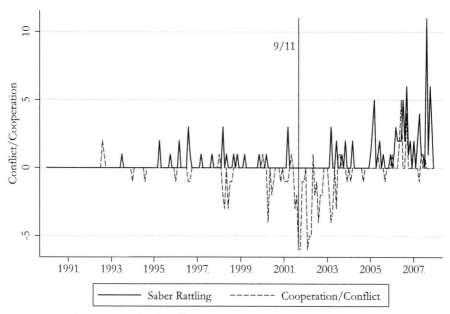

FIGURE 6.4. Iran cooperation/conflict.

Uday and Qusay, surrender and leave Iraq, giving them a forty-eight-hour deadline (*Public Papers of the Presidents,* March 17, 2003). About ninety minutes after the deadline expired on March 19, the United States began bombing Iraq. Presidential threats had failed to secure the desired foreign policy outcome, and the Iraq War commenced (Arms Control Association 2011b).

*Evaluating Iranian Cooperation/Conflict Graphically*
Relations with Iran were far less intense than with Iraq but suggest a similar pattern of failed presidential threats in achieving desired foreign policy outcomes. Figure 6.4 contains the time series plot for Iranian cooperation and conflict (dashed line). Again, presidential saber rattling toward Iran is superimposed onto the plot (solid line), and there is a vertical line for September 11.

As background, note that following the 1979 Iranian Revolution and hostage-taking, Iran was continuously viewed as an American adversary. In January 1984 the U.S. State Department declared it a state sponsor of terrorism. Under this designation, the president can restrict or require special licensing of sales of certain items to such countries. Arms exports and "dual-use" technologies, which have both civil and military applications, are also restricted.

Visual examination of the plot from 1990 through the Clinton administration again shows a pattern of increased Iranian conflict directed toward the

United States while the president was making threats. President George H. W. Bush made no public threats toward Iran, perhaps because he was preoccupied with the Persian Gulf War. President Clinton made numerous threats toward Iran. However, the intensity of his threats was not close to what we observed for Iraq.

On March 15, 1995, President Clinton issued Executive Order 12957 declaring "that the actions and policies of the Government of Iran constitute an unusual and extraordinary threat to the national security, foreign policy, and economy of the United States" (*Public Papers of the Presidents*, March 15, 1995). Sanctions were imposed prohibiting American companies and their foreign subsidiaries from doing business with Iran, in addition to any financing or development of its oil and gas sector. The following year, the president signed the Iran-Libya Sanctions Act (H.R. 3107), which imposed an embargo against non-American companies investing more than $20 million per year in Iran's oil and gas sector.

However, the 1998 Iranian elections resulted in a reformist president, which opened new prospects for rapprochement. Shortly after taking office, new President Mohammed Khatami called for a "dialogue among civilizations" (Amanpour 1998). President Clinton responded to the Iranian entreaty by toning down his threatening remarks. On March 17, 2000, Secretary of State Madeleine Albright delivered a speech apologizing for America's role in the 1953 overthrow of Mohammed Mossadeq (a democratically elected prime minister who threatened to nationalize Iran's oil fields). The Secretary acknowledged that the coup d'etat which installed the Shah "was clearly a setback for Iran's political development" (Albright 2000). Consistent with this more conciliatory tone, the Clinton administration partially lifted sanctions on Iran (but not for oil and gas). Nevertheless, theocratic leaders in Tehran responded with a denunciation of the American goodwill initiatives.

At the start of the George W. Bush administration, Figure 6.4 shows that the level of conflict from Iran increased sharply. Soon after assuming office, President Bush renewed President Clinton's 1995 executive order imposing sanctions on Iran (*Public Papers of the Presidents*, March 13, 2001). President Bush's executive order again asserted that Iran is a threat to U.S. national security, foreign policy, and the economy as a result of Iranian support for international terrorism, efforts to undermine the Middle East peace process, and efforts to acquire weapons of mass destruction. In addition, President Bush also signed an extension of the Iran-Libya Sanctions Act of 1995. From these early presidential actions forward, relations with Iran deteriorated.

Figure 6.4 shows that the Iranian response to President Bush's renewed hostility was rapid, with a step increase in Iranian conflict after the president's actions. Interestingly, the September 11 terrorist attacks also correspond closely with another sharp increase in Iranian conflict directed toward the United States. Again, we might speculate that this increase was due to Iranian sympathy with the terrorist actions. However, as with Iraq, it is also clear that Iranian behavior was not a result of increased presidential saber rattling. Between September 11, 2001, and January 2002, the president issued no threatening remarks toward Iran. As noted earlier, the president was more concerned during this period with Afghanistan, Al Qaida, and initiating a war on terror.

However, the president's 2002 State of the Union message again resumed presidential hostility, with Iran identified as part of an "axis of evil" (along with Iraq and North Korea) (*Public Papers of the Presidents,* January 29, 2002). Presidential attention also turned more intensely toward Iran after the March 19, 2003, invasion of Iraq, as it became increasingly evident that Iran was aiding the insurgency and obstructing reconstruction efforts. It increasingly through time trained, armed, and aided Shia militants in Iraq, and later the Taliban in Afghanistan.

Intermingled with these concerns for Iran's interference in Iraq and Afghanistan was concern over its ongoing nuclear program. In October 2003, European Union foreign ministers and Iranian officials in Tehran issued a statement in which Iran agreed to cooperate fully with the International Atomic Energy Agency (IAEA) and voluntarily suspend all uranium enrichment activities. However, the election of a theocratically supported president in 2005 altered this cooperation. After he took office, President Mahmoud Ahmadinejad promptly accused Iranian diplomats, who had negotiated the agreement, of treason and restarted Iran's nuclear activities.

Since this time the Iranian regime has gradually expanded its nuclear activities, regardless of presidential threats and increasing U.S. and international sanctions. Thus, similar to the Iraq case, the graphical evidence for Iran suggests that presidential threats were unsuccessful in achieving American foreign policy goals.

### Evaluating North Korean Cooperation/Conflict Graphically

Figure 6.5 contains the time series plot for cooperation and conflict from North Korea directed toward the United States (dashed line). As noted earlier, the number of cooperative events from North Korea toward the United States (148) exceeds the number of conflict events (118). This difference implies a more complex relationship than with the other two nations. Again, presidential saber rattling toward North Korea is superimposed onto the plot (solid line). Visual examination shows that presidential saber rattling toward North Korea was sparse relative to Iraq and Iran, especially before the George W. Bush administration. There is no line representing September 11 because there is no reason to believe this event affected U.S. relations with North Korea. Instead, text has been added to identify the major events associated with the largest spikes in the two time series.

Unlike for Iraq and Iran above, a single major issue divided the United States and North Korea from 1990 to 2008, North Korea's pursuit of nuclear weapons and delivery systems. As background, note that North Korea signed the Nuclear Non-Proliferation Treaty (NNPT) in December 1985. However, it did not complete a safeguards agreement for the treaty until after the United States withdrew its nuclear weapons from South Korea in September 1991 (Arms Control Association 2011a).

North Korea's signing of the NNPT and safeguards agreement did not, however, end conflict over its nuclear program. In March and again in June 1992, President George H. W. Bush imposed sanctions on North Korean companies for exporting missile technology to other countries. In September 1992 IAEA inspectors reported discrepancies in North Korea's initial report on its nuclear activities and asked for clarifications. In February 1993 the IAEA demanded inspections of North Korean sites storing nuclear wastes, under the suspicion that North Korea was cheating on its commitments under the NNPT. After the IAEA inspection demands, North Korea announced its intention to withdraw from the NNPT within three months (Arms Control Association 2011a).

However, after talks with the Clinton administration in June 1993, North Korea announced that it was reversing its decision to withdraw from the NNPT. At the same time, the United States promised not to use threats or force, including nuclear weapons. Despite North Korea's alleged adherence to the NNPT, U.S. intelligence agencies reported in late 1993 that North Korea had extracted enough plutonium to produce one or two nuclear weapons. Then, in June 1994 North Korea announced that it was withdrawing from the IAEA (a move distinct from withdrawing from the NNPT), meaning that inspectors would no longer be allowed into its nuclear facilities. At this point, former President Carter was sent by President Clinton to negotiate a deal with North Korea in which it agreed to freeze its nuclear programs and resume high-level talks (Arms Control Association 2011a).

Flowing from these talks in October 1994 was an "agreed framework" in which North Korea consented to eliminate its nuclear weapons programs in exchange for normalized diplomatic and economic relations with the United States, as well as help with proliferation resistant nuclear reactors. Thus, Figure 6.5 shows a large spike in North Korean cooperation at the time of the "agreed framework."

The period from 1994 through 2001 was characterized by continuing back and forth over North Korea's missile program and whether the two countries were living up to their mutual commitments under the "agreed framework." Throughout this period North Korea tested new missiles and exported missile technology to other countries, including Iran. At the same time, the United States was imposing sanctions for these activities and limiting the flow of economic aid to North Korea. As a result, the North Koreans claimed that the United States was not living up to its commitments to provide economic assistance and technological support for its peaceful nuclear programs under the "agreed framework" (Arms Control Association 2011a).

Between 1990 and 2001 Presidents George H. W. Bush and Clinton made only seven public threats toward North Korea. This period could be seen as one of negotiation based on mutually strategic advantage. In contrast, between

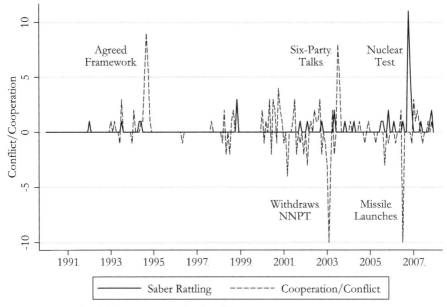

FIGURE 6.5. North Korea cooperation/conflict.

2001 and 2008, President George W. Bush made 36 public threats toward North Korea. This number of threats was roughly six times greater than during the previous two presidential administrations. Although the number of hostile presidential remarks toward North Korea was small relative to those directed toward Iraq and Iran, the shift of the Bush administration reflects an important change in the tone of relations between the two countries.

On March 7, 2001, before meeting with the South Korean president, President Bush stated that "any negotiation [with North Korea] would require complete verification of the terms of a potential agreement" (*Public Papers of the Presidents*, March 7, 2001). Six days later, North Korea reacted to the president's new tone by canceling ministerial-level talks with Seoul. Two days after that, the state news agency reported that Korea threatened to "take thousand-fold revenge" on the United States "and its black-hearted intention to torpedo the dialogue between north and south." It also called Washington's new policies "hostile" and noted that North Korea remained "fully prepared for both dialogue and war" (cited in Arms Control Association 2011a).

Continuing his hostility toward North Korea, President Bush singled it out again in his 2002 State of the Union address for "arming with missiles and weapons of mass destruction, while starving its citizens" (*Public Papers of the Presidents*, January 29, 2002). As noted earlier, he also characterized North Korea, along with Iraq and Iran, as part of an "axis of evil, arming to threaten the peace of the world."

In October 2002, the United States announced that North Korea had admitted to American diplomats that it had a clandestine program to enrich uranium for nuclear weapons (Arms Control Association 2011a). In response, North Korea officially withdrew in January 2003 from the NNPT. Accordingly, Figure 6.5 shows a large spike in North Korean conflict events associated with its withdrawal from the treaty. This event sent shockwaves throughout the East Asian and Pacific region, ultimately resulting in the first round of six-party talks between the two Koreas, China, Japan, Russia, and the United States. These talks continued periodically between 2003 and 2006 but with little success. As shown in Figure 6.5, the initial six-party talks produced a wave of North Korean cooperation that continued for some time. However, these cooperative acts were largely symbolic as North Korea continued its provocative behavior and pursuit of nuclear weapons (Arms Control Association 2011a).

In July 2006, North Korea test fired seven ballistic missiles into the Sea of Japan. The U.S. State Department described the launches as "provocative." Japan and South Korea punished North Korea for the tests, with Tokyo imposing sanctions and Seoul halting agricultural assistance. The U.N. Security Council adopted Resolution 1695, which condemned North Korea's missile launches and called for a resumption of the six-party talks (Arms Control Association 2011a).

The six-party talks resumed. However, North Korea conducted its first underground nuclear test on October 9, 2006. North Korea's Foreign Ministry stated that the "test was entirely attributable to the U.S. nuclear threat, sanctions, and pressure." North Korea "was compelled to substantially prove its possession of nukes to protect its sovereignty." The statement also indicated that North Korea might conduct further tests if the United States increased pressure (Korean Central News Agency October 11, 2006). Such pressure did in fact occur, both from the United States and the international community. And further nuclear tests occurred.

North Korea now possesses nuclear weapons and the means to deliver them. Thus, threats and hostile presidential rhetoric toward North Korea were no more successful than they were toward Iraq and Iran in altering an adversary's behavior. Presidential saber rattling failed as a foreign policy strategy.

### Multivariate Regression Analyses

The preceding graphical analyses suggest that modern presidential saber rattling is an ineffective tool of American foreign policy. As with French threats toward the early American republic, modern presidential threats have been met with either an absence of cooperation or increased conflict. However, we should also conduct more rigorous statistical analyses to enable drawing this conclusion.

Toward this end, three autoregressive regressions were run to partially capture the relations shown in Figure 6.1. Specifically, the dependent variables in these regressions were the Goldstein (1992) weighted cooperation/conflict time series shown in Figures 6.3 through 6.5. A lagged dependent variable was included in all analyses to capture the inertial nature of cooperation and conflict toward the United States. The independent variables in these analyses capture the theoretical nodes impinging on the cooperation/conflict node in Figure 6.1.

Specifically, variables are included for the president's domestic support, economic performance, war, and scandal. Indicators are included for the Clinton and George W. Bush administrations. However, the primary independent variables of interest are the new measures discussed earlier for terrorist actions toward U.S. interests and presidential saber rattling toward Iraq, Iran, and North Korea. If the preceding discussion is correct, then we should see consistent coefficients for these variables.

Table 6.1 contains the coefficients and *t* statistics from the three autoregressive regressions. Consider first the lagged dependent variables in the first row. These coefficients are positive and statistically significant for Iraq and Iran, but not for North Korea. They show that cooperation and conflict from Iraq and Iran was inertial, driven by past cooperation and conflict. Of course, Figures 6.3 and 6.4 show that these results are primarily due to continuing conflict rather than cooperation.

Contrary to predictions from threat credibility theory, strong domestic support for the president and a sound economy did not produce more cooperation and less conflict from these countries. In the seventh and eighth rows of Table 6.1, these relationships are either not statistically significant or in the wrong direction. Indeed, the statistically significant relation between domestic support for the president and Iranian cooperation/conflict is negative, indicating more conflict from Iran toward the United States when the president is strong domestically. The coefficients for scandal for Iraq and North Korea in the ninth row are nonsignificant. However, again for Iran there is a marginally significant negative relationship between presidential scandal and cooperation/conflict. The scandal coefficient suggests that the Iranians may have seized on presidential weakness (i.e., the Clinton impeachment) to engage in more conflict toward the United States.

Controlling for individual presidencies, the coefficient for war (in Afghanistan and Iraq) is not a statistically significant predictor of cooperation/conflict from any of the three countries. None of the countries reacted with greater conflict or cooperation. Rather, they were oblivious to U.S. interventions.

However, the indicators for the Clinton and George W. Bush presidencies show that the three countries reacted differently to each president. Iran reacted with increased conflict toward the Clinton presidency, relative to the George H. W. Bush presidency. Interestingly, all three countries reacted with increased conflict toward the George W. Bush presidency. Qualitatively, we know that George W. Bush adopted a much more confrontational stance relative to earlier presidents. Thus, the statistical analyses suggest that his bellicose tone was met with increased conflict from Iraq and Iran and marginally increased conflict from North Korea. The change in cooperation/conflict from North Korea is

TABLE 6.1. *Presidential Saber Rattling and Cooperation/Conflict with Foreign Actors*

| | Dependent Variable | | |
|---|---|---|---|
| Variable | Iraq Relations | Iran Relations | North Korea Relations |
| Cooperation/Conflict$_{t-1}$ | 0.19 | 0.14 | −0.03 |
| | (2.94) | (2.03) | (−0.43) |
| Terror | −1.69 | −0.09 | 0.25 |
| | (−1.19) | (−0.46) | (0.33) |
| Big Terror | 0.10 | 0.49 | 0.77 |
| | (0.02) | (0.55) | (0.24) |
| September 11 | −5.18 | −12.95 | 0.26 |
| | (−0.28) | (−5.01) | (0.03) |
| War | −7.09 | −0.42 | −0.33 |
| | (−1.16) | (−0.52) | (−0.11) |
| Presidential Saber Rattling$_{t-1}$ | −2.56 | −0.13 | 0.38 |
| | (−4.65) | (−0.85) | (0.55) |
| Domestic Support$_{t-1}$ | −0.11 | −0.06 | 0.02 |
| | (−0.84) | (−3.09) | (0.35) |
| Economic Conditions$_{t-1}$ | 0.21 | 0.24 | −0.05 |
| | (0.17) | (1.35) | (−0.08) |
| Scandal | 3.47 | −1.44 | −0.43 |
| | (0.63) | (−1.82) | (−0.15) |
| Clinton | −3.29 | −1.92 | 0.14 |
| | (−0.67) | (−2.69) | (0.05) |
| George W. Bush | −12.81 | −1.86 | −2.91 |
| | (−3.33) | (−3.28) | (−1.49) |
| Constant | 10.65 | 3.85 | −1.34 |
| | (1.24) | (2.98) | (−0.30) |
| *Diagnostics* | | | |
| N | 215 | 215 | 215 |
| $\sigma_e^2$ | 17.12 | 2.45 | 9.02 |
| Adjusted $R^2$ | 0.26 | 0.32 | 0.03 |

*Note:* The numbers in the table are coefficients and *t* statistics from regressions of Iraq, Iran, and North Korean relations on the variables indicated in the left column.

not statistically significant at conventional levels but certainly suggests greater hostility. Of course, these findings are consistent with the preceding graphical analyses.

The coefficients for terrorist actions reported in the second and third rows of Table 6.1 are not statistically significant. However, the strongly significant negative coefficient in the fourth row for the Iranian response to September 11 is consistent with the sharp negative break shown in Figure 6.3. Iran became considerably more bellicose toward the United States after the September 11 terrorist attacks. The estimated coefficient shows that following this event it directed roughly thirteen more conflict units on the Goldstein scale per month toward the United States. Furthermore, although September 11 did not produce a statistically significant increase in Iraqi conflict, as suggested by the preceding discussion surrounding Figure 6.3, the coefficient for this variable is substantively large. It suggests that following this event Iraq directed about five more conflict units on the Goldstein scale per month toward the United States.

Finally, consider how presidential saber rattling toward each of the three countries affected cooperation and conflict toward the United States. The coefficients in the fifth row of Table 6.1 show that, contrary to what would be predicted by realist and audience cost theory, public presidential threats produced no increased cooperation or reduced conflict from any of the three weaker countries. The coefficients for Iran and North Korea are not statistically significant, suggesting no response at all to presidential threats. In contrast, the coefficient for Iraq is large, statistically significant, but negative. In other words, the Iraqis increased their level of conflict in response to threatening presidential remarks.

Specifically, each instance of a presidential threat toward Iraq produced a decline of 2.56 units on the Goldstein scale. Given a mean of about 1.08 presidential threats toward Iraq per month and a standard deviation of about 2.40 threats per month, this coefficient suggests that on average presidential threats produced an increase of about 2.76 units in Iraqi conflict toward the United States with a standard deviation of about 6.14 units. Thus, presidential saber rattling toward Iraq was not only ineffective but produced a foreign policy result that was actually opposite from U.S. interests.

### A Near-VAR Analysis of Presidential Saber Rattling toward Iraq

Given the interesting results for Iraq, a Near-VAR analysis similar to those reported in Chapter 5 was also conducted for Iraq. The two estimated equations explaining presidential saber rattling and domestic support were the same as those reported for these theoretical nodes in Chapter 5. The equation for Iraqi cooperation/conflict is the same as that reported in Table 6.1, except that feedback is allowed and four lags of cooperation/conflict with Iraq are included in each equation. Also, a new terror index is included to form a separate terror equation in the Near-VAR analysis. The reformulated terror variable comprises a weighted sum of the three variables discussed earlier for Table 6.1.[8] Including the terror index endogenously enables the possibility that terrorist organizations may have responded to sponsoring regimes' level

---

[8] The index is constructed as follows. The terror variable drawn from the GTD is added to two standard deviations times the "big terror" indicator discussed earlier and three standard deviations times the "September 11" indicator. This weighting scheme is purely arbitrary but does enable treating terror as an endogenous factor that captures diversely important terrorist acts in a single variable. The precise weighting scheme used does not affect the reported results.

of hostility toward the United States or to threatening remarks toward those regimes by the U.S. president.

Figure 6.6 graphs the impulse responses from the Near-VAR analysis for Iraq. Again, the variables being shocked are along the diagonal, with the responses running from left to right in the rows. Consider first the responses to terrorist acts in the first row. A one standard error increase in the index of terrorist acts (row one, column one) produces no statistically significant change in presidential saber rattling toward Iraq (row one, column two). This non-finding is consistent with the evidence reported in Figures 6.3 through 6.5 for September 11. Presidents typically directed public threats toward the terrorists and Afghanistan in the aftermath of terror attacks, rather than toward the three countries alleged to be their state sponsors.

The response to terrorist acts for presidential approval (row one, column three) shows that presidents benefit from terrorist acts through increased public approval ratings. Similar to the emotional reactions to crisis events and presidential saber rattling reported in Chapter 5, people also responded emotionally to terror-related political drama. A one standard error simulated shock in the index of terrorist actions produces roughly a 1.25 percent average increase in presidential approval. This increased presidential approval due to terrorist acts typically lasts for about three months.

Finally, there is a small but statistically significant negative response of Iraqi cooperation/conflict (row one, column four) to terrorist actions. This negative movement confirms the graphical analysis reported earlier, but belies the nonsignificant responses to the three terror variables in Table 6.1. The Iraqi regime apparently cheered terrorism by increasing their level of conflict toward the United States.

Now consider the responses for presidential approval in the third row of graphs in Figure 6.6. Consistent with the analyses in Chapter 4 at Table 4.3, a one standard error increase in the president's approval ratings (row three, column three) produces a small decline in the presidential propensity to make target-specific threats (row three, column 2). Conversely, lower presidential approval ratings produce more presidential threats.

Increased presidential approval has no effect on the index of terrorist actions (row three, column one). However, increased presidential approval does have a marginal impact on cooperation and conflict from Iraq directed toward the United States (row three, column four). Similar to the analysis for Iran, the response of Iraqi cooperation/conflict shows a barely significant increase in conflict, but the duration of this effect is short. Thus, perceptions of presidential strength due to higher approval ratings do not increase the relative success of presidential threats. This effect is again inconsistent with predictions of realist and audience cost theories which argue that threat credibility should increase threat success.

Next, consider the responses to cooperation/conflict from Iraq in the fourth row of Figure 6.6. A one standard error increase in Iraqi cooperation/conflict

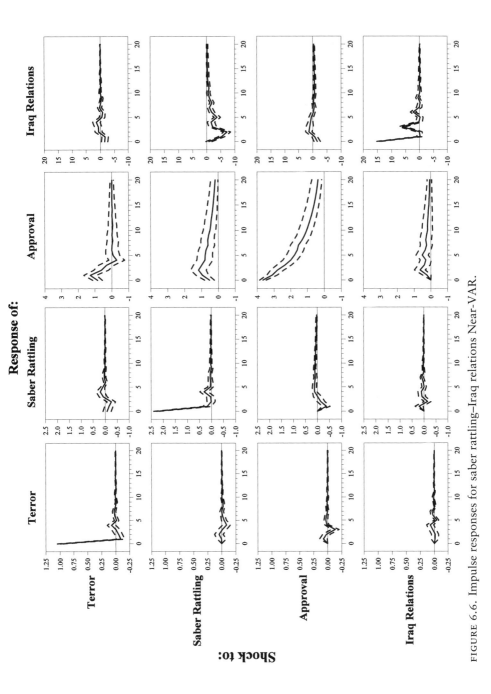

FIGURE 6.6. Impulse responses for saber rattling–Iraq relations Near-VAR.

(row four, column four) produces no significant change in terrorist actions (row four, column one) or presidential saber rattling (row four, column two). However, increased Iraqi cooperation or reduced conflict produces higher presidential approval ratings over a sustained period. In other words, presidents benefit domestically when their foreign policies are successful.

Finally, consider the key theoretical variable in the Near-VAR analysis, presidential saber rattling toward Iraq. The impulse responses in Figure 6.6 show that a one standard error increase in presidential saber rattling toward Iraq (row two, column two) produces significantly higher presidential approval ratings over an extended period (row two, column three). This prolonged increase is consistent with the statistical results reported in Chapter 5 at Table 5.1 and Figure 5.5. Thus, the analysis provides additional confirmation that presidents benefit domestically from making threats toward other countries.

Of course, although presidents are benefiting domestically from their threats, they may also be making relations worse with the target of those threats. In particular, presidential threats toward Iraq increased Iraqi conflict toward the United States. A one standard error shock in presidential saber rattling toward Iraq produced a decline of roughly seven units on the Goldstein scale. The magnitude of this effect is large, suggesting that American presidents were major contributors to the foreign policy failures leading to the U.S. invasion of Iraq in March 2003.

## Conclusions

The preceding analyses yield a coherent image for answering the research questions posed at the start of this chapter. They also provide insight about the efficacy of theories of international relations for understanding U.S. interactions with weaker adversaries.

Does presidential saber rattling increase cooperation or reduce conflict with other nations? The answer to this question is a definitive *no*. Hostile presidential rhetoric toward Iran and North Korea produced no meaningful response from these countries. At the same time presidents were directing threats toward Iran, it was reciprocating with increased conflict toward the United States. North Korean cooperation and conflict was largely independent of presidential threats, exhibiting a random pattern. Ultimately, North Korea developed nuclear capabilities, perhaps because it viewed the United States as a continuing threat. Consistent with the graphical evidence, the statistical analyses in this chapter showed no systematic relationship between presidential threats and the behavior of these two countries. Thus, presidential threats were an ineffective tool for altering their behavior.

Furthermore, hostile presidential rhetoric toward Iraq actually reduced cooperation and increased conflict with that country. As U.S. presidents became increasingly belligerent, Saddam Hussein became increasingly hostile. The statistical analysis for Iraq revealed that this negative reaction to presidential threats was large and significant. The impulse response analysis traced out the dynamics of the various responses, again confirming that presidential threats produced a negative Iraqi reaction. Thus, presidential saber rattling was actually counterproductive for relations with the Iraqi regime.

These statistical results are not consistent with predictions from realist and audience cost theories. According to these theories, stronger nations should be able to coerce weaker nations in an international system in which behavior is determined by power and threat credibility. The president's domestic strength, captured through presidential approval ratings and economic performance, should have increased the credibility of presidential threats. However, these factors had no systematic effect on adversary behavior. Furthermore, according to audience cost theory, the democratic leader of the free world should have been able to credibly threaten the three autocratic and weaker adversaries. However, presidential threats toward Iraq, Iran, and North Korea were ineffective. Thus, common theories of international relations are unsatisfactory instruments for predicting outcomes in the international system.

An exclamation point is added to this conclusion by considering cooperation and conflict from Iraq, Iran, and North Korea relative to the George W. Bush administration. He was well-known for "cowboy" diplomacy and hostile rhetoric toward American adversaries. Consistent with this assessment, the graphical analyses showed that the largest spikes in presidential bellicosity toward Iraq, Iran, and North Korea occurred during the George W. Bush administration. In turn, the statistical analyses in Table 6.1 show that all three nations directed significantly more conflict toward the United States during the Bush presidency. This result again implies that hostile presidential rhetoric toward weaker adversaries is counterproductive.

Does presidential saber rattling or an absence thereof diminish the frequency of terrorist acts or other nations' support for terrorist acts? Again, the answer to this question is a definitive *no*. Iraq, Iran, and North Korea were alleged by the United States to be state sponsors of terrorism. However, Iraqi and Iranian conflict toward the United States actually increased after the September 11 terror attacks. The period following the attacks was not characterized by increased presidential threats toward these countries. Furthermore, the Near-VAR analysis for Iraq confirmed a more general increase in conflict from Iraq in response to terrorist acts. We might speculate that these negative responses reflected these nations' sympathy with terrorism directed toward their archenemy, the United States. Regardless, presidential saber rattling had no effect on the behavior of alleged state sponsors or the future incidence of terrorist attacks.

More substantively, the results from this chapter suggest that U.S. foreign policy strategies since the late 1980s should be reconsidered. The strategy of "going public" with threats and intimidation of weaker adversaries clearly does not work. As with threats by the French toward America during the early American republic, modern threats and intimidation toward weaker nations often evoke negative, not positive, responses. Under this circumstance it might make more sense for presidents to "stay private" while working quietly behind the scenes to accomplish American foreign policy goals.

## Chapter 6 Appendix

The event forms for the cooperation and conflict data on Iraq, Iran, and North Korea extracted from the Integrated Data for Events Analysis (IDEA) database are as follows.

*Cooperation*

| | |
|---|---|
| \<AGAC\> | Agree or accept – Accept invitations and proposals, not otherwise specified. |
| \<ASSR\> | Assure – Assure or reassure that some promised or ongoing support or positive interest will continue. |
| \<CLAR\> | Acknowledge responsibility – Nonapologetically admit an error or wrongdoing, retract a statement without expression of remorse, or claim responsibility. |
| \<COLL\> | Collaborate – Form alliance, or associate with, merge, join, accompany, and coordinate activities; includes extraditions. |
| \<EEAI\> | Extend economic aid – Extending (must include the delivery) monetary aid and financial guarantees, grants, gifts and credit. The reported receipt of such aid constitutes an extend aid event with actors reversed. |
| \<EHAI\> | Extend humanitarian aid – Extending nonmilitary/noneconomic assistance, including civil training, development assistance, education, and training. The reported receipt of such aid constitutes an extend aid event with actors reversed. |
| \<EMAI\> | Extend military aid – Extending military and police assistance, including arms and personnel, includes both military and police peacekeeping. The reported receipt of such aid constitutes an extend aid event with actors reversed. |
| \<GASY\> | Grant asylum – The source of this interaction is the "protector" and the target of the interaction is the "protectee." |
| \<IMPR\> | Improve relations – Begin, improve or resume an activity or relations, extend diplomatic or other formal recognition. |
| \<NEGO\> | Engage in negotiation – Negotiate with other parties on particular issues. |
| \<OCOM\> | Optimistic comment – Comment on situation that is explicitly characterized as optimistic. |
| \<OPEN\> | Disclose information – Publicly reveal personal or sensitive information, to "out" someone. |

<PTMN>     Offer to negotiate – Propose or put forth plans to meet, negotiate, or discuss a situation or an issue.

<PTRU>     Offer peace proposal – Offer incentives for peace, suggest talks, propose resolution.

<RELE>     Release or return – Return, release, not otherwise specified.

<RRPE>     Return, release person(s) – Release people from detention, arrest or abduction.

<SOLS>     Solicit support – Request political support or solicit political influence, including electoral campaigning and lobbying.

<YIEL>     Yield – All yielding not otherwise specified.

<YORD>     Yield to order – Surrender, yield to order, submit to arrest, cede power.

### Conflict

<AERI>     Missile attack – Launching of intermediate- to long-range conventional ballistic missiles and aerial dropping of conventional explosive devices or bombs.

<BLAM>     Criticize or denounce – Blame, find fault, censure, rebuke, "whistle blowing," vilify, defame, denigrate, condemn and name-calling.

<BREL>     Break relations – Formal severance of ties, including declarations of independence, divorce, and protest resignations.

<CALL>     Call for action – Urge others to mobilize politically and calls for social action.

<CBIO>     Chem-bio attack – Use of chemical or biological weapons.

<CLAS>     Armed battle – Initiation of armed hostilities or engagement between two or more armed forces, includes truce violation (use as default for war and battles).

<DWAR>     Declare war – Formal or official statement that a state of war exists.

<FCOM>     Formally complain – Written and institutionalized protests and appeals and all petition drives and recalls.

<FORC>     Force use – All uses of physical force not otherwise specified. Includes material property destruction, acts of physical sabotage, and other acts of material damage not otherwise specified.

<GRPG>     Artillery attack – Use of short- to intermediate-range tank-mounted, ship-based, or field guns and cannons, mortars, and rocket-propelled grenades.

<INCC>     Security alert – The release of information relevant to citizen safety, generally initiated at the national level. This includes the issuing of Amber alerts, raising of the Terror Threat Level, precautionary evacuations of embassies, buildings, personnel, and

the like. This also relates to the discovery of any arms or dangerous situations (e.g., discovery of unexploded ordnance).

<MOBL>    Armed force activation – Activation of all or part of previously inactive armed forces.

<MTHR>    Armed force threats – All threats to use armed force.

<NMFT>    Other physical force threats – All threats to use nonarmed physical force.

<PASS>    Physical assault – All uses of nonarmed physical force in assaults against people not otherwise specified.

<PEXE>    Small arms attack – Shooting of small arms, light weapons, and small explosives, including the use of all handguns, light machine guns, rifles, and hand grenades.

<RAID>    Armed actions – Ambiguous initiation of the use of armed forces to fire on another armed force, population, or territory.

<RALL>    Refuse to allow – Disagree or object, refuse to allow or acknowledge, restrict or suspend liberties.

<RPMD>    Reject proposal to meet – Refuse to meet, discuss, or negotiate.

<TATT>    Threaten forceful attack – Explicit threat to use armed forces in an attack or invasion.

<TCBR>    Threaten biological or chemical attack – Explicit threat to use biological or chemical weapon against armed forces, a population, or a territory.

<THEN>    Threaten to halt negotiations – Threaten to halt unmediated discussions, negotiations, or meetings.

<THRT>    Threaten – All threats, coercive warnings not otherwise specified.

<TSAN>    Sanctions threat – Threats of nonmilitary, nonphysical force social, economic and political sanctions.

# 7

## The Bush War on Terror and Presidential Foreign Policy Representation

On the evening of September 20, 2001, President George W. Bush appeared before a joint session of Congress to address the nation on the American response to the September 11 attacks. The president's speech was laced with threats marking the start of the War on Terror. Much as President Adams's entire administration was consumed by the quasi-war with France, President Bush's entire administration was consumed by the War on Terror.

The president stated, "Our grief has turned to anger and anger to resolution.... On September 11th, enemies of freedom committed an act of war against our country." The president expressed further anger, and then identified those he believed had perpetrated the attacks. "The evidence we have gathered all points to a collection of loosely affiliated terrorist organizations known as Al Qaida.... This group and its leader, a person named Usama bin Laden, are linked to many other organizations in different countries ... The leadership of Al Qaida has great influence in Afghanistan and supports the Taliban regime in controlling most of that country."

Having identified those he believed were behind the September 11 attacks, the president then issued an ultimatum. "And tonight, the United States of America makes the following demands on the Taliban: Deliver to United States authorities all the leaders of Al Qaida who hide in your land.... The Taliban must act and act immediately. They will hand over the terrorists, or they will share in their fate."

The president correctly pointed to Osama bin Laden, Al Qaida, and Afghanistan as key players in the September 11 attacks. However, also embedded in the president's speech were remarks prescient of future U.S. actions. "Our War on Terror begins with Al Qaida, but it does not end there.... we will pursue nations that provide aid or safe haven to terrorism. Every nation, in every region, now has a decision to make. Either you are with us, or you are with the terrorists" (*Public Papers of the Presidents* September 20, 2001).

This part of the president's speech contained the seed for what was later to be called the Bush Doctrine. The president claimed a right to attack preemptively and unilaterally any nation deemed to be a threat to the security of the United States. President Bush declared later that the United States would actively seek to install democratic governments around the world, especially in the Middle East, as a strategy for combating the threat of future terrorism. From that point forward, regimes believed by the president to be harboring or supporting terrorists were at risk of attack.

The Bush Doctrine marked a sharp departure from past U.S. foreign policy. At this point in time there was a 212-year-old tradition that the United States did not attack other nations without a clear provocation. During the Cold War, U.S. policy had been to avoid war through deterrence and mutually assured destruction. The United States pursued proxy wars in Korea and Vietnam to contain the spread of communism, but both countries asked for American assistance. These wars were also supported by multilateral coalitions and international law. Following the Cold War, Presidents George H. W. Bush and Clinton continued the policy of containment and multilateralism.

After the terrorist attacks, two distinct foreign policy perspectives emerged within the Bush administration (Woodward 2002). Secretary of State Colin Powell and National Security Advisor Condoleezza Rice, as well as many State Department specialists, supported existing U.S. foreign policies. They advocated obtaining a multilateral consensus before undertaking military action against foreign adversaries and also sought increasingly harsh sanctions against problem states. In contrast, Vice President Dick Cheney, Secretary of Defense Donald Rumsfeld, and a number of influential Defense Department policy makers such as Paul Wolfowitz, and Richard Perle, held that direct unilateral action was justified in pursuing the War on Terror. Over the next several years, supporters of the Bush Doctrine prevailed, and preemptive unilateralism became the basis for U.S. foreign policy.

The Taliban did not respond favorably to the president's ultimatum. Thus, on October 7, 2001, less than a month after the terror attacks, the United States invaded Afghanistan without a multilateral coalition. The United States was joined only by the United Kingdom in the invasion, but extensive use was made of rebel Afghan forces. In Operation Enduring Freedom, massive U.S. air support was provided to U.S. and British Special Forces working with Afghan rebels to oust the Taliban regime. This initial phase of the operation was completed in a matter of weeks, as most senior Taliban leadership fled to Pakistan.

During the second phase, a democratic Islamic Republic of Afghanistan was declared, and expatriate Hamid Karzai was established as head of an interim government until elections could be held in 2004. It was only after the successful U.S. invasion that the U.N. Security Council gave its approval to the operation. It established an International Security Assistance Force (ISAF) soon after the invasion in December 2001. ISAF was intended to secure Kabul and surrounding areas. ISAF was transferred to NATO control in 2003, and included troops from 42 countries but with NATO members providing the bulk of the force.

Of course, a major purpose of the Afghan operation was to capture or kill Osama bin Laden and high-ranking Al Qaida members. It was also intended to destroy their terrorist organization. The operation apparently came close to getting bin Laden in mid-December 2001 during the Battle of Tora Bora. However, he narrowly escaped through mountain passes to Pakistan where Al Qaida reconstituted itself to continue an Afghan insurgency (Dalton 2009; Efran 2008; Lynch 2008). Osama bin Laden's escape left the Bush administration and public sensing that the War on Terror was far from over.

A month later in his 2002 State of the Union message, President Bush reaffirmed the administration's resolve. He stated "What we have found in Afghanistan confirms that, far from ending there, our war against terror is only beginning." The president then laid out future objectives. "First, we will shut down terrorist camps, disrupt terrorist plans, and bring terrorists to justice.... Our second goal is to prevent regimes that sponsor terror from threatening America or our friends and allies with weapons of mass destruction." The president then identified three nations as sponsors of terror. He stated "North Korea is a regime arming with missiles and weapons of mass destruction, while starving its citizens.... Iran aggressively pursues these weapons and exports terror, while an unelected few repress the Iranian people's hope for freedom.... The Iraqi regime has plotted to develop anthrax and nerve gas and nuclear weapons for over a decade.... States like these and their terrorist allies constitute an axis of evil, arming to threaten the peace of the world" (*Public Papers of the Presidents* January 29, 2002).

The president soon focused on Iraq as the next target for preemptive military action. Actually, many Bush administration appointees had viewed the removal of Saddam Hussein as a priority even before the September 11 attacks (Woodward 2004, chapter 1). However, after the rout of Al Qaida from Afghanistan, the president's advisors presented him with an idea for a second front in the War on Terror. According to recently declassified Bush administration documents, in November 2001 Defense Secretary Donald Rumsfeld ordered CENTCOM Commander General Tommy Franks to initiate planning for the "decapitation" of the Iraqi government and the installation of a "Provisional Government" (National Security Archive 2010a). White House interviews conducted by Bob Woodward (2004, prologue) confirm that the president had directed this initiative a mere 72 days after the September 11 attacks. President Bush met repeatedly with General Franks and his advisors starting in late December 2001 to plan the potential attack.

Woodward described a group of administration officials, including Vice President Dick Cheney and Defense Secretary Donald Rumsfeld, who advised the president early on to make war on Iraq. CIA director George Tenet claimed that the existence of weapons of mass destruction (WMD) in Iraq was a "slam dunk," and posed a serious threat if given to terrorist enemies (Woodward 2004, 249). Thus, the United States would pursue a new foreign policy of preventing a radical Middle Eastern state from ever acquiring WMD that might be given to terrorists. To achieve this objective, America was again to embrace a strategy of military preemption to remove the government of a rogue nation.

Contrary to the public face shown by the president and administration officials, the declassified documents show there was an early and concerted thrust toward war with Iraq. This was despite intelligence suggesting Iraq was a weak threat and the resulting difficulty of obtaining multilateral support (National Security Archive 2010b). However, what was most revealing from the declassified documents is what was "missing – any evidence that top Bush administration officials seriously considered an alternative to war" (National Security Archive 2010b). Among other findings, "the Bush administration sought to avoid the emergence of opposition to its actions by means of secrecy and deception, holding the war plan as a 'compartmented concept,' restricting information even from allies like the United Kingdom, and pretending that no war plans were being reviewed by the president" (National Security Archive 2010b).

Through all of 2002, President Bush and his administration sought to appear in public as pursuing diplomatic options, with war as a last resort. The president appeared before the United Nations (U.N.) General Assembly on September 12, 2002, calling for the organization to enforce its resolutions for disarming Iraq. The president strongly implied that if the U.N. did not act, the United States would (*Public Papers of the Presidents*, September 12, 2002). The Bush administration continued to press the U.N. for a new resolution calling for Iraq to give weapons inspectors complete access and authorizing the use of force for noncompliance. After considerable debate, the U.N. Security Council adopted a compromise resolution (Resolution 1441) that did not authorize using force.

The Bush administration propagandized the case for war throughout 2002. Starting in March, officials from the British and U.S. governments secretly "discussed 'the need for information' to be produced in support of plans for regime change in Iraq, leading to parallel white papers in the fall of that year. Although it was the British government that pushed hardest for efforts to manipulate political and public opinion – making this a condition of its participation in war – the Bush administration went furthest in making exaggerated claims about Iraqi WMD" (National Security Archive 2010c). Bush administration officials appeared frequently before the media making claims about the imminent danger to the United States from Iraqi WMD, ongoing Iraqi efforts to obtain nuclear materials, past and ongoing Iraqi support for Al Qaida and terrorists, and alleged connections between Iraq and the September 11 terror attacks (Matthews 2005).

President Bush wanted to initiate the Iraq war as early as January 2003 (Woodward 2004, 261). However, he was concerned about the implications for British Prime Minister Tony Blair and his domestic support without having built a stronger case before the international community. Blair asked him in January to seek a second U.N. resolution authorizing the use of force. Thus, the president postponed the invasion to pursue greater international support (Woodward 2004, 296–97).

Another problem with taking action against Iraq in January 2003 was that the invasion lacked strong public support. A Gallup poll conducted in January 2003 found that, despite administration efforts to legitimize the war, only a bare majority of Americans favored invading Iraq with U.S. ground troops to remove Saddam Hussein (Jones 2003). Further, a CBS News/*New York Times* poll in the same month showed that Americans wanted diplomatic efforts and U.N. inspections to run their course before an invasion. The poll found that 63 percent of Americans wanted President Bush to find a diplomatic solution to the problem of Saddam Hussein (Cosgrove-Mather 2003).

Recognizing that the case for an Iraqi invasion had not been made to either the international community or American public, President Bush personally requested Secretary of State Colin Powell to appear before the United Nations to lay out the arguments (Woodward 2004, 291). The secretary was initially opposed to using military force to overthrow the Iraqi dictator. In a press statement on February 24, 2001 Powell had even said the sanctions against Iraq had "worked. He has not developed any significant capability with respect to weapons of mass destruction. He is unable to project conventional power against his neighbors" (Powell, February 24, 2001). Powell had also tried to talk the president out of invading Iraq in a two-and-a-half-hour meeting (Baxter 2007). He told the president, "You are going to be the proud owner of 25 million people.... You will own all of their hopes, aspirations, and problems. You'll own it all" (Woodward 2004, 150).

However, the president wanted someone with Powell's credibility to present the evidence that Saddam Hussein had WMD and posed a threat. Although tentative about doing so, Powell agreed and appeared before a plenary session of the United Nations Security Council on February 5, 2003. Citing anonymous Iraqi defectors, Powell asserted, "there can be no doubt that Saddam Hussein has biological weapons and the capability to rapidly produce more, many more." Powell also stated that there was "no doubt in my mind" that Saddam was working to obtain key components to produce nuclear weapons. The secretary also alleged that a senior Al Qaida leader, Abu Musab al-Zarqawi, had gone to Baghdad in May 2002 for medical treatment and that during that time "nearly two dozen extremists converged on Baghdad and established a base of operations there.... These Al Qaida affiliates, based in Baghdad now coordinate the movement of people money and supplies into and throughout Iraq for [Zarqawi's] network, and they've now been operating freely in the capital for more than eight months." He also stated that the network, made up of 116 operatives, included the "ricin plotters" arrested in Britain (Powell, February 5, 2003).

Powell's speech was like a prosecution closing argument intended to persuade the American public, as well as the international community, that Saddam Hussein should be removed from power. The speech was broadcast live on all the major U.S. television networks.[1]

After Secretary Powell's speech the administration again attempted to gain international support for an invasion of Iraq. A new draft resolution was proposed at the United Nations, authored by the Bush administration and its allies Britain and Spain. The resolution declared, "Iraq will have failed to take the final opportunity afforded by Resolution 1441 unless, on or before March 17, 2003, the [U.N. Security] Council concludes that Iraq has demonstrated full, unconditional, immediate and active cooperation" (Department of State March 7, 2003). The draft was withdrawn from U.N. consideration on March 17, 2003, after it became obvious that it would not pass.

After Secretary Powell's speech the administration intensified its effort to garner public support for the war. The saber-rattling data reported in earlier chapters show that the president made thirty-seven public threats toward Iraq in the two months between the secretary's speech and the invasion. Here are excerpts from one of the president's war preparation speeches.

The Iraqi regime has actively and secretly attempted to obtain equipment needed to produce chemical, biological, and nuclear weapons. Firsthand witnesses have informed us that Iraq has at least seven mobile factories for the production of biological agents, equipment mounted on trucks and rails to evade discovery. Using these factories, Iraq could produce within just months hundreds of pounds of biological poisons.... And we have sources that tell us that Saddam Hussein recently authorized Iraqi field commanders to use chemical weapons.... One of the greatest dangers we face is that weapons of mass destruction might be passed to terrorists, who would not hesitate to use those weapons. Saddam Hussein has longstanding, direct, and continuing ties to terrorist networks.... Iraq has also provided Al Qaida with chemical and biological weapons training.... We also know that Iraq is harboring a terrorist network headed by a senior Al Qaida terrorist planner.... On September the 11th, 2001, the American people saw what terrorists could do by turning four airplanes into weapons. We will not wait to see what terrorists or terrorist states could do with chemical, biological, radiological, or nuclear weapons. (*Public Papers of the Presidents* February 6, 2003)

The president repeated these claims using similar or the exact same language in public remarks before the media on February 8, 13, 20, 26, March 1, 6, 8, and 15. The president's Weekly Radio Address on March 15, 2003, was perhaps the most demonizing of the president's war preparation speeches. He said:

We know from human rights groups that dissidents in Iraq are tortured, imprisoned, and sometimes just disappear; their hands, feet, and tongues are cut off; their eyes are

[1] Secretary Powell said later in a televised broadcast with Barbara Walters that his presentation to the United Nations will always be "a lasting blot on his record." He added that it was "devastating" to learn later that some intelligence agents knew the information he had was unreliable but did not speak up (Weisman 2005).

gouged out; and female relatives are raped in their presence.... We know from prior weapons inspections that Saddam has failed to account for vast quantities of biological and chemical agents, including mustard agent, botulinum toxin, and sarin, capable of killing millions of people.... There is little reason to hope that Saddam Hussein will disarm. If force is required to disarm him, the American people can know that our Armed Forces have been given every tool and every resource to achieve victory. (*Public Papers of the Presidents* March 15, 2003)

Two days later on March 17, 2003, President Bush again addressed the nation and demanded that Saddam Hussein and his two sons, Uday and Qusay, surrender and leave Iraq. He gave them a forty-eight-hour deadline to comply (*Public Papers of the Presidents*, March 17, 2003). About ninety minutes after the deadline expired on March 19, the president went on national television at 10:15 P.M. eastern standard time to announce the commencement of the U.S. bombing campaign. The bombing campaign that occurred before the ground attack was intended to instill "shock and awe" among Iraqi leaders and the population. The Iraq invasion had begun.

Three weeks later on April 9, 2003, U.S. forces took control of Baghdad. The televised media depicted Iraqi civilians cheering the advancing U.S. troops in a celebration of the end of Saddam Hussein's repressive rule. Iraqis, aided by U.S. Marines, toppled a large statue of Saddam in Baghdad's main square. No chemical or biological weapons were used by the Iraqis in their defense of the invasion. No evidence emerged, then or later, that Iraq had produced, was producing, or had the capability to produce weapons of mass destruction. No evidence was uncovered, then or later, of Iraqi support for or complicity with Al Qaida or the September 11 hijackers. Still, the Bush administration had achieved its goal, the removal of the Saddam Hussein regime.

Finally, on May 1, 2003, President Bush flew a Navy S-3B Viking aircraft onto the deck of the aircraft carrier USS *Abraham Lincoln* to give a victory speech. This was the first time a sitting president had made an arrested landing on an aircraft carrier (Lyke 2003). The president posed for photo-ops in his U.S. Navy flight suit with other pilots and members of the ship's crew. Like a conquering hero, he was there to announce that combat operations in Iraq were at an end. A few hours later, the president spoke to the nation beneath a large banner designed and constructed by the White House staff that read "MISSION ACCOMPLISHED."

## The Costs of the Iraq War

As we all know, the Iraq war continued through the remainder of the Bush administration and beyond. The 2008 election of President Barack Obama was undoubtedly affected in a major way by a war that had become increasingly unpopular through time, as well as a growing dislike of the American president. Roughly one month after assuming office, the newly elected president announced an eighteen-month withdrawal of all combat forces from Iraq.

On December 18, 2011, all American troops had been withdrawn (Arango and Schmidt 2011).

The cost of Bush's Iraq war in both economic and human terms remains an open sore for the nation and world. The economic costs of the war were grossly understated to the American public before the Iraq invasion. Vice President Dick Cheney reported in a *Meet the Press* interview with Tim Russert about a week before the invasion that the total cost of the war would be "at least $100 billion for a two-year involvement" (Russert 2003). However, a Congressional Research Service report released on March 29, 2011, estimated that total defense expenditures on the Iraq war had been $806 billion (Belasco 2011). Defense expenditures were only part of the price of U.S. operations. On October 24, 2007, Congressional Budget Office Director Peter Orszag testified that the long-term cost of the Iraq war to the nation would be about $1.9 trillion, an estimate that included veteran's health care and service on the increased federal debt through 2017 (Congressional Budget Office 2007). However, an independent assessment by economist Linda Bilmes and Nobel Laureate Joseph Stiglitz (2006) reported that this estimate grossly understates the true cost of the war. Their estimate of more than $3 trillion included costs to disabled veterans and macroeconomic effects for the U.S. economy. Whichever estimate one accepts, the economic costs of the Iraq war were huge.

The human costs were also high. The U.S. Department of Defense reported the total number of U.S. war dead at 4,421 as of January 18, 2012 (Department of Defense 2012). More than 4,000 of these occurred after Bush's "MISSION ACCOMPLISHED" speech. The Department of Defense also reported that 31,921 U.S. combatants had been wounded. Independent (antiwar) organizations put the casualty counts either somewhat or much higher depending on the source (e.g., see http://antiwar.com/casualties; http://icasualties.org/Iraq/index.aspx). Whatever the actual U.S. casualty count, the number is high.

The human costs of the war were also high for the Iraqis. A variety of sources have attempted to log the number of Iraqi casualties. The Associated Press reported a tally by the Iraqi government of 110,600 combat deaths (Associated Press 2009). This number is quite close to those reported by left-leaning organizations, such as Iraqi Body Count (http://en.wikipedia.org/wiki/Iraq_Body_Count_project) and Wikileaks (http://www.guardian.co.uk/news/datablog/2010/oct/23/wikileaks-iraq-data-journalism). The Congressional Research Service summarized the various reports of Iraqi civilian deaths for Congress (Fischer 2008). Estimates from those reports ranged from a low of about 35,000, based on media stories, to a high of almost 800,000, based on a study by epidemiologists relying on pre- and postwar Iraqi mortality rates. Of course, there is no good study evaluating other human costs to the Iraqi people such lost education, bad sanitation, malnutrition, and disease.

Beyond these direct economic and human costs, the United States also suffered indirect losses both economically and reputationally. Because of uncertainty in the Middle East, the price of oil quadrupled between 2002 and

2008. This change undoubtedly extracted a major toll on the U.S. economy. Some would argue that the soaring price of oil was a major contributor to the global economic recession that ensued near the end of the Bush administration.

Reputationally, there were questions about the legality of the Iraq war under international law. As a result, the United States lost moral authority within the community of nations. The Bush administration actions were also costly in terms of world public opinion. A BBC World Service poll of more than 26,000 people in 25 countries reported in January 2007 that 73 percent of the global population disapproved of U.S. handling of the Iraq war (BBC World Service 2007). Disapproval was highest among those in the Middle East (Zogby 2007). Thus, the United States lost significant credibility within the international community, and especially among those the administration most needed to influence.

### The Causes and Consequences of Bush's Saber Rattling

The Iraq invasion and its aftermath form a remarkable chain of events in the history of U.S. foreign policy. Because it is such a remarkable period, it is worth evaluating the nature of presidential representation through this period from the perspective of the theory developed in Chapter 2 and the empirical analyses reported in Chapters 3 through 6.

What were the causes of President Bush's saber rattling through this period? Was it grounded in just cause and a strong conception of the national interest? Was President Bush a wise and virtuous statesman acting as a trustee of the community? Or was President Bush's saber rattling rooted more in self-interest in its various dimensions?

### *Was George W. Bush a Statesman President?*

Just as we made an argument in the introductory chapter that John Adams behaved as a statesman in his dealings with France, we can also make an argument that George W. Bush behaved as a statesman during the War on Terror. First, the nation faced just cause for war. As noted in the introductory chapter, John Jay writing in Federalist #3 stated, "The JUST causes of war, for the most part, arise either from violation of treaties or from direct violence." America clearly experienced direct violence with the September 11 attacks, as well as with various other attacks before and after. President Bush saw his mission as preventing future terrorist attacks and followed a policy that he believed would do so.

The Bush administration viewed future terror attacks as likely. Accordingly, they set about sending a strong message to terrorists, and to states that would either support or harbor terrorists, that the United States would not tolerate these activities. As expressed by the president in his 2003 State of the Union message, "Before September 11th, many in the world believed that Saddam Hussein could be contained. But chemical agents, lethal viruses, and shadowy terrorist networks are not easily contained. Imagine those 19 hijackers with other weapons and other plans, this time armed by Saddam Hussein. It would take one vial, one canister, one crate slipped into this country to bring a day of horror like none we have ever known. We will do everything in our power to make sure that that day never comes" (*Public Papers of the Presidents* January 28, 2003).

Bush's invasion of Iraq was presented to the world and American public as a preemptive war. Saddam Hussein allegedly posed a clear and present danger to the security of the United States. However, it is more likely that within the administration it was viewed more as a preventive war. A preemptive war is initiated against another party when it is perceived that an attack by the other party is imminent. In contrast, a preventive war is initiated to prevent another party from attacking when an attack by that party is not known to be imminent or planned (Walt 2006, 224). By its very nature, it is not possible to know whether terror attacks are imminent or planned. Therefore, the Iraq invasion was a preventive rather than preemptive war.

Under the modern framework of international law, a preventive war undertaken without the approval of the United Nations is illegal (Brownlie 2008, 734; Shaw 2008, 1140). A preventive war constitutes an act of aggression under the United Nations charter. However, a preemptive war is legal under international law. It is widely accepted as an act of self-defense. Bush administration officials argued that the illegality of preventive war is an outdated concept, given the relative invisibility of terrorist activities (e.g., see Yoo and Delahunty 2009). Nevertheless, the Bush administration wanted to be perceived as pursuing a legal war, so they sold the Iraq war to the international community as a preemptive war rather than a preventive one.

Was the president acting on behalf of the community in the War on Terror? Various left-wing critics argued that the Iraq war was motivated by oil interests or the pro-Israel lobby (e.g., see Mekay 2004; Moyers and Winship 2008). Iraq sits atop a large proportion of the world's known oil reserves. Both the president and vice president had strong ties to the oil industry. Furthermore, Saddam Hussein launched scud missiles against Israel during the 1990–1991 Persian Gulf War. Thus, it was feared that if he obtained a nuclear weapon or other WMD, he might use them against Israel. Some notable international relations scholars (e.g., see Mearsheimer and Walt 2007, chapter 8) have argued that the pro-Israel lobby was important and that the Bush administration wanted to secure the Middle East by spreading democracy.

However, the former president denied these claims in his memoir *Decision Points*. He stated, "those theories were false. I was sending our troops into combat to protect the American people" (Bush 2010, 253). He further claimed, "my most meaningful accomplishment as president" is that "the homeland" suffered no large terrorist attack in the seven and one-half years that remained of his administration after September 11, 2001 (Bush 2010, 181). The Bush memoir gives the impression that the former president genuinely believed this was a result of his tough decisions to go on the offensive and fight the bad guys where they live rather than wait for them to come to us.

There is also evidence that the president believed he was not influenced by public opinion or reelection in his decision to make war on Iraq. In an interview with Bob Woodward on December 11, 2003, Bush stated, "I am prepared to risk my presidency to do what I think is right. I was going to act. And if it could cost the presidency, I fully realized that. But I felt so strongly that it was the right thing to do that I was prepared to do so." Woodward then asked the president if he had earlier said in one of his meetings, "I would like to be a two-term president, but if I am a one-term president, so be it." The president responded "That's right." Woodward replied "And if the decision costs you the election?" The president responded, "The presidency – that's just the way it is.... Fully prepared to live with it" (Woodward 2004, 443).

There can be little doubt that George W. Bush viewed himself as morally bound to protect the American people from a vicious terrorist enemy. However, he may also have been motivated by a spiritual belief that he was ordained by God to do so. When asked by Bob Woodward about whether he had sought advice from his father, former President George H. W. Bush, on going to war with Iraq, he stated, "He is following the news now. And so I am briefing him on what I see. You know, he is the wrong father to appeal to in terms of strength. There is a higher father that I appeal to" (Woodward 2004, 421).

The day the Iraq invasion began, Woodward reports that the president said, "It was emotional for me. I prayed as I walked around the circle. I prayed that our troops be safe, be protected by the Almighty, that there be minimal loss of life.... Going into this period, I was praying for strength to do the Lord's will.... I'm surely not going to justify war based upon God. Understand that. Nevertheless, in my case I pray that I be as good a messenger of His will as possible" (Woodward 2004, 379).

George W. Bush was a self-professed "born-again" Christian who prayed regularly, attended Bible study, and often invoked the biblical concepts of good versus evil in his public rhetoric. Reportedly, he also took biblical prophecy into account in his decision to invade Iraq. In 2003, while lobbying world leaders to gather an international coalition, President Bush spoke to French President Jacques Chirac. He told a story about how the biblical creatures Gog and Magog were at work in the Middle East and how they must be defeated. Bush also reportedly told Chirac, "This confrontation is willed by God, who wants to use this conflict to erase his people's enemies before a New Age begins." Chirac confirmed these reports in a book published in France in 2009 (Maurice 2009).

Former Palestinian foreign minister Nabil Shaath also reported that Bush told him and Palestinian President Mahmoud Abbas, "I'm driven with a mission from God. God would tell me, 'George, go and fight those terrorists in Afghanistan.' And I did, and then God would tell me, 'George go and end the tyranny in Iraq,' and I did." Confirming this report in an interview with

BBC, Mr. Abbas recalled how the U.S. president told him he had a "moral and religious obligation" to act (but see BBC News 2005; BBC Two 2005).

An article published in the *New York Review of Books* by Pulitzer Prize–winning historian Garry Wills claims to show the extent to which religion drove the Bush White House.

The White House was alive with piety. Evangelical leaders were in and out on a regular basis. There were Bible study groups in the White House. . . . Over half of the White House staff attended the meetings. One of the first things David Frum heard when he went to work there as a speech writer was: 'Missed you at the Bible study.' . . . Aside from Rove and Cheney, Bush's inner circle are all deeply religious. [Condoleezza] Rice is a minister's daughter, chief of staff Andrew Card is a minister's husband, Karen Hughes is a church elder, and head speechwriter Michael Gerson is a born-again evangelical, a movement insider. . . . The deputy undersecretary for defense intelligence, General William (Jerry) Boykin . . . made headlines during the Iraq war with a slide show lecture he gave in churches. . . . He asked audiences . . . Ask yourself this: why is this man in the White House? The majority of Americans did not vote for him. Why is he there?. . . I tell you this morning he's in the White House because God put him there for such a time as this. God put him there to lead not only this nation but to lead the world, in such a time as this. (Wills 2006)

In light of the preceding discussion, an argument can readily be made that George W. Bush believed he invaded Iraq from a desire to protect the American people from evil. One of those evils was Saddam Hussein, a dictator who allegedly had the temperament and potential resources to supply terrorists with WMD. It does not matter whether the president's drive to protect Americans was rooted in his presidential oath under the Constitution, strongly held religious beliefs, or both. Either way, the president was doggedly determined to protect the nation. Viewed in this light, President Bush can be viewed as serving community interests by guarding against perceived external threats.

### Was George W. Bush Motivated by Support Seeking, Passion, or Partisanship?

An argument can also be made that President Bush's behavior was driven by support seeking, passion, and partisanship. Consider first some factual evidence in this regard. At the time of the September 11 attacks, the U.S. State Department listed seven nations as state sponsors of terrorism. These were Iran, Iraq, North Korea, Libya, Sudan, Syria, and Cuba. Many nations were considered by the U.S. State Department to be harboring and aiding terrorists. Bush identified three of these in his 2002 "axis of evil" speech: North Korea, Iran, and Iraq.

According to the 2001 State Department Country Reports, "Iran remained the most active state sponsor of terrorism in 2001. Iran's Islamic Revolutionary Guard Corps (IRGC) and Ministry of Intelligence and Security (MOIS) continued to be involved in the planning and support of terrorist acts and supported a variety of groups that use terrorism to pursue their goals. . . . There are . . . reports that Arab Afghans, including al-Qaida members, used Iran as a transit route to enter and leave from Afghanistan" (Department of State 2001). Thus, the case for regime change in Iran was just as strong, or stronger, than it was for Iraq. Iran's theocracy was more dangerous to regional peace and stability than was Saddam Hussein who had been weakened by war and a decade of sanctions. Although neither country had a provable official connection to Al Qaida or the September 11 attacks, Iran had a real record of promoting terrorism abroad and was actually working to develop nuclear capabilities. Why not choose Iran for an object lesson in American power?

President Bush also identified North Korea in his "axis of evil" speech as a sponsor of global terrorism. As discussed in the previous chapter, by the time of the Iraq invasion North Korea had pulled out of the Nuclear Non-Proliferation Treaty and was well underway toward actually producing a nuclear WMD. Indeed, declassified documents show that as early as the mid-1980s there was official concern over North Korea's pursuit of nuclear weapons (National Security Archive 2003). The 1993 National Intelligence Estimate even implied that North Korea already possessed one or two nuclear weapons (Sigal 1998, 90). In April 2003, one month after the start of the Iraq invasion, North Korea announced that it possessed a nuclear arsenal (Sanger 2003). If North Korea was also part of Bush's "axis of evil," then why not choose North Korea as an object lesson in American power?

Why did George W. Bush choose Iraq from among the many terror-sponsoring nations as a target for his preventive war? It can be argued that the real reason was rooted in passion and his personal hatred for Saddam Hussein. Saddam had allegedly attempted to assassinate the president's father with a car bomb during a visit to Kuwait in April 1993. Through interviews with the suspects and examination of the bomb's circuitry and wiring, the FBI established that the plot had been directed by the Iraqi Intelligence Service (Inspector General 1997). The attempted killing of one's father can evoke powerful emotions. Thus, George W. Bush may have been predisposed toward hating Saddam Hussein. He even admitted as much during a campaign speech in September 2002. Bush cited a number of reasons for why Saddam Hussein should be removed. Among these, he said, "After all, this is the guy who tried to kill my dad" (*Public Papers of the Presidents* September 26, 2002a).

Of course, George W. Bush was not alone in disliking Saddam Hussein. Althaus and Largio (2004) reported extensive survey evidence showing that Americans were also predisposed toward disliking Saddam Hussein, even before the September 11 attacks. Nearly seven months before the attacks, an Opinion Dynamics poll showed that 73 percent of Americans said it was very or somewhat likely that "Saddam Hussein will organize terrorist attacks on United States" (Althaus and Largio 2004, 799). In multiple polls taken immediately after the September 11 attacks, "open-ended questions showed that Americans were not spontaneously blaming Iraq for the attacks. But forced-choice questions showed that as many as 8 in 10 Americans thought that

Hussein was probably behind them." Upon being presented with this possibility immediately after the September 11 attacks, a very large majority of
Americans were "already prepared to believe that Saddam was to blame long
before the administration began building popular support for the war" (Althaus
and Largio 2004, 799). Thus, the president may also have been motivated by
public passions in his thrust toward war.

Consistent with these arguments, Bush's "axis of evil" speech was originally
focused only on Iraq and used the phrase "axis of hatred." Michael Gerson,
the president's evangelical speech writer, had asked David Frum, a conservative
staff member, "to come up with a sentence or two summing up the case for
going after Iraq." He called it an "axis of hatred." This phrase was later
changed to "axis of evil" to make the notion broader and more sinister. The
original speech had focused only on drawing a nexus between Saddam Hussein
and the terrorists, with no reference to Iran or North Korea. However, Secretary
of State Rice and National Security Advisor Stephen Hadley worried that such
a focus would "appear a declaration of war." Therefore, they suggested adding
Iran and North Korea (Woodward 2004, 86–88).

Reelection may have been another motivation for George W. Bush to link
Saddam Hussein with the War on Terror. As suggested in the introductory
chapter, President Adams may have engaged in war talk toward the French
Directory to increase his public approval and chances for reelection in 1800.
We showed in Chapter 4 through statistical analyses that modern presidents
are more prone toward saber rattling as elections approach. We also showed in
Chapter 5 that presidential saber rattling can substantially increase a president's
approval ratings. Thus, although President Bush denied this motivation in his
interview with Bob Woodward (2004, 443), the Bush administration push
for an Iraq invasion could have been influenced by support seeking and the
upcoming election.

Bush had observed firsthand the pain his father had experienced from his
reelection defeat in 1992. Many in the former president's administration left
office with a sense of rejection and unfinished business. The president and his
team desperately wanted to avoid the same fate. For the president, it was a
matter of family honor and prestige to not be another one-term president. For
members of the president's team it was a matter of validation and finishing
what was started with the Persian Gulf War.

A quick victory in Iraq would enable the president to "chest pound" as he did
wearing his Navy flight suit aboard the USS *Abraham Lincoln* and later under
the "MISSION ACCOMPLISHED" banner. Although Bush had earlier failed
to kill or capture Osama bin Laden, the removal of Saddam Hussein would
enable him to claim at least a partial victory in the War on Terror. Furthermore,
a protracted war might even be good for the president's reelection prospects.
No president in American history who ran for reelection during a war had ever
been defeated (Weisberg and Christenson 2007).

Officially, administration officials predicted a short war. Donald Rumsfeld stated, "The war could last six days, six weeks. I doubt six months." Air Force General Richard Myers, chairman of the Joint Chiefs of Staff, remarked to reporters "What you'd like to do is have it be a short, short conflict. . . . Iraq is much weaker than they were back in the '90s," when its forces were routed from Kuwait. Vice President Dick Cheney, on NBC's *Meet the Press*, stated "I think things have gotten so bad inside Iraq, from the standpoint of the Iraqi people, my belief is we will, in fact, be greeted as liberators. . . . I think it will go relatively quickly, . . . weeks rather than months" (Page 2003).

Although the official prediction was for a short war, there were also subtle indications they thought the war could last longer. As noted earlier, Vice President Dick Cheney reported in a *Meet the Press* interview with Tim Russert about a week before the invasion that the total cost of the war would be "at least $100 billion *for a two-year involvement*" (Russert 2003, emphasis added). If it lasted two years, then it would still be going on at the time of the 2004 election. On March 30, 2003, Joint Chiefs of Staff chair Myers stated on *Meet the Press* "Nobody should have any illusions that this is going to be a quick and easy victory. This is going to be a tough war, a tough slog yet, and no responsible official I know has ever said anything different once this war has started" (Page 2003).

It is probably true that the administration intended the war to be short. However, it is also true that George W. Bush benefited politically from the war during the 2004 election. During the election campaign the Iraq invasion bolstered the president's image among fellow partisans who overwhelmingly supported the war. This approach worked well and resulted in a large turnout among the Republican base. However, with the war going badly, by election time a majority of Americans disapproved of the president's handling of the war. Exit polls in the 2004 election showed that those who approved of Bush's handling of the War on Terror were more likely to vote for Bush, whereas those disapproving of Bush's handling of the Iraq war were more likely to vote for Kerry (Weisberg 2005). In the end, as stated by Weisberg (2007), "The War on Terrorism gave George Bush the legitimacy that the 2000 election had not conferred on him. It allowed him to run as the incumbent Commander-In-Chief in 2004." As a result, he successfully mobilized his Republican base to pull off a narrow victory.

Another potential influence on presidential behavior was the media frenzy following the September 11 attacks. We showed in Chapter 4 that media frenzy is a powerful predictor of presidential bellicosity through time. As media frenzies become more intense, presidents become more prone to making foreign policy threats. The post–September 11 media frenzy was intense and prolonged. At a minimum during this period, the Bush administration did not face serious media scrutiny that questioned the War on Terror or the inclusion of Iraq in that war. The post–September 11 media environment also failed to thoroughly vet administration claims about Iraqi WMD or their alleged associations of Saddam Hussein with the September 11 hijackers. Just the opposite, the media was uncritically prowar before the Iraq invasion.

Rendall and Broughel (2003) found that the network news disproportionately relied on prowar sources and avoided antiwar sources in the lead-up to the invasion. According to their analysis, 64 percent of total news sources were pro-invasion, and antiwar sources comprised only 3 percent in the United States. As a result of this media bias, Kull et al. (2003) found that 57 percent of mainstream media viewers believed the falsehood that Iraq had provided substantial support to Al Qaida or was directly involved in the September 11 attacks. Around 69 percent believed the falsehood that Saddam Hussein was personally involved in the September 11 attacks. After the invasion 22 percent believed the falsehood that WMD had been found in Iraq, with 21 percent believing they had been used against U.S. troops. In a combined analysis, 80 percent of Fox News watchers had one or more of these misperceptions compared with 27 percent for NPR/PBS audience.

We can also say definitively that gaining and keeping media support was important to the Bush administration. Otherwise, it would not have tried so hard to influence the media before the Iraq invasion. A less supportive and more conflict-ridden media environment would have spelled trouble for the Bush war plans. Thus, media coverage of the War on Terror and its effect on the public were probably influential of the president's behavior toward Iraq.

Finally, the president may have been motivated by partisanship as he attempted through vilification and threats to connect the Iraqi dictator with the War on Terror. As shown by the analyses in Chapters 3 and 4, Republicans are more prone to aggressive foreign policy behavior than Democrats. As a cowboy and gun-toter, this strategy may have been consistent with the president's own personal preferences. Furthermore, feeding fellow partisans and the partisan media a steady supply of "red meat" was a surefire strategy for mobilizing the Republican base in the lead-up to the 2004 election.

### The Neoconservatives and Bush's Motivations for the Iraq Invasion
Of course, President Clinton had also consistently argued that Saddam Hussein posed a threat to the United States and world peace. He said on February 4, 1998, "The best way to stop Saddam from building nuclear, biological, or chemical weapons is simply to get the international inspectors back to work with no restraints.... But I will say again, one way or the other, we are determined to deny Iraq the capacity to develop weapons of mass destruction and the missiles to deliver them" (*Public Papers of the Presidents* February 4, 1998).

Recognizing that diplomatic efforts were limited, on October 31, 1998, President Clinton signed the Iraq Liberation Act (P.L. 105–338). This legislation originated in the U.S. House of Representatives where it passed by a vote of 360 to 38. In the Senate the legislation passed unanimously. This legislation called for the removal of Saddam Hussein and required the president to provide all necessary support to opposition groups within Iraq. However, what the legislation did not do was authorize the president to use U.S. military force. President Clinton and many Democrats did not believe that the U.S. military should be used to remove Saddam Hussein. Rather, Clinton believed that the problem should be solved without direct U.S. intervention.

In contrast, many Republicans believed that the Clinton policy of containment and isolation was not working. Simply providing support to opposition groups within Iraq was unlikely to produce the desired result. Thus, starting in 1997 a group of neoconservative Republicans began pushing for the use of military force against Iraq. Their founding organization, the Project for the New American Century (PNAC), was a Washington-based think tank intended to promote American hegemony around the world (Donnelly 2000).

Among the stated goals of its founders, William Kristol and Robert Kagan, were the following: place permanently based forces in southern Europe, Southeast Asia, and the Middle East; modernize U.S. forces, including enhanced fighter aircraft, submarine, and surface fleet capabilities; develop and deploy a global missile defense system; develop a strategic dominance of space; control the "International Commons" of cyberspace; increase defense spending to a minimum of 3.8 percent of gross domestic product, up from the 3 percent currently spent (Donnelly 2000).

However, the most disturbing aspect of the PNAC statement of purpose was the described Core Missions for U.S. Military Forces. The group advocated that the United States "fight and decisively win multiple, simultaneous major theater wars" and "perform the 'constabulary' duties associated with shaping the security environment in critical regions." It also wanted to "transform U.S. forces to exploit the 'revolution' in military affairs." In pursuing these ideas, the group wanted America to "retain its militarily dominant status for the coming decades" (Donnelly 2000).

In pursuit of its mission, the PNAC sent a letter on January 26, 1998, to President Clinton urging the president to use military force to remove Saddam Hussein (Project for the New American Century 1998). The letter stated:

We urge you to seize [the] opportunity, and to enunciate a new strategy that would secure the interests of the U.S. and our friends and allies around the world. That strategy should aim, above all, at the removal of Saddam Hussein's regime from power.... The policy of "containment" of Saddam Hussein has been steadily eroding... As a result, in the not-too-distant future we will be unable to determine with any reasonable level of confidence whether Iraq does or does not possess such weapons.... The only acceptable strategy is one that eliminates the possibility that Iraq will be able to use or threaten to use weapons of mass destruction. In the near term, this means a willingness to undertake military action as diplomacy is clearly failing. In the long term, it means removing Saddam Hussein and his regime from power. That now needs to become the aim of American foreign policy. (Project for the New American Century 1998)

The 1998 PNAC letter to President Clinton was signed by Donald Rumsfeld, Paul Wolfowitz, Richard Perle, Richard Armitage, Elliott Abrams, William J. Bennett, John Bolton, Robert Zoellick, Peter Rodman, and Zalmay Khalilzad. In addition, Vice President Dick Cheney and his Chief of Staff I. Lewis "Scooter" Libby were signers of the PNAC Statement of Principles issued on June 3, 1997 (Project for the New American Century 1997). Of course, all of these names should be familiar as important foreign policy officials of the Bush administration.

In the area of foreign policy, newly elected President George W. Bush was tabula rasa (a blank slate; e.g., see Woodward 2006, chapter 1). As former governor of Texas he had no foreign policy experience. Many thought the new president lacked the intellectual curiosity to learn about foreign policy on his own. However, as with many Republicans, Bush idolized former President Reagan who had cast an aura of "Wild West" diplomacy in dealing with Grenada, Libya, the former Soviet Union, and Middle Eastern terror. President Bush's father had also followed an aggressive path, unilaterally invading Panama to remove the dictator Manuel Noriega. His father had also led the international coalition against Iraq during the Persian Gulf War. Thus, George W. Bush was probably predisposed toward an aggressive foreign policy. Thus, the new president was a willing blank slate waiting to be indoctrinated by his neoconservative PNAC appointees.

Many of the Bush PNAC appointees had been former officials of his father's presidency, as well as of the Reagan administration. Therefore, it was natural that they would join the Bush team as trusted advisors. However, other appointees from his father's administration did not buy in to the PNAC philosophy. As noted earlier, National Security Advisor Condoleeza Rice tempered the administration's thrust toward war, preferring the policies of containment and isolation associated with the George H. W. Bush and Clinton administrations. Additionally, Secretary of State Colin Powell was reluctant to go along with the neoconservative plans, at one point even calling them "lunacy" (Woodward 2004, 22).

A *Washington Post* reporter interviewed top military officials, including some members of the Joint Chiefs of Staff, and concluded that many favored a more cautious approach to dealing with Saddam Hussein. "The senior officers' position – that the risks of dropping a successful containment policy for a more aggressive military campaign are so great that it would be unwise to do so – was made clear in the course of several interviews with officials inside and outside the Pentagon" (Ricks 2002).

Other former officials of the George H. W. Bush administration were also opposed to the Iraq invasion. Former National Security Advisor Brent Scowcroft editorialized in the *Wall Street Journal* that a military attack on Saddam Hussein would detract from the broader fight against terrorism and the Israeli-Palestinian conflict, which should be the highest administration priorities in the Middle East (Scowcroft 2002).

Despite this opposition, the evidence strongly suggests that a highly partisan group of neoconservatives within the administration dominated the president's thinking after the September 11 attacks (Woodward 2002, 2004, 2006). The president was already predisposed in this direction by his Republican partisanship and affinity for Ronald Reagan and his own father. However, the neoconservatives were also probably a decisive factor in Bush's hostile rhetoric toward Saddam Hussein and his decision to invade Iraq in March 2003.

## Pretended Presidential Saber Rattling

Whether George W. Bush was driven by perceptions of community interest or self-interest, we know beyond question that the president reported as fact many falsehoods, which he either knew to be false or did not know to be fact at the time. Many of these falsehoods have been documented by the nonpartisan Center for Public Integrity (Lewis and Reading-Smith 2008) and are made available via a searchable online database (http://projects.iwatchnews.org/index.htm/ projects.publicintegrity.org/WarCard/Defaulte193.html?src=project_home). Among the 935 falsehoods promulgated by the president are the following:

- On September 7, 2002, in remarks at Camp David, President Bush referenced an IAEA report claiming that Saddam Hussein was only "six months away from developing [a nuclear] weapon" (Milbank 2002). No such IAEA report existed.
- On September 25 and 26, 2002, the president asserted that Saddam Hussein and Al Qaida "work in concert" and that the Iraqi regime "has longstanding and continuing ties to terrorist organizations, and there are [Al Qaida] terrorists inside Iraq" (*Public Papers of the Presidents* September 25, 2002, September 26, 2002b). However, a Defense Intelligence Agency assessment issued three months earlier had found an absence of "compelling evidence demonstrating direct cooperation between the government of Iraq and Al Qaeda" (Lewis and Reading-Smith 2008).
- In his weekly radio address on September 28, 2002, the president said, "The Iraqi regime possesses biological and chemical weapons, is rebuilding the facilities to make more and, according to the British government, could launch a biological or chemical attack in as little as 45 minutes after the order is given" (Lewis and Reading-Smith 2008; *Public Papers of the Presidents* September 28, 2002). The British government had provided no such information.
- In an address to the nation on October 7, 2002, the president stated "We've learned that Iraq has trained Al Qaida members in bombmaking and poisons and deadly gases" (*Public Papers of the Presidents* October 7, 2002). However, according to Louis Fischer (2003), the president's own intelligence officials doubted the veracity of this information at the time of the president's speech.

- Bush administration officials promoted a rumor about Mohammed Atta, leader of the September 11 terror attacks, having met with an Iraqi intelligence officer in Prague in April 2001. However, Czech President Vaclav Havel and his intelligence service said there was no evidence of such a meeting (Green 2002; Risen 2002a, 2002b). CIA Director George Tenet later informed Congress that his agency had no information to show that Atta was in Prague or met with Iraqi intelligence officials (Fischer 2003).
- In his January 2003 State of the Union address, Bush stated, "The British government has learned that Saddam Hussein recently sought significant quantities of uranium from Africa. Our intelligence sources tell us that he has attempted to purchase high-strength aluminum tubes suitable for nuclear weapons production." However, two weeks before the president's speech a State Department analyst had sent an e-mail to the intelligence community explaining why he believed the uranium-purchase agreement "probably is a hoax" (Lewis and Reading-Smith 2008; *Public Papers of the Presidents* January 28, 2003).

From these and many other examples, we know that President Bush deceived the international community and nation about the capabilities and motivations of the Iraqi regime before the March 19, 2003, invasion. What we do not know is *why* the president chose to do so.

Was he behaving in the community interest, really believing that Saddam Hussein posed an immediate threat to American national security? Or was he motivated by passion, reelection, media hysteria, or partisanship? We will never be able to answer these questions without getting inside the former president's mind.

Nevertheless, whether one believes that the president was motivated by community-interest or self-interest, George W. Bush engaged in pretended saber rattling. Under a community-interest interpretation he engaged in pretended saber rattling because he truly believed he was protecting the nation. Under a self-interest interpretation he engaged in pretended saber rattling because he was motivated to do so by his hatred of Saddam Hussein, reelection incentives, media hysteria, or partisanship. In either case, questions should remain about whether President Bush behaved as a statesman.

Statesmen are also supposed to be leaders who possess both *wisdom* and *virtue*. We turn to the importance of presidential wisdom and virtue in the final chapter.

# 8

# Wisdom, Virtue, and Presidential Foreign Policy Representation

The Founders had a clear vision for the types of individuals who should occupy the presidency and how they should behave while in office. They wanted leaders with *wisdom* and *virtue* who always behaved as representatives of the entire nation. As expressed by James Madison in Federalist #57, "The aim of every political Constitution is, or ought to be, first to obtain for rulers men who possess most wisdom to discern, and most virtue to pursue, the common good of the society" (Madison 1788a).

"Wisdom is a deep understanding and realizing of people, things, events or situations, resulting in the ability to...consistently produce optimum results...Wisdom is also the comprehension of what is true or right coupled with optimum judgment as to action" (Wikipedia 2011b). The Founders were schooled in ancient political philosophy and understood well Plato's concept of wisdom in *The Republic* in which the leaders of his utopia were to be philosopher kings who understood The Good and possessed the courage and independence to act accordingly (Plato 2007). Thus, the Founders wanted leaders who have the knowledge, experience, and judgment to independently follow what is objectively the best course for the community.

"Virtue is a behavior showing a high moral standard and is a pattern of thought and behavior based on high moral standards" (Wikipedia 2011a). The Founders would also have been familiar with Aristotle's *Nicomachean Ethics* (2009), which argues that "A virtuous person is naturally disposed to behave in the right ways and for the right reasons, and to feel pleasure in behaving rightly" (SparkNotes Editors 2003). Thus, the Founders wanted leaders not only to be wise but also to use that wisdom in such a way as to reflect moral judgment. They viewed moral judgment as a prerequisite for keeping faith with the community and would have condemned immoral behavior occurring for whatever reason.

However, the Founders also had a keen understanding that their vision of presidential leadership was just an "ideal type." They did not believe that future leaders would always live up to their ideal. As stated by Madison in Federalist #10, "Enlightened statesmen will not always be at the helm" (Madison 1788b). John Jay, writing as Publius in Federalist #4, was particularly skeptical about the prospects for always having wise and virtuous leaders. He stated:

It is too true, however disgraceful it may be to human nature, that nations in general will make war whenever they have a prospect of getting anything by it; nay, absolute monarchs will often make war when their nations are to get nothing by it, but for the purposes and objects merely personal, such as thirst for military glory, revenge for personal affronts, ambition, or private compacts to aggrandize or support their particular families or partisans. These and a variety of other motives, which affect only the mind of the sovereign, often lead him to engage in wars not sanctified by justice or the voice and interests of his people. (Jay 1788a)

Jay was skeptical about the motivation of absolute monarchs for engaging in war or other hostile activities. However, Jay's remarks also pertain to all leaders who do not face the persistent scrutiny of countervailing forces. His remarks pertain to dictators and autocrats not positioned within an appropriate institutional framework. His remarks also include the American president if left unconstrained by other forces.

Thus, as noted in Chapter 2, the Founders intended the U.S. president to share foreign policy authority with Congress. Shared power with Congress should theoretically be a check on the president's inherent wisdom, virtue, or lack thereof. Also, a First Amendment–enabled free media has an obligation to present all sides of an issue so that it can be fully aired by the community. As a last resort, free elections should enable people to show their pleasure or displeasure with the president's revealed wisdom, virtue, or lack thereof. However, even in a democracy presidential leadership can stray.

If the electorate does not select for its leader an individual who is innately wise and virtuous, then an election is unlikely to magically imbue a president with these qualities. Rather, presidents, like absolute rulers, require the checks of countervailing institutions. They must be constrained by the prospect that Congress will intervene. They must understand that the media will expose miscreant behavior. And leaders straying from the path of wisdom and virtue must fear that they will be turned from office by an electorate that sees their deviation from the true path of community interest.

### The Causes of Presidential Saber Rattling

The analyses reported in this book show that the Founders were right to be skeptical about presidential motivations as they pursue American foreign policy. Presidents have historically engaged in both just and pretended behaviors.

Certainly there have been times when presidents behaved as statesmen responding to threats from external actors. Fascism and communism were real threats to American national security from World War II through the 1980s. Terrorist attacks starting in the 1980s were also real, threatening American interests abroad as well as the security of the nation and its citizens. Thus, the systematic analyses in Chapters 3 and 4 revealed that presidential threats toward other nations increased as a function of war and other critical events.

Furthermore, the case studies of the Adams and Bush administrations in Chapters 1 and 7 suggested that these presidents responded to real threats to the nation's security. The French were really attacking American shipping between 1795 and 1799, and terrorists had really attacked the World Trade Center and Pentagon on September 11, 2001. Thus, both presidents were responding to direct violence perpetrated against the nation and its citizens.

However, the analyses in Chapters 3 and 4 also suggest that presidents have often engaged in pretended saber rattling when there were no such threats or violence. The systematic analyses in Chapter 4 showed that presidential threats toward other nations increased sharply during periods when presidents were seeking reelection. The spectral time series analyses showed a strong election cycle pattern in presidential saber rattling of all types, general, and target-specific of various types. The multivariate analyses confirmed these increases due to elections, after statistical controls, for saber rattling of all types and general saber rattling. Thus, the statistical evidence is strong that presidents use bellicose rhetoric in an attempt to build their domestic support when elections are approaching.

The analyses in Chapters 3 and 4 also showed evidence that presidential saber rattling may be rooted in partisanship. Republican presidents are more bellicose than Democrats, perhaps because this is expected by their constituencies. However, increased presidential saber rattling by Republicans seemingly started with the Reagan administration, perhaps because of his more aggressive style. The analyses in Chapter 3 showed that presidents after Reagan were far more hostile than earlier presidents. Even after controlling for war, critical events, and domestic factors, Republican presidents have consistently used more general saber rattling directed at no particular foreign target. Presidents Clinton and George W. Bush engaged in far more target-specific saber rattling than other presidents, probably reflecting their respective efforts to contain and topple Saddam Hussein.

The case study evidence for the Bush administration in Chapter 7 also suggests a more sinister dimension of partisanship. Extreme partisanship within a political party can be important to presidential behavior. During the Bush administration, many Republicans both inside and outside the administration favored continuing the policy of containment and isolation of Saddam Hussein. This was the policy initiated during the prior George H. W. Bush presidency and continued through the Clinton administration. However, three full years before George W. Bush took office, many neoconservative Bush administration appointees had already decided to remove Saddam Hussein using military force. The president was predisposed in this direction because of his Republican partisanship and admiration for Ronald Reagan and his own father. The September 11 terror attacks provided a convenient excuse for removing Saddam Hussein militarily as part of the War on Terror. As a result, it was simply a matter of planning the invasion and persuading an already-primed American public that an invasion was appropriate. Viewed in this light, the president and his neoconservative appointees engaged in pretended saber rattling to facilitate their already planned invasion of Iraq.

The statistical analyses in Chapter 4 also showed that the mass media have an outsize effect on presidential foreign policy behavior. Since the Iran hostage crisis the mass media have regularly hyperbolized foreign policy crises for the American public. These media frenzies have involved round-the-clock coverage intended to capture larger viewing audiences. Their activities affect the mass public by creating an environment of excitement and elevated attention. The mass media profit from large audiences and public excitement, and have strong incentives to continue these activities.

Persistent media frenzies have starkly increased the public salience of foreign policy crises and events that have occurred through time. In an environment of hype and heightened salience, presidents have no longer had the option of staying private to settle foreign policy disputes. Rather, their actions have forced visibility as the media and citizenry hunger to know how their leaders will respond.

As shown by the statistical analyses in Chapter 4, the result of these media frenzies has been increased presidential saber rattling through time. Presidents respond, perhaps to take advantage of heightened issue salience in the ongoing foreign policy drama. Presidents want to appear strong during a crisis to improve their standing with the public. For whatever reason, the statistical analyses in Chapter 4 showed that media frenzies have resulted in large increases in presidential threats toward other nations. Moreover, the effect of the mass media on the propensity of presidents to issue threats is of about the same magnitude as that for the presence of war. This is a large effect, suggesting that the role of the mass media in resolving foreign policy crises is not constructive.

Of course, the media frenzy following the September 11 terror attacks involved an especially long and intense period. It lasted well beyond the Iraq invasion in March 2003. Media and public passions were high during this period. Accordingly, the case study evidence in Chapter 7 suggested that the Bush administration took advantage of the resulting high public excitement to push their invasion of Iraq. The media hardly questioned whether the Iraq invasion was an appropriate action as part of the War on Terror. Furthermore, the mass public, although wanting the administration to pursue diplomatic solutions, was not adamantly opposed to the Iraq invasion. Indeed, as reported in Chapter 7, many Americans believed the Bush administration propaganda that Saddam Hussein was an immediate threat, had WMD, was training and likely to provide WMD to terrorists, and was involved in the September 11 terror attacks. Thus, as with the systematic analyses in Chapter 4, the case study evidence in Chapter 7 suggests that the media frenzy facilitated the Bush administration's saber rattling toward Iraq.

## The Consequences of Presidential Saber Rattling

The analyses in this book also reveal why the Founders wanted presidents to be foreign policy statesmen rather than support seekers driven by self-interest, passion, or partisanship. Presidents have benefited personally from their non-statesman behavior, while the community has suffered.

The statistical analyses in Chapter 5 showed that presidents have consistently achieved a stronger public standing through saber rattling. Presidents exert a psychological influence on the American public. People look to the president for strength and leadership. Making threats projects such an image of strength and leadership. Thus, controlling for war and important foreign policy crises, media coverage, and economic variables, the results reported in Chapter 5 showed that presidents significantly increased their public approval ratings after they used threatening rhetoric. Furthermore, the increases in the president's domestic support were not short-term increases but lasted for many months.

The systematic analyses in Chapter 5 are again bolstered by the case study evidence for the Adams and Bush presidencies reported in Chapters 1 and 7. Although we have no quantitative measure of President Adams's public approval ratings, the historical evidence suggests strongly that he experienced a surge in public adulation following the release of the XYZ dispatches and after he began speaking publicly of war with France. As reported by Ferling, people paraded on Adams's behalf. Patriotic marches were played in the president's honor at concerts and before theater performances. When Adams traveled, he was accorded "every mark of distinguished attention." According to one Federalist, when he went to New York in the summer of 1798 he received the "most splendid" reception ever given a political leader, former President Washington notwithstanding. Some people believed that Adams's stature was now equal to Washington and that "no man . . . will go down to posterity with greater luster." President Adams reveled in this adulation and began to appear in a full military uniform with a sword strapped to his side (Ferling 1992, 352).

Similarly, George W. Bush benefited from his saber rattling following the September 11 terror attacks and subsequent invasions of Afghanistan and Iraq. Between August and October 2001, President Bush's monthly public approval ratings increased from 57 to 88 percent, a shift of 31 percent. Although much of this increase was undoubtedly due to the terror attack itself, some of it was also due to the president's response to the attacks. Bush presented the public with a

"Wild West" heroic image of the presidency. He issued numerous threats and vowed to bring those who had perpetrated the attacks to justice.

Following the Afghan invasion, the president received no bump in public approval, perhaps because it was already about as high as it could get because of the terror attacks. However, by the time of the Iraq invasion the president's public approval ratings had fallen back to around 57 percent. On March 17, 2003, Bush issued the ultimatum to Saddam Hussein and his sons. After the ultimatum and consequent commitment of U.S. forces, the president's approval ratings increased again to more than 70 percent. Interestingly, the president also received about a 7 percent bump in his foreign policy approval rating just after he delivered the "MISSION ACCOMPLISHED" speech in his U.S. Navy flight suit aboard the aircraft carrier USS *Abraham Lincoln*. Thus, Bush benefited personally through higher approval ratings as a result of his saber rattling and wartime rhetoric.

The president presented the public with an image following September 11 and the military conquests of Afghanistan and Iraq that was later helpful to his reelection campaign. During the 2004 campaign, he pushed his image as leader of the War on Terror. This approach worked well with his fellow partisans and resulted in a large turnout among the Republican base. In the end, the War on Terror gave George Bush the legitimacy he had not achieved from the 2000 election, and he pulled off a narrow victory in the 2004 election.

Although presidents have benefited personally from their saber rattling, the statistical evidence in Chapter 5 also suggests that the community has often suffered from this behavior. Presidential saber rattling has had unanticipated and undesirable economic consequences. Economic actors are not fully rational and rely on cues from their information environment to inform their decision making. They make forecasts of the economic future and its relative certainty based on these cues. Under normal conditions, presidents are a major source of economic cues. However, they are even more so during times of foreign policy crisis.

Increased presidential saber rattling produces uncertainty for economic actors. In turn, they become more anxious about the economic future and more reluctant to spend and borrow. Because the U.S. economy depends on a continuous flow of consumption and borrowing, such behavioral changes ultimately affect U.S. economic performance. Wood (2009b) showed that presidential saber rattling can substantially reduce annual economic growth, personal consumption expenditures, and risk taking by both consumers and investors and increase perceptions of negative economic news. Thus, although presidents may benefit personally from their foreign policy threats, the community is hurt economically by these activities.

Furthermore, the statistical analyses in Chapter 6 showed that public presidential threats are not an effective foreign policy strategy. Presidential saber rattling does not increase cooperation or reduce conflict with other nations. Hostile presidential rhetoric toward Iran and North Korea between 1990 and

2008 produced no meaningful response from these countries. At the same time presidents were directing threats toward Iran, that country was reciprocating with increased conflict directed toward the United States. North Korean cooperation and conflict was largely independent of presidential threats, exhibiting a random pattern. Thus, presidential threats were not an effective tool for altering their behavior.

Hostile presidential rhetoric toward Iraq between 1990 and 2008 actually reduced cooperation and increased conflict with that country, ultimately resulting in a war. As U.S. presidents became increasingly hostile, Saddam Hussein became increasingly belligerent. In other words, presidential saber rattling was a counterproductive strategy for the community if the goal was to change an adversary into a nation friendly to American interests.

Of course, the case study of the Bush administration in Chapter 7 again reinforces this conclusion. George W. Bush became increasingly hostile toward Iraq after his 2002 "axis of evil" speech. This speech was part of the administration's campaign of pretended saber rattling to target Iraq as part of the War on Terror. The campaign of presidential threats continued through March 19, 2001, with ever-increasing intensity and vitriol. Yet Saddam Hussein did not back down from the American president. He was insolent up to the time of the invasion. Presidential threats only served to make him more hostile and less compliant with U.S. demands and those of the international community.

Bush's pretended saber rattling toward Iraq precipitated a war that ultimately became the most costly in U.S. history. As noted in Chapter 7, the Congressional Research Service reported that total defense expenditure on the Iraq war through early 2011 had been about $806 billion. These expenditures were not financed through war bonds, as with past wars, but through current deficit financing. As a result, the national debt grew substantially during the Bush administration and beyond. Furthermore, Congressional Budget Office Director Peter Orszag testified that the long-term cost of the Iraq war would be about $1.9 trillion through 2017 (Congressional Budget Office 2007). Independent analyst Linda Bilmes and Nobel Laureate Joseph Stiglitz (2006) reported that the true cost was more than $3 trillion when one considers the additional costs to disabled veterans and macroeconomic effects for the U.S. economy.

The human costs were also high. As noted in Chapter 7, the total number of U.S. war dead as of January 18, 2012, was at 4,421 (Department of Defense 2012). This number is considerably higher than the number killed on September 11. The Department of Defense also reported that 31,921 U.S. combatants had been wounded. Independent organizations put the casualty counts either somewhat or much higher depending on the source.

Reputationally, there are also questions about the legality of the Iraq invasion under international law. Preventive war is illegal under the international system, and there was little evidence that Saddam Hussein posed an imminent threat to U.S. national security. More generally, the image of the United States as a bastion of justice was tarnished. The world overwhelmingly disapproved of Bush's invasion of Iraq. Given that the international community was not supportive, the American community suffered a reputational loss as a result of President Bush's pretended saber rattling and the ensuing Iraqi invasion.

Furthermore, as history will undoubtedly judge, the Iraq invasion and subsequent war involved neither wise nor virtuous judgment. The president's judgment was not wise because of the unanticipated economic, human, and reputational costs to the nation. These are costs we are still paying and will continue to pay into the future. The president's judgment was not virtuous because the Iraq invasion was initiated under false pretenses. Iraq posed no immediate threat to U.S. national security, and the United States had never made an unprovoked attack on another nation in its 214-year history. Such behavior is widely viewed as aggression. Therefore, the president's behavior was neither wise nor virtuous.

### A Final Perspective on Statesman Presidential Representation

Presidential foreign policy behavior motivated by self-interest, passion, or partisanship can be harmful to the nation. We observed these harmful effects empirically in preceding chapters. However, a more theoretical argument can also be made about the desirability of statesman presidential representation.

Self-interest, passion, and partisanship are all rooted in emotions. They derive from deep within the human psyche. Self-interest is rooted in egotism. All individuals possess egotism to a greater or lesser extent. Egotism compels an individual to act selfishly rather than altruistically. Yet altruism is required for presidents to represent the community as a whole. There are times when a president must accept personal losses to do what is best for the community. An individual who is unwilling to do so is unlikely to be a good community representative.

Passion is by definition a powerful or compelling feeling for something or someone, such as anger, fear, or hate. People are often at the mercy of their passions and find them difficult to control. Passion is not a rational response but is rooted in human evolution. Such feelings as anger, fear, and hate usually lead to automatic responses. In other words, responses are programmed rather than well thought out. As a result, an individual who is controlled by his or her passions is unlikely to be a good community representative.

Partisanship typically entails rigid and sometimes blind adherence to a set of ideological principles. Ideology may also not have a rational basis but be rooted in a person's religious, family, or educational orientations. Strong partisans tend to adopt shortcuts, rather than clear reasoning, in determining their issue stances and behaviors. Partisan representation is often grounded in cues and an incomplete analysis of data. Partisanship also tends to favor a subset of the community. Therefore, behavior rooted in partisanship may be irrational and also not coincide with community interests.

Consistent with these theoretical arguments, we should again consider the normative rationale of the intellectuals who founded our republic. As noted in Chapter 2, Alexander Hamilton, discussing the presidency in Federalist #71, stated:

The republican principle demands that the deliberate sense of the community should govern the conduct of those to whom they intrust the management of their affairs; but it does not require an unqualified complaisance to every sudden breeze of passion, or to every transient impulse which the people may receive from the arts of men, who flatter their prejudices to betray their interests. (Hamilton 1788)

Here Hamilton argued that presidents should not be overly influenced by external forces in their conduct of the presidency. They should not be swayed by "sudden breeze of passion" or "transient impulse" from people deceived by "the arts of men." Of course, such external forces commonly emanate from passion-driven partisans. They may also derive from a partisan media or an overly excited public.

President Washington expressed similar views on presidential representation in his letter to the Selectmen of Boston on July 28, 1795:

In every act of my administration, I have sought the happiness of my fellow citizens. My system for the attainment of this object has uniformly been to overlook all personal, local, and partial considerations; to contemplate the United States as one great whole; to confide that sudden impressions, when erroneous, would lead to candid reflection; and to consult only the substantial and permanent interests of our country. (Fitzpatrick 1931)

Here Washington argued that a president should put aside "sudden impressions," personal considerations, and partisanship (i.e., emotion-driven responses) to engage in "candid reflection" on what is in the community interest. In other words, Washington was advocating that presidents exercise wise and virtuous judgment.

Yet, as noted in the first part of this chapter, the Founders were also well aware that leaders such as Washington would not always be present. As a result, the potential for nonstatesman behavior needs to be controlled. In Federalist #51 Madison laid out the problem as follows:

But what is government itself, but the greatest of all reflections on human nature? If men were angels, no government would be necessary. If angels were to govern men, neither external nor internal controls on government would be necessary. In framing a government which is to be administered by men over men, the great difficulty lies in this: you must first enable the government to control the governed; and in the next place oblige it to control itself. A dependence on the people is, no doubt, the primary control on the government; but experience has taught mankind the necessity of auxiliary precautions. (Hamilton 1788)

Thus, Madison argued that executive power needs to be counterbalanced through "auxiliary precautions." He viewed periodic elections as one such precaution. Shared power with Congress was another. A constitutionally authorized free press should also shed light on the relative efficacy of presidential behavior.

These solutions to the problem of statesman presidential representation seem straightforward enough. Whenever possible, the community should elect wise and virtuous leaders. When the community fails to do so, or when elected leaders cease being so, then auxiliary precautions such as elections, congressional oversight, and media scrutiny should come into play.

However, there is an obvious problem with the Founders' prescription. How do the electorate, Congress, and media know presidential motivations and their likely outcomes? Indeed, how do presidents themselves know when they are behaving as statesmen versus self-interested, passion-driven, partisans? All presidents self-righteously claim to represent the nation at large. They may even persuade themselves that their behavior is in pursuit of the community interest when others think differently. Thus, presidential behavior which is pretended may be difficult to distinguish from behavior that is wise and virtuous.

This distinction has been problematic since the beginning of the republic. President Washington said he was pursuing the Jay Treaty to protect the nation from a renewed war with Britain. Such a war would have been harmful to a fledgling American economy and political system. However, he was also accused of Federalist partisanship supporting Northeastern merchants who wanted to trade with Britain. How do we know whether Washington was a wise and virtuous statesman versus a self-interested partisan?

Similarly, as we observed in the introductory chapter, President Adams sought to avoid war with France through negotiation and presenting a strong defense posture. His preference for negotiation, rather than war, ultimately led to his reelection failure in 1800. Thus, he could easily have been regarded as a statesman. However, President Adams was also accused of partisanship in his saber rattling toward the French out of hatred, self-interest, and Federalist ideology. How do we know whether Adams was a wise and virtuous statesman versus a self-interested partisan?

Finally, our case study of the Bush presidency also demonstrated the difficulty of distinguishing statesmanship from behavior driven by self-interest, passion, or partisanship. George W. Bush may have genuinely believed that Saddam Hussein posed an immediate threat to the national security of the United States. If so, then he was justified in wanting to remove the Iraqi dictator from power. However, it might also be argued that doing so militarily was problematic. The Iraqi invasion has been viewed widely as due to contrived motivations. It was also of questionable legality, and the nation paid very high costs for its military intervention. Thus, how do we know whether Bush was a wise and virtuous statesman versus a self-interested partisan?

Obviously, people can disagree about what factors motivated these presidents. Thus, we must ultimately rely on trust that the electorate will choose wise and virtuous leaders. Failing this, we must trust Congress and the media to act as countervailing forces that temper the tendency of presidents to pursue pretended behavior. As the analyses in this book demonstrate, these countervailing institutions have not always been successful. However, they may become more so in the future with continued social science research on these topics.

# References

Akaike, Hirotogu. 1973. "Information Theory and the Extension of the Maximum Likelihood Principle." Paper read at 2nd International Symposium on Information Theory, at Budapest.

Albright, Madeleine K. 2000. "Remarks by Madeleine K. Albright on American-Iranian Relations." Washington, DC: U.S. Department of State.

Aldrich, John 1983. "A Downsian Spatial Model with Party Activism." *American Political Science Review* 77 (4):974–90.

Althaus, Scott L., and Devon M. Largio. 2004. "When Osama Became Saddam: Origins and Consequences of the Change in America's Public Enemy #1." *PS: Political Science and Politics* 37 (4):795–99.

Amanpour, Christiane. 1998. "Transcript of Interview with Iranian President Mohammed Khatami." *Cable News Network*, January 7.

Arango, Tim, and Michael S. Schmidt. 2011. "Last Convoy of American Troops Leave Iraq." *New York Times*, December 18.

Aristotle. 2009. *Nicomachean Ethics*. New York: World Library Classics.

Arms Control Association. 2011a. *Chronology of U.S.-North Korean Nuclear and Missile Diplomacy*. Available at http://www.armscontrol.org/factsheets/dprkchron.

———. 2011b. *Iraq: A Chronology of U.N. Inspections*. Available at http://www.armscontrol.org/act/2002_10/iraqspecialoct02.

Arrow, Kenneth J. 1951. *Social Choice and Individual Values*. New York: John Wiley and Sons.

Associated Press. 2009. "AP Exclusive: Secret Tally Has 87,215 Iraqis Dead." *Boston Herald*, April 23.

Austin-Smith, David, and Jeffrey Banks. 1988. "Elections, Coalitions, and Legislative Outcomes." *American Political Science Review* 82 (2):405–22.

Bache, Benjamin Franklin. In *Aurora*, ed. B. F. Bache. Philadelphia.

Bartels, Larry M. 2002. "Beyond the Running Tally: Partisan Bias in Political Perceptions." *Political Behavior* 24 (2):117–50.

Baum, Matthew A. 2004. "Going Private: Public Opinion, Presidential Rhetoric, and the Domestic Politics of Audience Costs in U.S. Foreign Policy Crises." *Journal of Conflict Resolution* 48 (5):603–31.

Baxter, Sarah. 2007. "Powell Tried to Talk Bush Out of War." *The Sunday Times,* July 8.

BBC News. 2005. "White House Denies Bush God Claim." *BBC News,* October 6.

BBC Two. 2005. "Program 3: Sharon (2003–2005)." In *Elusive Peace.* London: BBC.

BBC World Service. 2007. "World View of US Role Goes from Bad to Worse." London: BBC World Service.

Beck, Nathaniel. 1991. "The Illusion of Cycles in International Relations." *International Studies Quarterly* 35 (2):455–76.

Belasco, Amy. 2011. "The Cost of Iraq, Afghanistan, and Other Global War on Terror Operations Since 9/11." Washington, DC: Congressional Research Service.

Bennett, W. Lance. 1990. "Toward a Theory of Press-State Relations in the United States." *Journal of Communication* 40 (2):103–25.

Berelson, Bernard R., Paul F. Lazarsfeld, and William N. McPhee. 1954. *Voting: A Study of Public Opinion Formation in a Presidential Campaign.* Chicago: University of Chicago Press.

Beschloss, Michael. 2007. *Presidential Courage: Brave Leaders and How They Changed America 1789–1989.* New York: Simon & Schuster.

Bilmes, Linda, and Joseph Stiglitz. 2006. "The Economic Costs of the Iraq War: An Appraisal Three Years after the Beginning of the Conflict." Cambridge, MA: National Bureau of Economic Research.

Blumenthal, Sidney. 1982. *The Permanent Campaign.* New York: Simon & Schuster.

Bond, Doug, Joe Bond, Churl Oh, J. Craig Jenkins, and Charles Lewis Taylor. 2003. "Integrated Data for Events Analysis (IDEA): An Events Typology for Automated Events Data Development." *Peace Research* 40 (6):733–45.

Box-Steffensmeier, Janet M., David C. Kimball, Scott R. Meinke, and Katherine Tate. 2003. "The Effects of Political Representation on the Electoral Advantages of House Incumbents." *Political Research Quarterly* 56 (3):259–70.

Brace, Paul, and Barbara Hinckley. 1992. *Follow the Leader: Opinion Polls and Modern Presidencies.* New York: Basic Books.

Brody, Richard A. 1991. *Assessing the President: The Media, Elite Opinion, and Public Support.* Stanford, CA: Stanford University Press.

Brody, Richard A., and Benjamin I. Page. 1975. "The Impact of Events on Presidential Popularity: The Johnson and Nixon Administrations." In *Perspectives on the Presidency,* ed. A. Wildavsky. Boston: Little, Brown.

Brownlie, Ian. 2008. *Principles of Public International Law.* New York: Oxford University Press.

Bullock, John G. 2009. "Partisan Bias and the Bayesian Ideal in the Study of Public Opinion." *Journal of Politics* 71 (3):1109–24.

Burke, Edmund. 1774. "Speech to the Electors of Bristol." In *The Works of the Right Honorable Edmund Burke.* Available at the Project Gutenberg Web site: http://www.gutenberg.org/ebooks/15198.

Bush, George W. 2010. *Decision Points.* New York: Crown.

Caballero, R. J. 1991. "Earnings Uncertainty and Aggregate Wealth Accumulation." *American Economic Review* 81 (4):859–71.

Cameron, A. Colin, and Pravin K. Trivedi. 1998. *Regression Analysis of Count Data.* 2nd ed. New York: Cambridge University Press.

Campbell, Angus, Philip Converse, Warren Miller, and Donald Stokes. 1960. *The American Voter.* New York: John Wiley and Sons.

Canes-Wrone, Brandice. 2006. *Who Leads Whom? Presidents, Policy, and the Public.* Chicago: University of Chicago Press.

Canes-Wrone, Brandice, Michael C. Herron, and Kenneth W. Schotts. 2001. "Leadership and Pandering: A Theory of Executive Policymaking." *American Journal of Political Science* 45 (July):532–50.

Canes-Wrone, Brandice, William G. Howell, and David E. Lewis. 2008. "Toward a Broader Understanding of Presidential Power: A Reevaluation of the Two Presidencies Thesis." *Journal of Politics* 70 (1):1–16.

Canes-Wrone, Brandice, and Kenneth W. Shotts. 2004. "The Conditional Nature of Presidential Responsiveness to Public Opinion." *American Journal of Political Science* 48 (October):690–706.

Card, Andrew. 2011. "No One Likes Article II, but Article II." October 13. Presentation to the American Politics Program at Texas A&M University.

Carroll, C. D. 1994. "How Does Future Income Affect Current Consumption?" *Quarterly Journal of Economics* 109 (1):111–47.

———. 1997. "Buffer-Stock Saving and the Life Cycle/Permanent Income Hypothesis." *Quarterly Journal of Economics* 110 (1):1–55.

Carroll, C. D., and A. A. Samwick. 1997. "The Nature of Precautionary Wealth." *Journal of Monetary Economics* 40 (1):41–71.

———. 1998. "How Important Is Precautionary Savings?" *Review of Economics and Statistics* 80 (3):410–19.

Cassino, Dan, and Milton Lodge. 2007. "The Primacy of Affect in Political Evaluations." In *The Affect Effect: Dynamics of Emotion in Political Thinking and Behavior,* ed. W. R. Neuman, G. E. Marcus, A. N. Crigler, and M. MacKuen. Chicago: University of Chicago Press.

Chappell, Henry W., and William R. Keech. 1985. "A New View of Political Accountability for Economic Performance." *American Political Science Review* 79 (1):10–27.

Clarke, Harold D., and Marianne C. Stewart. 1994. "Prospections, Retrospections, and Rationality: The "Bankers" Model of Presidential Approval Reconsidered." *American Journal of Political Science* 38 (4):1104–23.

Cohen, Jeffrey E. 1991. "A Historical Reassessment of Wildavsky's 'Two Presidencies' Thesis." *Social Science Quarterly* 63 (3):549–55.

———. 1999. *Presidential Responsiveness and Public Policy-Making: The Public and the Policies that Presidents Choose.* Ann Arbor: University of Michigan Press.

Conference Board. 2001. *Business Cycle Indicators Handbook.* New York: The Conference Board.

Congressional Budget Office. 2007. "Statement of Peter Orszag, Director, Estimated Costs of U.S. Operations in Iraq and Afghanistan and of Other Activities Related to the War on Terrorism." In *Committee on the Budget, U.S. House of Representatives.* Washington, DC: U.S. Government Printing Office.

Conover, Pamela Johnson, and Stanley Feldman. 1986. "Emotional Reactions to the Economy: I'm Mad as Hell and I'm Not Going to Take It Anymore." *American Journal of Political Science* 30 (1):50–78.

———. 1989. "Candidate Perceptions in an Ambiguous World: Campaigns, Cues, and Inference Processes." *American Journal of Political Science* 33 (3):917–40.

Cooper, Phillip J. 2002. *By Order of the President: The Use and Abuse of Executive Direct Action*. Lawrence: University of Kansas Press.

Cosgrove-Mather, Bootie. 2003. "Poll: Talk First, Fight Later." CBS News.com, January 23.

Cotton, Timothy Y. C. 1987. "War and American Democracy: Electoral Costs of the Last Five Wars." *The Journal of Conflict Resolution* 30 (December):616–35.

Curtin, Richard T. 2000. *Psychology and Macroeconomics: Fifty Years of the Surveys of Consumers*. Special Report, Surveys of Consumers, University of Michigan. Available after public login at http://www.sca.isr.umich.edu/.

Dalton, Fury. 2009. *Kill Bin Laden: A Delta Force Commander's Account of the Hunt for the World's Most Wanted Man*. New York: St. Martin's Griffin.

Davis, O. A., and Melvin A. Hinich. 1966. "A Mathematical Model of Policy Formulation in a Democratic Society." In *Mathematical Applications in Political Science II*, ed. J. L. Bernd. Dallas, TX: Southern Methodist University Press.

Davis, O. A., Melvin A. Hinich, and Peter Ordeshook. 1970. "An Expository Development of a Mathematical Model of the Electoral Process." *American Political Science Review* 64 (2):426–48.

DeConde, Alexander. 1966. *The Quasi-War: The Politics and Diplomacy of the Undeclared War with France, 1797–1801*. New York: Charles Scribner and Sons.

DeRouen, Karl. 1995. "The Indirect Link: Politics, the Economy, and the Use of Force." *Journal of Conflict Resolution* 39 (4):671–95.

_____. 2000. "Presidents and the Diversionary Use of Force: A Research Note." *International Studies Quarterly* 44 (2):317–28.

Diggins, John Patrick. 2003. *John Adams*. New York: Henry Holt.

Donnelly, Thomas. 2000. "Rebuilding America's Defenses: Strategy, Forces and Resources for a New Century." Washington, DC: Project for the New American Century.

Dorussen, Han, and Jongryn Mo. 2001. "Ending Economic Sanctions: Audience Costs and Rent-Seeking as Commitment Strategies." *Journal of Conflict Resolution* 45 (4):395–426.

Dovi, Suzanne. 2006. "Political Representation." In *Stanford Encyclopedia of Political Philosophy*, ed. E. N. Zalta. Stanford, CA: The Metaphysics Research Lab.

Downs, Anthony. 1957. *An Economic Theory of Democracy*. New York: Harper and Row.

Edelman, Murray. 1964. *The Symbolic Uses of Politics*. Urbana: University of Illinois Press.

Edwards, George C., III. 1983. *The Public Presidency: The Pursuit of Popular Support*. New York: St. Martin's Press.

_____. 1986. "The Two Presidencies: A Reevaluation." *American Politics Quarterly* 14 (3):247.

_____. 2003. *On Deaf Ears: The Limits of the Bully Pulpit*. New Haven, CT: Yale University Press.

Edwards, George C., III, William Mitchell, and Reed Welch. 1995. "Explaining Presidential Approval: The Significance of Issue Salience." *American Journal of Political Science* 39 (1):108–34.

Edwards, George C., III, and B. Dan Wood. 1999. "Who Influences Whom? The President and the Public Agenda." *American Political Science Review* 93 (2):327–44.

Efran, Shawn. 2008. "Army Officer Recalls Hunt for Bin Laden." *60 Minutes*, CBS News, October 5.

Elkins, Stanley, and Eric McKitrick. 1993. *The Age of Federalism*. New York: Oxford University Press.

Enders, Walter, and Todd Sandler. 2000. "Is Transnational Terrorism Becoming More Threatening?" *Journal of Conflict Resolution* 44 (2):307–32.

Enelow, James M., and Melvin J. Hinich. 1981. "A New Approach to Voter Uncertainty in the Downsian Spatial Model." *American Journal of Political Science* 25 (3):483–93.

————. 1982. "Ideology, Issues, and the Spatial Theory of Elections." *American Political Science Review* 76 (3):493–501.

————. 1984. *The Spatial Theory of Voting: An Introduction*. New York: Cambridge University Press.

Entman, Robert M. 1991. "Framing U.S. Coverage of International Affairs: Contrasts in Narratives of the KAL and Iran Air Incidents." *Journal of Communication* 51 (4):6–27.

Erikson, Robert S., Michael B. MacKuen, and James A. Stimson. 2002. *The Macro Polity*. Boston: Cambridge University Press.

Fearon, James. 1994. "Domestic Political Audiences and the Escalation of International Conflict." *American Political Science Review* 88 (3):577–92.

Fearon, James D. 1997. "Signaling Foreign Policy Interests." *Journal of Conflict Resolution* 41 (1):68–90.

Feldman, Noah. 2006. "Our Presidential Era: Who Can Check the President?" *New York Times*, January 8.

————. 2007. "Our Presidential Era: Who Can Check the President?" *New York Times*, February 4.

Ferling, John. 1992. *John Adams: A Life*. New York: Oxford University Press.

Finkel, Steven E. 1993. "Reexamining the 'Minimal Effects' Model in Recent Presidential Campaigns." *Journal of Politics* 55 (1):1–21.

Fiorina, Morris P. 1981. *Retrospective Voting in American National Elections*. New Haven, CT: Yale University Press.

Fischer, Hanna. 2008. "Iraqi Civilian Deaths Estimates." Washington, DC: Congressional Research Service.

Fisher, Louis. 2003. "Deciding on War against Iraq: Institutional Failures." *Political Science Quarterly* 118 (3):389–410.

————. 2006. "The Sole Organ Doctrine." In *Studies on Presidential Power in Foreign Relations*. Washington, DC: The Law Library of Congress.

————. 2007a. "Invoking Inherent Powers: A Primer." *Presidential Studies Quarterly* 37 (1):1–22.

————. 2007b. "The Law: Presidential Inherent Power: The 'Sole Organ' Doctrine." *Presidential Studies Quarterly* 37 (1):139–52.

————. 2007c. "Signing Statements: Constitutional and Practical Limits." *William and Mary Bill of Rights Journal* 16:183–210.

————. 2007d. Statement by Louis Fisher appearing before the House Committee on the Judiciary, "Constitutional Limitations on Domestic Surveillance," June 7. Washington, DC: Library of Congress. Available at http://loc.gov/law/help/usconlaw/pdf/tsp-house-judiciary.pdf.

———. 2007e. "Treaty Negotiation: A Presidential Monopoly." *Presidential Studies Quarterly* 38 (1):144–58.

———. 2008a. "Extraordinary Rendition: The Price of Secrecy." *American University Law Review* 57:1405.

———. 2008b. Statement by Lewis Fisher before the Subcommittee on the Constitution of the Senate Committee on the Judiciary, "Restoring the Rule of Law," September 16. Washington, DC: Library of Congress. Available at: http://loc.gov/law/help/usconlaw/pdf/senate%20judiciary%20sept_16_%202008.pdf.

Fitzpatrick, John C., ed. 1931. *The Writings of George Washington from the Original Manuscript Sources, 1745–1799*. Vol. 34. Washington, DC: U.S. Government Printing Office.

Fleisher, Richard, and Jon R. Bond. 1988. "Are There Two Presidencies? Yes, but Only for Republicans." *The Journal of Politics* 50 (3):747–67.

———. 2000. "The Demise of the Two Presidencies." *American Politics Quarterly* 28 (1):3.

Fordham, Benjamin. 1998a. "Partisanship, Macroeconomic Policy, and U.S. Uses of Force, 1949–1994." *Journal of Conflict Resolution* 42 (4):418–39.

———. 1998b. "The Politics of Threat Perception and the Use of Force: A Political Economy Model of U.S. Uses of Force, 1949–1994." *International Studies Quarterly* 42 (3):567–90.

———. 2002. "Another Look at "Parties, Voters, and the Use of Force Abroad." *Journal of Conflict Resolution* 46 (4):572–96.

Freeman, John R., John T. Williams, and Tse-min Lin. 1989. "Vector Autoregression and the Study of Politics." *American Journal of Political Science* 33 (November):842–77.

Friedman, Milton. 1957. *A Theory of the Consumption Function*. Princeton, NJ: Princeton University Press.

Gelpi, Christopher F., and Michael Griesdorf. 2001. "Winners or Losers? Democracies in International Crisis, 1918–94." *The American Political Science Review* 95 (3):633–47.

George, Alexander L. 2009. "Coercive Diplomacy." In *The Use of Force: Military Power and International Politics*, ed. R. J. Art and K. N. Waltz. New York: Rowman and Littlefield.

Gerber, Alan, and Donald P. Green. 1997. "Rational Learning and Partisan Attitudes." *American Journal of Political Science* 42 (3):794–818.

———. 1999. "Misperceptions about Perceptual Bias." *Annual Review of Political Science* 2 (1):189–210.

Gergen, David. 2000. *Eyewitness to Power: The Essence of Leadership*. New York: Simon & Schuster.

Global Terrorism Database. Available at http://www.start.umd.edu/gtd. Accessed on February 7, 2010. College Park, MD: National Consortium for the Study of Terrorism and Responses to Terrorism (START), University of Maryland.

Goldstein, Joshua S. 1992. "A Conflict-Cooperation Scale for WEIS Events Data." *Journal of Conflict Resolution* 36 (2):369–85.

Gowa, Joanne. 1998. "Politics at the Water's Edge: Parties, Voters, and the Use of Force Abroad." *International Organization* 52 (2):307–24.

Granger, Clive W. J. 1969. "Investigating Causal Relations by Econometric Models and Cross-Spectral Models." *Econometrica* 37 (July):424–38.

Green, Peter S. 2002. "Havel Denies Telephoning U.S. on Iraq Meeting." *New York Times*, October 23.

Greene, Joyce A. 2009. Presidential Signing Statements, 2001–present. Available at http://www.coherentbabble.com/faqs.htm.

Grimmett, Richard F. 2001. "The War Powers Resolution: After Twenty-Eight Years." Washington, DC: Congressional Research Service.

Haller, H. Brandon, and Helmut Norpoth. 1994. "Let the Good Times Roll: The Economic Expectations of U.S. Voters." *American Journal of Political Science* 38 (3):625–50.

Halstead, T. J. 2007. "Presidential Signing Statements: Constitutional and Institutional Implications." Washington: U.S. Government Printing Office.

Hamilton, Alexander. 1788. The Duration in Office of the Executive, from the New York Packet. *Federalist Papers* No. 71. Available at the Avalon Project Web site: http://avalon.law.yale.edu/18th_century/fed71.asp.

Hibbs, Douglas A., Jr. 1974. "Problems of Statistical Estimation and Causal Inference in Time Series Regression Models." In *Sociological Methodology, 1973–74*, ed. H. L. Costner. San Francisco: Jossey-Bass.

———. 1987. *The American Political Economy: Macroeconomics and Electoral Politics*. Cambridge, MA: Harvard University Press.

Hill, Kim Quaile, and Patricia A. Hurley. 1999. "Dyadic Representation Reappraised." *American Journal of Political Science* 43 (1):109–37.

Houghton Mifflin. 1996. *American Heritage Dictionary of the English Language*, 3rd Edition. Boston: Houghton Mifflin. Available online at http://dictionary.reference.com/browse/saber-rattling.

Howell, William G. 2003. *Power without Persuasion: The Politics of Direct Presidential Action*. Princeton, NJ: Princeton University Press.

Howell, William G., and Jon C. Pevehouse. 2005. "Presidents, Congress, and the Use of Force." *International Organization* 59 (1):209–32.

———. 2007. *While Dangers Gather: Congressional Checks on Presidential War Powers*. Princeton, NJ: Princeton University Press.

Huddy, Leonie, Stanley Feldman, and Erin Cassese. 2007. "On the Distinct Political Effects of Anxiety and Anger." In *The Affect Effect: Dynamics of Emotion in Political Thinking and Behavior*, ed. W. R. Neuman, G. E. Marcus, A. N. Crigler, and M. MacKuen. Chicago: University of Chicago Press.

Inspector General. 1997. "FBI Laboratory: An Investigation into Laboratory Practices and Alleged Misconduct in Explosives-Related and Other Cases." Washington, DC: Office of the Inspector General, Department of Justice. Available at http://www.justice.gov/oig/special/9704a/.

Jacobs, Lawrence R., and Robert Y. Shapiro. 2000. *Politicians Don't Pander*. Chicago: University of Chicago Press.

Jacoby, William G. 1988. "The Impact of Party Identification on Issue Attitudes." *American Journal of Political Science* 32 (2):643–61.

James, Patrick, and Athanasios Hristoulas. 1994. "Domestic Politics and Foreign Politics: Evaluating a Model of Crisis Activity for the United States." *Journal of Politics* 56 (2):327–48.

James, Patrick, and James Oneal. 1991. "The Influence of Domestic and International Politics on the President's Use of Force." *The Journal of Conflict Resolution* 35 (2):307–32.

Jay, John. 1788a. The Same Subject Continued: Concerning Dangers from Foreign Force and Influence, for the Independent Journal. *Federalist Papers* No. 3. Available at the Avalon Project Web site: http://avalon.law.yale.edu/18th_century/fed03 .asp.

———. 1788b. Concerning Dangers from Foreign Force and Influence, for the Independent Journal. *Federalist Papers* No. 4. Available at the Avalon Project Web site: http://avalon.law.yale.edu/18th_century/fed04.asp.

Jones, Jeffrey M. 2003. "Public Support for Invasion of Iraq Holds Steady." *Gallup News Service*, February 28.

Katona, George. 1951. *Psychological Analysis of Economic Behavior*. New York: McGraw-Hill.

———. 1960. *The Powerful Consumer: Psychological Studies of the American Economy*. New York: McGraw-Hill.

———. 1964. *The Mass Consumption Society*. New York: McGraw-Hill.

———. 1975. *Psychological Economics*. New York: Elsevier.

Kernell, Samuel J. 1978. "Explaining Presidential Popularity: How Ad Hoc Theorizing, Misplaced Emphasis, and Insufficient Care in Measuring One's Variables Refuted Common Sense and Led Conventional Wisdom Down the Path of Anomalies." *American Political Science Review* 72 (June):506–22.

———. 1997. *Going Public: New Strategies of Presidential Leadership*, 3rd ed. Washington DC: CQ Press.

Kimball, M. S. 1990. "Precautionary Saving in the Small and in the Large." *Econometrica* 58 (1):53–73.

Korean Central News Agency. 2006. "DPRK Foreign Ministry Spokesman on U.S. Moves Concerning Its Nuclear Test." Korean Central News Agency, October 11. Available at: http://www.youtube.com/watch?v=YDiK_Qu6AaY.

Kull, Stephen, Clay Ramsay, and Evan Lewis. 2003. "Misperceptions, the Media, and the Iraq War." *Political Science Quarterly* 118 (4):569–98.

Kunda, Ziva. 1987. "Motivation and Inference: Self-Serving Generation and Evaluation of Evidence." *Journal of Personality and Social Psychology* 53:636–47.

———. 1990. "The Case for Motivated Political Reasoning." *Psychological Bulletin* 108 (3):480–98.

Kurizaki, Shuhei. 2007. "Efficient Secrecy: Public versus Private Threats in Crisis Diplomacy." *The American Political Science Review* 101 (3):543–58.

Laver, Michael. 1981. *The Politics of Private Desires: The Guide to the Politics of Rational Choice*. New York: Penguin Books.

Lebo, Matthew J., and Daniel Cassino. 2007. "The Aggregated Consequences of Motivated Reasoning and the Dynamics of Partisan Presidential Approval." *Political Psychology* 28 (6):2007.

LeLoup, Lance T., and Steven A. Shull. 1979. "Congress Versus the Executive: The 'Two Presidencies' Reconsidered." *Social Science Quarterly* 59 (4):704–19.

Leventoğlu, Bahar, and Ahmer Tarar. 2005. "Prenegotiation Public Commitment in Domestic and International Bargaining." *The American Political Science Review* 99 (3):419–33.

Levy, Jack S. 1987. "Domestic Politics and War." *Journal of Interdisciplinary History* 18 (4):653–73.

———. 1989. "The Causes of War: A Review of Theories and Evidence." In *Behavior, Society, and Nuclear War*, ed. P. E. Tetlock, J. L. Husbands, R. Jervis, P. C. Stern, and C. Tilly. New York: Oxford University Press.

Lewis, Charles, and Mark Reading-Smith. 2008. *The War Card: Orchestrated Deception on the Path to War.* Center for Public Integrity. Available at http://projects. iwatchnews.org/index.htm/projects.publicintegrity.org/WarCard/Defaulte193.html? src=project_home.

Lewis, David. 1997. "The Two Rhetorical Presidencies." *American Politics Quarterly* 25 (3):380.

Lewis, David E. 2003. *Presidents and the Politics of Agency Design.* Palo Alto, CA: Stanford University Press.

Lewis, David E., and William G. Howell. 2002. "Agencies by Presidential Design." *Journal of Politics* 64 (4):1095–114.

Lodge, Milton, and Ruth Hamill. 1986. "A Partisan Schema for Political Information Processing." 82 (3):737–61.

Lodge, Milton, and Charles S. Taber. 2000. "Three Steps Toward a Theory of Motivated Political Reasoning." In *Elements of Reason: Cognition, Choice, and the Bounds of Rationality,* ed. A. Lupia, M. McCubbins, and S. L. Popkin. New York: Cambridge University Press.

———. 2005. "Automaticity of Affect for Political Candidates, Parties, and Issues: An Experimental Test of the Hot Cognition Hypothesis." *Political Psychology* 26 (3):455–82.

Lyke, M. L. 2003. "Commander in Chief's Visit Sets Aircraft Carrier's Crew Abuzz." *Seattle Post Intelligenser,* May 1.

Lynch, Stephen. 2008. "The Most Dangerous Game: What Went Wrong in the Hunt for bin Laden." *New York Post,* October 5.

MacKuen, Michael B. 1983. "Political Drama, Economic Conditions, and the Dynamics of Presidential Popularity." *American Journal of Political Science* 27 (2):165–92.

MacKuen, Michael B., Robert S. Erikson, and James A. Stimson. 1992. "Peasants or Bankers? The American Electorate and the U.S. Economy." *American Political Science Review* 86 (3):597–611.

MacKuen, Michael, George E. Marcus, W. Russell Neuman, and Luke Keele. 2007. "The Third Way: The Theory of Affective Intelligence and American Democracy." In *The Affect Effect: Dynamics of Emotion in Political Thinking and Behavior,* ed. W. R. Neuman, G. E. Marcus, A. N. Crigler, and M. MacKuen. Chicago: University of Chicago Press.

Madison, James. 1788a. The Alleged Tendency of the New Plan to Elevate the Few at the Expense of the Many in Connection with Representation, from the New York Packet. *Federalist Papers* No. 57. Available at the Avalon Project Web site: http://avalon.law.yale.edu/18th_century/fed57.asp.

———. 1788b. The Same Subject Continued: The Union as a Safeguard Against Domestic Faction and Insurrection, from the New York Packet. *Federalist Papers* No. 10. Available at: http://avalon.law.yale.edu/18th_century/fed10.asp.

———. 1911. "August 17, 1787." In *The Records of the Federal Convention of 1787,* ed. M. Farrand. New Haven, CT: Yale University Press.

Mansbridge, Jane. 2003. "Rethinking Representation." *American Political Science Review* 97 (4):515–28.

Marcus, George E. 1988. "The Structure of Emotional Response: 1984 Presidential Candidates." *American Political Science Review* 82:737–81.

Marcus, George E., and Michael B. MacKuen. 1993. "Anxiety, Enthusiasm, and the Vote: The Emotional Underpinnings of Learning and Involvement in Presidential Campaigns." *American Political Science Review* 87:672–85.

Marcus, George E., W. Russell Neuman, and Michael MacKuen. 2000. *Affective Intelligence and Political Judgment*. Chicago: University of Chicago Press.

Markus, Gregory. 1988. "The Impact of Personal and National Economic Conditions on the Presidential Vote: A Pooled Cross-Sectional Analysis." *American Journal of Political Science* 32 (1):137–54.

Markus, Gregory B., and Philip E. Converse. 1979. "A Dynamic Simultaneous Equation Model of Electoral Choice." *American Political Science Review* 73 (4):1055–70.

———. 1982. "Political Attitudes during an Election Year: A Report on the 1980 NES Panel Study." *American Political Science Review* 76 (2):538–60.

Marshall, Bryan W., and Richard L. Pacelle, Jr. 2005. "Revisiting the Two Presidencies." *American Politics Research* 33 (1):81–105.

Matthews, Chris. 2005. "Road to War: How the Bush Administration Sold the War to the American People." *Hardball*, MSNBC TV, November 8.

Maurice, Jean-Claude. 2009. *Si vous le répétez, je démentirai... Chirac, Sarkozy, Villepin*. Paris: Plon.

Mayer, Kenneth R. 1999. "Executive Orders and Presidential Power." *Journal of Politics* 61:445–66.

———. 2001. *With the Stroke of a Pen: Executive Orders and Presidential Power*. Princeton, NJ: Princeton University Press.

McCullough, David. 2001. *John Adams*. New York: Simon & Schuster.

McGraw, Kathleen M., Mark Fischle, Karen Stenner, and Milton Lodge. 1996. "What's in a Word? Bias in Trait Descriptions of Political Leaders." *Political Behavior* 18 (3):263–87.

McGraw, Kathleen M., Milton Lodge, and Jeffrey M. Jones. 2002. "The Pandering Politicians of Suspicious Minds." *Journal of Politics* 64 (2):362–83.

Mearsheimer, John J. 2001. *The Tragedy of Great Power Politics*. New York: Norton.

Mearsheimer, John J., and Stephen M. Walt. 2007. *The Israel Lobby and American Foreign Policy*. New York: Macmillan.

Meernik, James. 1994. "Presidential Decision Making and the Political Use of Military Force." *International Studies Quarterly* 39 (1):121–38.

Meernik, James, and Peter Waterman. 1996. "The Myth of the Diversionary Use of Force by American Presidents." *Political Research Quarterly* 49 (3):573–90.

Mekay, Emad. 2004. "9/11 Commission Director: Iraq War Launched to Protect Israel." antiwar.com: Inter Press Service.

Milbank, Dana. 2002. "For Bush, Facts Are Malleable." *Washington Post*, October 22.

Modigliani, F., and R. Brumberg. 1954. "Utility Analysis and the Consumption Function: An Interpretation of Cross-Section Data." In *Post-Keynesian Economics*, ed. K. Kurihara. Piscataway, NJ: Rutgers University Press.

Monroe, Kristen R. 1978. "Economic Influences on Presidential Popularity." *Public Opinion Quarterly* 42 (Autumn):360–69.

Morgan, Clifton T., and Kenneth N. Bickers. 1992. "Domestic Discontent and the External Use of Force." *Journal of Conflict Resolution* 36 (1):25–52.

Moyers, Bill, and Michael Winship. 2008. "It Was Oil, All Along." *Bill Moyers Journal*. Available at http://www.pbs.org/moyers/journal/blog/2008/06/bill_moyers_michael_winship_it.html.

Mueller, John. 1970. "Presidential Popularity from Truman to Johnson." *American Political Science Review* 65 (1):18–34.

————. 1973. *War, Presidents, and Public Opinion.* New York: John Wiley & Sons.

National Security Archive. 2003. "North Korea and Nuclear Weapons: The Declassified Record." In *National Security Archive Electronic Briefing Book No. 87,* ed. R. A. Wampler. Washington, DC: George Washington University. Available at http://www .gwu.edu/~nsarchiv/NSAEBB/NSAEBB87/.

————. 2010a. "THE IRAQ WAR – PART I: The U.S. Prepares for Conflict, 2001." In *National Security Archive Electronic Briefing Book No. 328,* ed. J. Prados and C. Ames. Washington, DC: George Washington University. Available at http://www .gwu.edu/~nsarchiv/NSAEBB/NSAEBB326/index.htm.

————. 2010b. "THE IRAQ WAR – PART II: Was There Even a Decision?" In *National Security Archive Electronic Briefing Book No. 328,* ed. J. Prados and C. Ames. Washington, DC: George Washington University. Available at http://www.gwu.edu/~ nsarchiv/NSAEBB/NSAEBB328/index.htm.

————. 2010c. "THE IRAQ WAR – PART III: Shaping the Debate." In *National Security Archive Electronic Briefing Book No. 328,* ed. J. Prados and C. Ames. Washington, DC: George Washington University. Available at http://www.gwu.edu/~ nsarchiv/NSAEBB/NSAEBB330/index.htm.

Nixon, Richard M. 1973. Message Vetoing House Joint Resolution 542, A Joint Resolution Concerning the War Powers of Congress and the President. October 24.

Norpoth, Helmut. 1996. "Presidents and the Prospective Voter." *Journal of Politics* 58 (3):776–92.

Olson, Mancur, Jr. 1965. *The Logic of Collective Action.* Cambridge, MA: Harvard University Press.

Ornstein, Norman, and Thomas Mann, eds. 2000. *The Permanent Campaign and Its Future.* Washington, DC: American Enterprise Institute and the Brookings Institution.

Ostrom, Charles W., Jr., and Brian Job. 1986. "The President and the Political Use of Force." *American Political Science Review* 80 (2):541–66.

Ostrom, Charles W., Jr., and Renee Smith. 1993. "Error Correction, Attitude Persistence, and Executive Rewards and Punishments: A Behavioral Theory of Presidential Approval." *Political Analysis* 4:127–84.

Page, Benjamin I., and Robert Y. Shapiro. 1985. "Presidential Leadership through Public Opinion." In *The Presidency and Public Policy Making,* ed. G. C. I. Edwards, S. A. Shull, and N. C. Thomas. Pittsburgh, PA: University of Pittsburgh Press.

————. 1992. *The Rational Public: Fifty Years of Trends in American's Policy Preferences.* Chicago: University of Chicago Press.

Page, Susan. 2003. "Confronting Iraq: Prewar Predictions Coming Back to Bite." *USA Today.*

Partell, Peter J., and Glenn Palmer. 1999. "Audience Costs and Interstate Crises: An Empirical Assessment." *International Studies Quarterly* 43 (2):389–405.

Pennock, J. Roland, and John Chapman, eds. 1968. *Representation.* New York: Atherton Press.

Pitkin, Hanna Fenichel. 1967. *The Concept of Representation.* Los Angeles: University of California Press.

Plato. 2007. *The Republic.* New York: Penguin Classics.

Powell, Colin L. February 24, 2001. "Remarks by Secretary of State Colin L. Powell and Foreign Minister of Egypt Amre Moussa Ittihadiya Palace Cairo, Egypt February 24, 2001." Available at http://usembassy-israel.org.il/publish/peace/archives/2001/ february/meo224b.html.

————. February 5, 2003. "Remarks to the United Nations Security Council." Available at http://web.archive.org/web/20070109235502/http:/www.state.gov/secretary/former/powell/remarks/2003/17300.htm.

Project for the New American Century. 1997. "Statement of Principles." Washington, DC: Project for the New American Century. Available at http://www.newamerican century.org/statementofprinciples.htm.

————. 1998. "Letter to President Clinton, January 26, 1998." Washington, DC: Project for the New American Century. Available at http://www.newamericancentury .org/iraqclintonletter.htm.

*Public Papers of the Presidents.* March 17, 2003. "Address to the Nation on Iraq." Washington, DC: U.S. Government Printing Office.

————. March 15, 2003. "The President's Radio Address." Washington, DC: U.S. Government Printing Office.

————. February 6, 2003. "Remarks on the Iraqi Regime's Noncompliance with United Nations Resolutions." Washington, DC: U.S. Government Printing Office.

————. January 28, 2003. "Address Before a Joint Session of the Congress on the State of the Union." Washington, DC: U.S. Government Printing Office.

————. October 7, 2002. "Address to the Nation on Iraq from Cincinnati, Ohio." Washington, DC: U.S. Government Printing Office.

————. September 28, 2002. "The President's Radio Address." Washington, DC: U.S. Government Printing Office.

————. September 26, 2002a. "Remarks at a Reception for Senatorial Candidate John Cornyn in Houston, Texas." Washington, DC: U.S. Government Printing Office.

————. September 26, 2002b. "Remarks Following a Meeting with Congressional Leaders." Washington, DC: U.S. Government Printing Office.

————. September 25, 2002. "Remarks Prior to Discussions with President Alvaro Uribe of Colombia and an Exchange with Reporters." Washington, DC: U.S. Government Printing Office.

————. September 12, 2002. "Address to the United Nations General Assembly in New York City." Washington, DC: U.S. Government Printing Office.

————. January 29, 2002. "Address Before a Joint Session of the Congress on the State of the Union." Washington, DC: U.S. Government Printing Office.

————. September 20, 2001. "Address Before a Joint Session of the Congress on the United States Response to the Terrorist Attacks of September 11." Washington, DC: U.S. Government Printing Office.

————. March 13, 2001. "Notice-Continuation of Iran Emergency." Washington, DC: U.S. Government Printing Office.

————. March 7, 2001. "Remarks Prior to Discussions with President Kim Dae-jung of South Korea and an Exchange with Reporters." Washington, DC: U.S. Government Printing Office.

————. February 4, 1998. "Remarks Announcing the High Hopes for College Initiative." Washington, DC: U.S. Government Printing Office.

————. November 8, 1996. "Presidential Documents, Week Ending November 8, 1996." Washington, DC: U.S. Government Printing Office.

————. March 15, 1995. "Executive Order 12957 – Prohibiting Certain Transactions with Respect to the Development of Iranian Petroleum Resources." Washington, DC: U.S. Government Printing Office.

———. January 21, 1981. "Swearing In Ceremony for White House Staff." Washington, DC: Government Printing Office.

Rahn, Wendy M. 1993. "The Role of Partisan Stereotypes in Information Processing about Political Candidates." *American Journal of Political Science* 37 (2):472–96.

Ramsay, Kristopher W. 2004. "Politics at the Water's Edge: Crisis Bargaining and Electoral Competition." *The Journal of Conflict Resolution* 48 (4):459–86.

Redlawsk, David P. 2002. "Hot Cognition or Cool Consideration: Testing the Effects of Motivated Reasoning on Political Decision Making." *Journal of Politics* 64 (4):1021–44.

Rendall, Steve, and Tara Broughel. 2003. "Amplifying Officials, Squelching Dissent." In *FAIR: Fairness and Accuracy in Reporting*. New York: FAIR.

Richardson, James D., ed. 1907a. John Adams, Special Session Message, May 16, 1797. Vol. 1, Section 2. Available at the Project Gutenberg Web site: http://www.gutenberg .org/files/10894/10894-h/10894-h.htm.

———, ed. 1907b. John Adams: First Annual Address, November 22, 1797. Vol. 1, Section 2. Available at the Project Gutenberg Web site: http://www.gutenberg.org/ files/10894/10894-h/10894-h.htm.

———, ed. 1907c. John Adams: Message to Congress, March 19, 1798. Vol. 1, Section 2. Available at the Project Gutenberg Web site: http://www.gutenberg.org/files/10894/ 10894-h/10894-h.htm.

Ricks, Thomas E. 2002. "Some Top Military Brass Favor Status Quo in Iraq: Containment Seen Less Risky than Attack." *Washington Post*, July 28.

Riker, William H., and Peter Ordeshook. 1973. *An Introduction to Positive Political Theory*. Englewood Cliffs, NJ: Prentice-Hall.

Risen, James. 2002a. "How Politics and Rivalries Fed Suspicions of a Meeting." *New York Times*, October 21.

———. 2002b. "Prague Discounts an Iraqi Meeting." *New York Times*, October 21.

Roosevelt, Franklin D. 1937. Second Inaugural Address. January 20.

Roosevelt, Theodore. 1901. Speech at the Minnesota State Fair. September 2 Available at http://www.theodore-roosevelt.com/images/research/txtspeeches/678.pdf.

———. 1913. *The Autobiography of Theodore Roosevelt, Centennial Edition*. New York: Charles Scribner's Sons.

Rumsfeld, Donald. 2011. *Known and Unknown: A Memoir*. New York: Penguin.

Russert, Tim. 2003. Interview with Vice-President Dick Cheney. *Meet the Press*, NBC News, March 16.

Russett, Bruce. 1989. "Economic Decline, Electoral Pressure, and the Initiation of Interstate Conflict." In *Prisoners of War: Nation States in the Modern Era*, ed. C. Gockman and A. N. Sabrosky. Boston: Heath.

Sanger, David E. 2003. "North Korea Says It Now Possesses Nuclear Arsenal." *New York Times*, April 25.

Schelling, Thomas. 1960. *The Strategy of Conflict*. Cambridge, MA: Harvard University Press.

Schultz, Kenneth A. 1998. "Domestic Opposition and Signaling in International Crises." *The American Political Science Review* 92 (4):829–44.

———. 2001a. *Democracy and Coercive Diplomacy*. New York: Cambridge University Press.

———. 2001b. "Looking for Audience Costs." *Journal of Conflict Resolution* 45 (1):32–60.

Schwartz, Nancy. 1988. *The Blue Guitar: Political Representation and Community.* Chicago: University of Chicago Press.

Schwartz, Randal L., Erik Olson, and Tom Christiansen. 1997. *Learning PERL on Win32 Systems.* Cambridge, MA: O'Reilly.

Scowcroft, Brent. 2002. "Don't Attack Saddam." *Wall Street Journal,* August 15.

Sharp, James Roger. 1993. *American Politics in the Early Republic.* New Haven, CT: Yale University Press.

Shaw, Malcolm. 2008. *International Law,* 6th ed. Cambridge, United Kingdom: Cambridge University Press.

Shepsle, Kenneth A. 2010. *Analyzing Politics: Rationality, Behavior, and Institutions,* 2nd ed. New York: W. W. Norton.

Sigal, Leon V. 1998. *Disarming Strangers: Nuclear Diplomacy with North Korea.* Princeton, NJ: Princeton University Press.

Sigelman, Lee. 1979. "A Reassessment of the Two Presidencies Thesis." *The Journal of Politics* 41 (4):1195–205.

Simon, Dennis M., and Charles W. Ostrom. 1989. "The Impact of Televised Speeches and Foreign Travel on Presidential Approval." *Public Opinion Quarterly* 53 (1):58–82.

Simon, Herbert A. 1947. *Administrative Behavior.* New York: Free Press.

Sims, Christopher A. 1980. "Macroeconomics and Reality." *Econometrica* 48 (January):1–48.

Sims, Christopher A., and T. Zha. 1999. "Error Bands for Impulse Responses." *Econometrica* 67 (5):1113–56.

Smith, Alastair. 1996. "Diversionary Foreign Policy in Democratic Systems." *International Studies Quarterly* 40 (1):133–53.

———. 1998. "International Crises and Domestic Politics." *American Political Science Review* 92 (3):623–38.

Souleles, Nicholas S. 2001. "Consumer Sentiment: Its Rationality and Usefulness in Forecasting Expenditure-Evidence from the Michigan Micro Data." National Bureau of Economic Research Working Paper W8410.

SparkNotes Editors. 2003. "Sparknote on Nicomachean Ethics." Available at http://www.sparknotes.com/philosophy/ethics.

Stimson, James A. 1991. *Public Opinion in America: Moods, Cycles, and Swings.* Boulder, CO: Westview Press.

Stimson, James A., Michael B. MacKuen, and Robert S. Erikson. 1995. "Dynamic Representation." *American Political Science Review* 89 (September):543–65.

Taber, Charles S., and Milton Lodge. 2006. "Motivated Skepticism in the Evaluation of Political Beliefs." *American Journal of Political Science* 50 (3):755–69.

Tarar, Ahmer, and Bahar Leventoğlu. 2009. "Public Commitment in Crisis Bargaining." *International Studies Quarterly* 53 (3):817–39.

Tomz, Michael. 2007. "Domestic Audience Costs in International Relations: An Experimental Approach." *International Organization* 61 (Fall):821–40.

Tulis, Jeffrey. 1987. *The Rhetorical Presidency.* Princeton, NJ: Princeton University Press.

U.S. Department of Defense. 2012. "Operation Iraqi Freedom (OIF) Casualty Status." Washington, DC: Department of Defense. Available at http://www.defense.gov/news/casualty.pdf.

U.S. Department of State. 2001. "Overview of State Sponsored Terrorism." Washington, DC: U.S. Government Printing Office. Available at http://www.state.gov/documents/organization/10296.pdf.

———. 2003, March 7. "Spain, United Kingdom of Great Britain and Northern Ireland and United States of America: Draft Resolution." New York: United Nations Security Council. Available at http://www.un.org/news/dh/iraq/iraq-blue-res-052103en.pdf.

———. 2011. "Country Reports on Terrorism." Washington, DC.

Walt, Stephen M. 2006. *Taming American Power*. New York: W. W. Norton.

Waltz, Kenneth N. 1979. *Theory of International Politics*. Reading, MA: Addison-Wesley.

Weeks, Jessica L. 2008. "Autocratic Audience Costs: Regime Type and Signaling Resolve." *International Organization* 62 (Winter):35–64.

Weisberg, Herbert F. 2005. "The U.S. Presidential and Congressional Elections, November 2004." *Electoral Studies* 24 (3):777–84.

Weisberg, Herbert F., and Dino P. Christenson. 2007. "Changing Horses in Wartime? The 2004 Presidential Election." *Political Behavior* 29 (2):279–304.

Weisman, Stephen. 2005. "Powell Calls His UN Speech a Lasting Blot on His Record." *New York Times*, September 9.

Western Standard Publishing Company. 2000. *American Reference Library* [CD-ROM]. Available at http://www.OriginalSources.com.

Wikipedia. 2011a. "Virtue." Available at wikipedia.org. Available at http://en.wikipedia.org/wiki/Virtue.

———. 2011b. "Wisdom." Available at wikipedia.org. Available at http://en.wikipedia.org/wiki/Wisdom.

Wildavsky, Aaron. 1966. "The Two Presidencies." *Trans-Action* 4:7–14.

Wills, Garry. 2006. "A Country Ruled by Faith." *The New York Review of Books*, November 16. Available at http://www.nybooks.com/articles/archives/2006/nov/16/a-country-ruled-by-faith/?pagination=false.

Wittman, Donald. 1983. "Candidate Motivation: A Synthesis of Alternatives." *American Political Science Review* 77:142–57.

Wlezien, Christopher. 1996. "Dynamics of Representation: The Case of U.S. Spending on Defense." *British Journal of Political Science* 26 (1):81–103.

Wood, B. Dan. 2000. "Weak Theories and Parameter Instability: Using Flexible Least Squares to Take Time-Varying Relationships Seriously." *American Journal of Political Science* 44 (3):603–18.

———. 2007. *The Politics of Economic Leadership*. Princeton, NJ: Princeton University Press.

———. 2009a. *The Myth of Presidential Representation*. New York: Cambridge University Press.

———. 2009b. "Presidential Saber Rattling and the Economy." *American Journal of Political Science* 53 (3).

Wood, B. Dan, and Angela Hinton Andersson. 1998. "The Dynamics of Senatorial Representation." *Journal of Politics* 60 (3):705–36.

Wood, B. Dan, Brandy M. Durham, and Chris T. Owens. 2005. "Presidential Rhetoric and the Economy." *Journal of Politics* 67 (3):627–45.

Wood, B. Dan, and Han Soo Lee. 2009. "Explaining Presidential Liberalism: Pandering, Partisanship, or Pragmatism." *Journal of Politics* 71 (4):1–16.

Wood, B. Dan, and Jeffrey S. Peake. 1998. "The Dynamics of Foreign Policy Agenda Setting." *American Political Science Review* 92 (1):173–84.

Wood, B. Dan, and Arnold Vedlitz. 2009. "Information Processing, Focusing Events, and the Public Response to Global Climate Change." Paper presented at the annual meeting of the Southern Political Science Association, New Orleans, LA.

Woodward, Bob. 2002. *Bush at War*. New York: Simon & Schuster.

———. 2004. *Plan of Attack*. New York: Simon & Schuster.

———. 2006. *State of Denial: Bush at War Part III*. New York: Simon & Schuster.

Yoo, John C., and Robert J. Delahunty. 2009. "The 'Bush Doctrine': Can Preventive War Be Justified?" *Harvard Journal of Law and Public Policy* 32 (3):843–46.

Yoon, M. Y. 1997. "Explaining U.S. Intervention in Third World Internal Wars, 1945–89." *Journal of Conflict Resolution* 41 (4):580–602.

Zaller, John R. 1992. *The Nature and Origins of Mass Opinion*. Boston: Cambridge University Press.

Zeger, S. L., and B. Qaqish. 1988. "Markov Regression Models for Time Series: A Quasi-Likelihood Approach." *Biometrics* 44:1019–31.

Zellner, Arnold. 1962. "An Efficient Method of Estimating Seemingly Unrelated Regression Equations and Tests for Aggregation Bias." *Journal of the American Statistical Association* 57 (June):348–68.

Zogby, James. 2007. "Four Years Later: Arab Opinion Troubled by Consequences of Iraq War." Washington, DC: Arab American Institute.

# Index